THE AMBULANCE DRIVERS

BY JAMES McGRATH MORRIS

Eye on the Struggle: Ethel Payne, The First Lady of the Black Press

Pulitzer: A Life in Politics, Print, and Power

The Rose Man of Sing Sing: A True Tale of Life, Murder, and Redemption in the Age of Yellow Journalism

Jailhouse Journalism: The Fourth Estate Behind Bars

THE
AMBULANCE
DRIVERS

Hemingway, Dos Passos, and
a Friendship Made and Lost in War

James McGrath Morris

DA CAPO PRESS

Designed by Jeff Williams

Set in 11.5 point Dante MT by Perseus Books

Library of Congress Cataloging-in-Publication Data

Names: Morris, James McGrath author.
Title: The ambulance drivers : Hemingway, Dos Passos, and a friendship made and
    lost in war / James McGrath Morris.
Description: Boston : Da Capo Press, 2017.
Identifiers: LCCN 2016043398| ISBN 9780306823831 (hardcover) | ISBN
    9780306823848 (ebook)
Subjects: LCSH: Hemingway, Ernest, 1899–1961—Criticism and interpretation. |
    Dos Passos, John, 1896–1970—Criticism and interpretation. | Hemingway,
    Ernest, 1899–1961—Friends and associates. | Dos Passos, John,
    1896–1970—Friends and associates. | World War, 1914–1918—Literature and
    the war.
Classification: LCC PS3515.E37 Z74318 2017 | DDC 813/.52—dc23
LC record available at https://lccn.loc.gov/2016043398

Published by Da Capo Press, an imprint of Perseus Books, LLC, a subsidiary of Hachette Book Group, Inc.

www.dacapopress.com

Da Capo Press books are available at special discounts for bulk purchases in the U.S. by corporations, institutions, and other organizations. For more information, please contact the Special Markets Department at Perseus Books, 2300 Chestnut Street, Suite 200, Philadelphia, PA 19103, or call (800) 810-4145, ext. 5000, or e-mail special.markets@perseusbooks.com.
10 9 8 7 6 5 4 3 2 1

To our children
Stephanie, Benjamin, and Alexander
and to our grandchildren.
May they never know war.

In writing you have a certain choice
that you do not have in life.

—ERNEST HEMINGWAY

Life doesn't often hold out her hand to you—
I think you should take it when she does and
let the consequences take care of themselves,
rather than ask if she wears gloves or not.

—JOHN DOS PASSOS

PROLOGUE

IN THE EARLY SUMMER OF 1924 TWO AMERICAN WRITERS SAT IN A PARIS café. One author came armed with a dictionary, believing that reading the small type would improve his vision. The other brought a King James edition of the Bible. They took turns reading passages aloud from the Old Testament. The Chronicles and Kings were their favorites, along with the Song of Deborah.

The café where they sat, La Closerie des Lilas, straddled the corner of the boulevard St. Michel and the boulevard du Montparnasse and took its name from the white and purple lilac bushes encircling its terrace. As in most Paris cafés, the garçons had become accustomed to delivering café crème to tables populated by American expatriates swarming the City of Light. As the day wore on, the orders would change to vermouth cassis or the more potent absinthe, a green liqueur that turned milky white when mixed with water.

Of the two men at the table that day, John Dos Passos was the more famous and more accomplished. His last novel had been widely read and much talked about. At this moment he had a multibook contract with a New York publishing house. His straight black hair was already receding at age twenty-eight, giving him a kind of professorial look, which was accented by thick-lensed glasses and the gray suits he favored. When he spoke he did so in a halting tentative fashion with a mild stammer.

In contrast, the man sitting across the table from Dos Passos exuded confidence. With a full head of brown lustrous hair, chiseled features, and a broad-shouldered body made taut by vigorous exercise, Ernest Hemingway possessed looks that invariably drew attention, especially from women. But when it came to writing, he was struggling to make ends meet. So far, twenty-five-year-old Hemingway had paid the bills by working as a stringer for a Canadian newspaper and with monthly remittances from his wife's trust fund.

A prestigious annual collection had included one of his stories but misspelled his name. Such was his anonymity. However, a boutique Paris publisher had just printed a slim volume of Hemingway's stories and poems—with his name correctly spelled, this time—that brought his literary promise to the attention of American expatriate writers in Paris.

There were a good number of them. The magnetism of Paris made the city irresistible to writers as well as to artists and composers. Popular novelist Fannie Hurst told *Washington Post* readers in 1924 that Paris was like a beautiful woman. "And America," she added, "with a sentiment that is characteristic, worships the lovely creature."

Paris represented everything their homeland was not for the generation of American writers like Hemingway and Dos Passos who had come of age during the Great War. An incomprehensible number of people—more than 17 million—had been killed, and as many as 20 million had been maimed. It seemed to these young aspiring writers that the United States, which counted only fifty-three thousand combat deaths, refused to recognize that the world was no longer the same and never would be again. In their minds their country obdurately clung to its straitlaced ways, extending its Puritanism to a war on liquor and even to book burning, such as the four hundred copies of the legally banned *Ulysses* by James Joyce that were condemned to bonfires.

So they fled and came to Paris, described by those who watched as members of a lost generation creating a massive literary party and seeking new forms of expression for the reality of a fractured world. "Indeed, to young writers like ourselves," said Malcolm Cowley, who also went to Paris, "a long sojourn in France was almost a pilgrimage to Holy Land." By the time Dos Passos and Hemingway sat that summer day at La Closerie des Lilas, Paris's American population had topped thirty thousand. "It was not what France gave you," said Gertrude Stein, literary grande dame of the city, "but what it did not take away from you that was important."

The expatriates created a colony in Montparnasse, the Left Bank quartier of Émile Zola and Anatole France. Most of the flats were without running water and many without heat. These American artists wrote in cafés by day, populated clubs at night, drank with abandon, and relished the city's liberated sexual life.

Money—or, more precisely, its unequal exchange—fueled the migration. Foreign currency was the equivalent of being wealthy because the franc was worth so little. American writers, said one expatriate author, flocked to Europe like crows to a cornfield.

Even getting to Paris had become affordable. Steamship companies responding to draconian restrictions on immigration rapidly spruced up and converted their steerage class to Tourist Third Class. Promising a romantic crossing with a bohemian touch, the liners advertised these tickets to students, artists, teachers, and tourists.

✦

In the midst of this Parisian literary colony Hemingway and Dos Passos delighted in each other's company. "Ernest was always looking for someone who could really talk with him and on his level, and with the same interests," his wife Hadley said. "John Dos Passos was one of the few people at certain times whom Ernest could really talk to."

The two Chicago natives, however, were very different from each other. Whereas Hemingway was egotistical, certain of himself, willing to get ahead at the expense of others, apolitical, and athletic, the Harvard-educated Dos Passos was timid, questioning, considerate to a fault, a committed left-wing pacifist, and incapable in all sports aside from hiking. Their common pursuit, however, trumped their differences: they were plotting a literary revolution. To them the war had made traditional writing styles inadequate. Their generation needed its own voice, not one that imitated another from the past.

Dos Passos was deep into a new manuscript that used an innovative pastiche of visual imagery and cinematic jump cuts. For his part, Hemingway worked like a jeweler on paragraph-long unadorned stories, as he would later say, trying to pen "the truest sentence that you know." For now, in 1924, Dos Passos was ahead in their mutual pursuit for a new means of expression.

In the late afternoon on the days they met at La Closerie des Lilas the two writers would put down their glasses, pay their tab, and stroll back to Hemingway's place. In the small walk-up flat Dos Passos lent a hand to Ernest and Hadley in bathing their baby son and tucking him into bed. Afterward, when the housemaid arrived to babysit, Ernest, Hadley, and Dos Passos went out into the Paris night for dinner, and literary discussion renewed.

"They had a lot to say to each other," Hadley recalled. "There wasn't anyone else around for Ernest like that." Their nascent friendship rose out of a unique common bond. Like the other ambitious Americans drawn to the cafés of Montparnasse or even their colleagues who had remained in the United States, they too dreamed of penning the great books of their generation. But Hemingway and Dos Passos were different from the rest. They were almost alone among American writers of their age in having witnessed the war that defined their generation.

Dos Passos and Hemingway had held front-row seats as part of a cadre of men who volunteered for ambulance duty on the killing fields of Europe. In fact, Hemingway still carried shrapnel in his body. The men had confronted hardships and danger to a lesser degree than the soldiers, but they had also been afforded a greater view than that seen from the trenches. It was exhilarating and harrowing. "The war created in young men a thirst for abstract danger," recalled Cowley, who also had served as an ambulance driver, "not suffered for a cause but courted for itself."

Now, six years after the end of the conflict, John Dos Passos and Ernest Hemingway burned to put on paper what they had seen and experienced. The Great War was over, but not for them. Not yet.

1

ON THE MORNING OF OCTOBER 14, 1916, JOHN RODERIGO DOS PASSOS'S father accompanied him to the *Espagne*, moored in lower Manhattan. The latest war news unnerved those boarding the Europe-bound ship. After reading about the recent close calls with German U-boats, ninety-five passengers had canceled their reservation.

Since graduating from Harvard University in May, the twenty-year-old Dos Passos had been like a foal confined in too small a paddock. Stuck for the summer at his father's expansive Virginia estate along the Potomac River, he endured the mugginess, stirring only to turn the page of a book. He worked his way through the ten-volume novel *Jean-Christophe* by the French writer Romain Rolland, who had won the Nobel Prize for Literature the previous year. But what inspired Dos Passos most was Walt Whitman's poem "Song of the Open Road." The poet's invitation to set out on a journey roused Dos Passos. "I wanted to see the war, to paddle up undiscovered rivers, to climb unmapped mountains," he said. "I was frantic to be gone."

He spotted his chance for escape when he learned that men his age were being recruited for ambulance duty in Europe. When the Great War broke out in the summer of 1914 American expatriates living in Paris obtained ambulances and ferried the wounded from the front back to the well-equipped American hospital. Their actions inspired Richard Norton, an American archaeologist living in Paris at the time, who set about launching an organized ambulance service. The son of noted Harvard art history professor Charles Eliot Norton, the socially well-connected younger Norton found ready support for his plan. French millionaire H. Herman Harjes wrote large checks, and the venture was named the Norton-Harjes Ambulance Corps.

The Norton-Harjes Ambulance Corps pursued drivers as if it were looking for candidates for membership in an elite men's club rather than for service in a war zone. "A volunteer must be a man of good disposition possessed of self-control—in short, a gentleman," said one recruitment letter. From a practical point of view, targeting the American elite for recruitment made sense: the prerequisite ability to speak French and the skill to operate a car were talents acquired primarily by members of the upper class. It also took money to join—recruits were expected to pay for their passage and expenses. Ivy League campuses, with their wealthy students, were choice picking grounds. Soon more than 800 Ivy League volunteers headed to France, 348 from Harvard alone.

Dos Passos decided that being an ambulance driver would bring him to the warfront without serving the war-making powers he despised. But his father soon put the kibosh on any ideas his son might have about joining a team of gentleman drivers dashing about European battlefields. Instead, he told him he would send him to study Spanish in Madrid, safely south of the battlefields. Dos Passos consented to his father's plan when he realized his Iberian confinement would last only until January 1917 when he turned twenty-one. "Then in spring I shall go to Paris and make every endeavor to get to the front by hook or crook," he confided to a friend.

At the dock father and son said their good-byes by the breezy water's edge in the fall coolness. "We had no regrets to express to each other, and no sighs were made," the father wrote to a friend soon after. "It was simply a kiss and *au revoir*." Later in the afternoon, looking out from the window of his law office, the father watched as the ocean liner carried his son out of New York City's harbor.

✦

It had been an unconventional father-son relationship. The son had been born in a Chicago hotel on January 14, 1896, the product of an affair between the well-known but married New York City attorney John

Randolph Dos Passos and Lucy Addison Sprigg Madison, a widow from a socially prominent Petersburg, Virginia, family. Dos Passos and Madison were in love, but a divorce was out of the question for him. A Catholic, he knew his wife would not consent. So the child was named John Roderigo Madison Jr. His childhood was lived out in hotels in Brussels, Biarritz, and Boulogne-sur-Mer, places where his parents could meet openly. But time with his father remained rare. "I came to know him," the son said, "through the turbulence of conflicting currents of love and hate that mark many men's feelings for their fathers."

John R. Dos Passos's wife died in 1910, and he soon after married Lucy Madison. Their son was consigned to Choate, a small and exclusive Connecticut boarding school. It was a miserable life, one that Dos Passos hated. Small, skinny, younger than his classmates, wearing thick glasses, and speaking with a stutter, he was bullied by the testosterone-infused bullies who ruled the student bodies of New England prep schools like Choate. "I have no friends—there is no one who cares a rap about me," he wrote in his diary. Books became Dos Passos's dependable companions. They stirred his ambition. Someday, he told his diary, he would be so successful that his classmates would say, "'I went to school with John R. Dos Passos' (If I ever do assume that name.)" In time his mother and father did change his last name so he could affect the guise of being a stepson. Despite the name change and the marriage of his parents, Dos Passos passed the remainder of his childhood devoid of genuine family life.

When sixteen-year-old Dos Passos walked into Harvard Yard in the fall of 1912, he stepped out from a childhood in which he had been unable to fit in anywhere into a world willing to accept him on his own terms. True, many of Harvard's students were the scions of wealth whose place at the university was assured by birthright. But the faculty, unequaled in any other place in the United States, supported an intellectual meritocracy that rewarded excellence rather than social standing. Despite his unhappy years at Choate, the school had well prepared Dos Passos for his studies.

At last in a setting suitable for a poor-sighted shy teenager, Dos Passos drew enough courage to begin planning a life of his choosing. He elected to study art, poetry, and literature, thereby dashing his father's hopes that he would pursue instruction in law. The prodigious reading he had done at Choate grew even more expansive. The new authors he encountered beguiled him. It seemed as if he sought to devour Harvard's entire collection of books. He read, in the original French, authors such as Flaubert, Rimbaud, Verlaine, and Voltaire, and he worked his way through British writers like Oscar Wilde, H. G. Wells, and Laurence Sterne as well as a full repast of Victorian poets and classic writers such as Ovid, Virgil, and Horace, reading these in Latin, of course.

Eager to become a published writer himself, Dos Passos submitted a short story at the end of his first year to the *Harvard Monthly*. It was only the first. The magazine took twenty-eight other of his stories along with many poems over the next few years. One could not pick up an issue of the *Harvard Monthly* without finding the Dos Passos byline.

At the close of his junior year in May 1915 Dos Passos opened a letter from his family's housekeeper. His mother's long-term battle with ill health had taken a turn for the worse. Next came a telegram from his father. "Your mother," he wrote, "is gradually sinking and we must prepare for the worse." She died a few days later.

Dos Passos returned home. Devastated by the loss of his one steadfast parent, he even considered not returning to Harvard for his final year. Grieving, he sought to distract himself by taking a trip to the World's Fair in San Francisco. On the *Shasta Limited* train Dos Passos met a fifteen-year-old student from St. Paul's School, an elite prep school in New Hampshire, who was traveling with his brother and cousin. It was like meeting a younger version of himself. Walter Rumsey Marvin, who went by his middle name, had spent time in European schools; spoke French, loved history, the classics, and reading and writing poetry; and came from wealth. They linked paths again at the World's Fair and in San Diego, where they passed a lazy day under Southern California's sun swimming and climbing the Sunset Cliffs. When they parted for the last time, promises were made to remain in touch.

"Dear Rummy," Dos Passos wrote from the train taking him back east. "When our roads divided the other morning I had quite reconciled myself to not meet any of you people again—because, you know—you never do meet people again that you want to." In Rummy Dos Passos had found a younger brother to mentor, a confidant with whom to share intimate thoughts in the privacy of letter writing, a kindred soul. The summer that had begun with death now sparkled with renewal.

When it came to the deep sorrow over his mother's death, Cambridge also proved to be a tonic. He was elected to the board of the *Harvard Monthly*. The publication's office, upstairs in the Harvard Union, was a mecca for students who loved to write and talk about books. There Dos Passos gravitated to poets Robert Hillyer, Dudley Poore, and Edward Estlin Cummings, who went by his initials E. E. and who was already experimenting with form, punctuation, and spelling. When work on the magazine was done, the men moved to Dos Passos's room in Thayer Hall overlooking the Yard for literary debates that stretched well into the night, fueled by an ample supply of alcohol.

He was once again busy, engaged in his studies, and full of life.

+

By the end of 1916 the literary and poetic pleasures of Harvard, the culinary delights of the streets of Cambridge, and liquor were a crumbling bulwark to the outside world. The Great War and the clamor of the interventionists could no longer be kept at bay. "The sounds of marching feet came dimly through the walls of the sanctum upstairs in the Harvard Union," Dos Passos said. "Franco-British propaganda was beating the drums for American intervention. The professors were losing their minds; hating the Huns became a mania."

It was a war that few in America had seen coming and no one in Europe had sought, but once unleashed, it could not be stopped. Military treaties, like the tacky silk of spiderwebs, pulled heavily armed nations into battle following the 1914 assassination of the Archduke Franz Ferdinand, the presumptive heir to the Austro-Hungarian throne. A radical's single gunshot from a pocket-sized pistol set off a continental conflagration of immensity never before seen. Germany and Austria-Hungary, which led off the fighting, and Britain, France, and Russia, the main allies on the other side, were all convinced the war would be over in a matter of months. It was a bad gamble. Stubbornness, misjudgment, and alliances created an inextinguishable explosive mixture. By Christmas 1914 more than six hundred thousand French and German soldiers had died, and five hundred miles of trenches from the Swiss Alps to the North Sea carved out a killing field on soil blackened by bombardment.

The American warmongers gained ground in public opinion as the war dragged on. But they did not sway Dos Passos. Rather, he was inspired by the same kind of pacifism advocated by John Reed, the radical journalist who had graduated from Harvard in 1910. Dos Passos, in the company of E. E. Cummings, made sure to attend Reed's campus speech against US military involvement in Mexico. He carried his admiration for Reed to the *Harvard Monthly*, where he published two praising reviews of Reed's books. Dos Passos envied and emulated Reed's style of blending facts and impressions in capturing the war in Mexico and Europe. To put the injustices of the world on the page, for Dos Passos this seemed the great power of a writer.

Upon graduation in 1916 Dos Passos confined himself to his father's place in Virginia until he departed for Spain. He consumed books as if he were still in college, and he wrote essays. "Always against something, always the voice crying in the wilderness," he said. But writing was not enough. "I wanted to see the world," he said. "The world was the war."

✤

In Spain Dos Passos waited to turn twenty-one years old and be free of his father's rule. But his January 14, 1917, birthday was soon followed by loss. John R. Dos Passos had been found unconscious on the floor of his bathroom; he died a few hours later of pneumonia. The death of his father brought Dos Passos back to the United States. His mother and father now gone, he had no family aside from a distant half-brother and a maternal aunt. With no one left to stop him, Dos Passos enlisted in the Norton-Harjes Ambulance Corps. It was a well-timed decision that permitted him to escape the newly instituted military draft triggered by the US entry into the war on April 6, 1917.

Dos Passos prepared for the work ahead by learning some basic first aid and training to operate an ambulance at a New York City automobile driving school. The skill to drive an ambulance was not easy to acquire. The vehicle had levers below the steering wheel. One served as an accelerator, and the other controlled the spark that ignited the combustion gas inside the engine's cylinders. As the ambulance sped or slowed, the driver had to change the timing of the spark. Too much adjustment either way, and the engine would knock or overheat. All the while the driver had to use his feet, like an organist, to operate three pedals that controlled the transmission's various speeds or put the car in reverse.

When not training, Dos Passos attended leftist political rallies and went out with a new covey of radical friends that included Max Eastman, the editor of the magazine *The Masses*. But leftist politics were risky off campus. Authorities were increasingly clamping down on dissent now that the nation had declared war on Germany. One night Dos Passos barely escaped arrest when the police raided a Greenwich Village apartment of radicals where he was attending an avant-garde dance recital.

He was happy to be among this crowd. "Every day I become more red," Dos Passos wrote to a friend. "I think we are all of us a pretty milky lot—don't you?—with our tea-table convictions and our radicalism that keeps so consistently within the bounds of decorum. Dammit, why couldn't one of us have refused to register and gone to jail and made a general ass of himself?" he wrote. "Until Widener [library] is blown up and A. Lawrence Lowell [president of Harvard] assassinated and the Business School destroyed—and its site sowed with salt—no good will come out of Cambridge."

Leaving the United States was a wise move. Congress would soon put the final touches on an Espionage Act that would make such antiwar utterances a criminal offense.

✛

Under a brazen sun on Wednesday morning, June 20, 1917, Dos Passos lugged his heavy duffle bag along the dock at Pier 57 on the west side of lower Manhattan. Moored before him was the SS *Chicago*. For nine years the French-owned 508-foot liner had carried passengers in its well-appointed cabins across the Atlantic Ocean. But now it had been enlisted to bring American troops to war.

Above him French sailors scurried about the deck, making final preparations for a crossing to Bordeaux, France. On the pier, among the crates and a pair of long guns destined for the ship's hold, a crowd of well-wishers swayed to a band's peppy, if unauthentic, rendition of Hawaiian music. Women, in summer dresses and colorful hats, waved white handkerchiefs. Then hundreds of men, clad in khaki uniforms, pulled free of clasped hands and embraces, swung their gear over their shoulders, fell into line, and climbed the gangplanks like ants on a tree trunk.

Among them were two of Theodore Roosevelt's children, Theodore Jr. and his younger brother Archibald. President Woodrow Wilson had denied their bellicose father's application to lead a battalion to war. Instead, Roosevelt offered his sons to the nation. A few weeks earlier he had written to General John J. Pershing, commander of the American Expeditionary Forces, requesting that he take Theodore and Archibald to France. "I apply on behalf of my sons that they may serve under you as enlisted men, to go to the front with the first troops sent over," wrote the former president who was convinced the fight would be a short one now that American troops were being called into battle.

The soldiers were also led to believe that what lay ahead would be a brief adventure. A collective hubris, fed by a compliant press and amplified by the government's propaganda, left the uniformed young men blind to the caldron of death across the ocean. The war had already taken more than 4 million European lives. In just four months the first of many telegrams would begin to be sent to 116,516 American families. Their opening words would be: *Deeply regret to inform you . . .*

Dos Passos reached the top of the gangplank and pushed his way across the ship's deck. It teemed with soldiers who smelled of sweat and beer and were shouting their good-byes to friends and family on the dock below. He found his assigned stateroom and his two cabin mates, also ambulance corps volunteers. Dos Passos stowed his gear and waited. The hot day wore on. Shortly after five o'clock the mooring lines holding the *Chicago* fast to the pier were slipped off their bollards and the Hudson's water bubbled as the ship's propellers came to life. "Hurrah—the whistle's blowing and the old tub is starting to move," Dos Passos scribbled furiously on a letter to Rummy. At last he was off on the adventure he had sought since graduating from Harvard a year earlier.

Dos Passos sealed the last of the letters he had dashed off. With his missives in hand, he went up on deck and found the harbor pilot, who agreed to post the letters when he returned to shore. Later, before joining the crowd heading to the bar and smoking rooms, Dos Passos took one last look at New York City outlined by the setting sun in the west. "Rosy yellow and drab purple," he thought, "the buildings of New York slid together into a pyramid above brown smudges of smoke standing out in the water, linked to the land by the dark curves of the bridges."

Ahead lay France, which he loved and knew well from his itinerant childhood in Europe's posh locales, and the great unknown of war.

2

AS THE *CHICAGO*, WITH DOS PASSOS ON BOARD, CUT THROUGH THE GRAY-blue waters of the Atlantic Ocean in the summer of 1917, a Model T Ford was churning up a wake of brown dust on the bumpy dirt roads of northern Michigan. At the steering wheel Dr. Clarence Edmonds Hemingway was doing his best to dodge the wheel-busting potholes. In the backseat his wife, Grace, held their two-year-old son on her lap and competed for space with the luggage. By his side in the front seat sat his six-foot-tall, seventeen-year-old son, Ernest.

The group was on its way to Windemere, the family's summer cottage on Walloon Lake. This year the four Hemingway daughters had taken the boat, but the two sons, mother, and father were adventurously traveling the 450 miles of rough roads using $8.32 of gas and oil and spending $11.95 for four nights of lodgings and meals. It was an arduous trip, and the car required on-the-road repairs. But for Ernest Hemingway each bumpy mile brought him closer to a boy's paradise.

Hemingway knew that when the chores were done he would be free to dangle worms in front of pike and pickerel with a bamboo pole in clear deep waters, hunt partridge with a single-barrel twenty-gauge shotgun, swim in the lake, paddle a canoe, and lollygag in a hammock with a book. It was a Huck Finn existence complete with a straw hat.

He was leaving behind the family's hometown of Oak Park, Illinois, a straitlaced sober Chicago suburb whose blue laws prevented anything entertaining from interfering with the Sabbath, that was so dotted with Protestant churches it was nicknamed "Saints' Rest." A few weeks earlier he had marked the end of a youth of churchgoing, steady meritorious schoolwork, and modest athletic success with his graduation from high school.

+

Ernest Miller Hemingway had been born on July 21, 1899, in a gabled Queen Anne house, one of many set back on the wide lawns that lined Oak Park's shaded streets. His parents were an unusual couple for the staid community, as they were both professionals. His father, Clarence, was a physician, and his mother, Grace, a musician. Hemingway and his siblings came home each day from school to a house that doubled as a place of business where the father saw patients and the mother gave lessons.

The medical practice grew into a moderately prosperous affair. Using income from it and Grace's lessons, along with an inheritance, the family built a three-story house. Large even by Oak Park standards, it was abundant with modern conveniences and designed both for family life and lavish entertainment. Its eight bedrooms held the couple, their six children, an uncle who visited frequently, and a pair of servants.

Grace ruled the homestead. Housework was done by servants and, in their absence, her physician husband. In fact, he shopped, canned vegetables and fruits, and tended the chickens and rabbits in the backyard. Beset with migraine headaches, Grace exempted herself from the duties of housewifery. She liked to remind her family that had she chosen the stage instead of Clarence, her name would be on posters outside the New York Metropolitan Opera.

The parents welcomed time apart from each other. For Clarence the outdoors provided a permissible escape from his domestic life. He shared his enthusiasm for his pastimes with Ernest. Once when his son was ten, Clarence took Ernest quail shooting. In a thicket some distance from his father Ernest found a dead quail still warm to the touch; an errant pellet from his father's gun apparently had felled it. Ernest looked around to see if anyone could see him. Then he aimed his shotgun at the dead bird at his feet, closed his eyes, and pulled the trigger. The explosion of the twin barrels kicked Ernest back against a tree, his ears ringing and nose bleeding. He got to his feet, picked up the quail carcass, and went to find his father.

"Did you get one, Ernie?" asked his father upon spotting his son coming out of the brush.

Ernest held up the dead bird.

"It's a cock. See his white throat? It's a beauty," said his father on examining it.

Ernest went to bed that night in tears, his head under the pillow. "I had lied to him," he confessed years later. "If he would have waked up I would have told him. I think. But he was tired and sleeping heavily."

+

Summers in northern Michigan also included work. This year there were a large number of house repairs to be done. "To Hemingway chores of that kind were pretty much torture," said Bill Smith, who summered a few miles away. Smith and his two siblings were orphans who lived with an aunt in St. Louis in the winters and escaped north in the summer. Ernest and Bill enjoyed fishing together and shared a love for reading. But it was his sister Katharine who most intrigued Ernest. Slim and small breasted, Katy was not a striking beauty at first glance. Yet when she brushed back her flyaway hair, her green eyes were bewitching. But she was four years his senior, had a boyfriend, and was maddeningly condescending.

Autumn had invariably meant a return to school. The four-story Oak Park and River Forest Township High School, with a palatial front door at the top of the curved stone staircase, was the pride of the village. It succeeded so well in preparing its students that most of them met the admission standards of Yale, Amherst, or Williams and dominated the list of scholarships given by the University of Chicago to the region's students.

Hemingway plowed his way through plane geometry and algebra, biology and zoology, ancient and American history, three years of Latin, and a heavy dose of applied and orchestral music, and he thrived in five classes of English. A cadre of talented English teachers provided topflight instruction. In his first two years they guided Hemingway through *The*

Rime of the Ancient Mariner, Twelfth Night, Pilgrim's Progress, David Copper-field, and *Silas Marner*, among a wide assortment of classical texts. The emphasis in introducing the students to literature was placed on narrative.

Hemingway read *Old Testament Narratives*, an unusual compilation assembled for class instruction by Charles Elbert Rhodes, a Buffalo, New York, high school principal. In explaining his purpose Rhodes praised the "directness and simplicity of the Biblical style," particularly its narrative that grew from its origins as an oral tale. "Hence, short and simple sentences dominate" with a vocabulary of "concrete words, since they produce immediate and vivid impressions." This examination of the literary aspects of the Old Testament, familiar to him as a religious work from Sunday services at the Third Congregational Church, found a receptive audience in the teenager. "That's how I learned to write by reading the Bible," Hemingway told a friend a few years after leaving Oak Park High.

Later came works by Milton, Pope, Spencer, Chaucer, Wordsworth, Shelley, Keats, and Browning. American authors, with the exception of Benjamin Franklin's *Autobiography*, were absent from class as well as in the library. Of the British writers that dominated the prescribed reading lists, Hemingway most liked Rudyard Kipling, who favored an economical style of storytelling. It was not long before he could quote Kipling passages verbatim.

+

Hemingway's work spilled from the class onto the pages of the school's magazine. He made his literary debut with a gruesome tale set in the northern woods. An Indian leaves a bear trap for his white partner, whom he believes stole his money. The man steps into the trap and is consumed by wolves. Realizing he had wrongly accused his partner, the Indian rushes back but is too late. Snagged by another bear trap, he reaches for his rifle to end his life before the wolves return to do it for him. Hemingway followed this story with one about boxing and a third one about a fugitive Indian who killed the game warden and, in turn, meets his death on railroad tracks near Wallon Lake. "The Père Marquette Limited," he wrote, "removed all the traces."

The school newspaper the *Trapeze* also benefited from young Hemingway's skill. A faculty member, recently given the responsibility for the school paper, sought to transform it from an occasionally sloppy publication to a weekly of decent quality. Looking for reporters, the teacher approached Hemingway, having heard of his writing ability from other students.

From his third-floor bedroom Hemingway pounded out contributions on a secondhand typewriter. He began first by accepting an assignment to cover club meetings and school debates before graduating to sports, mimicking the style of Ring Lardner, the famed sportswriter for the *Chicago Tribune*. Writing for the *Trapeze* made for some of Hemingway's happiest hours of his high school years.

By the end of his senior year Hemingway was no longer the underweight, scrawny teenager he had been when he first climbed the stone steps leading into Oak Park High. Tall and with a barrel chest, he caught the attention of girls, exuding confidence from his academic and social prowess. One girl in his class, who confessed to admiring Hemingway's looks, classified him as "egotistical, dogmatic, and somewhat obnoxious." However, she added, "he unquestionably had 'personality plus.'"

On commencement day in June 1917 Hemingway was asked to deliver the class prophecy, a traditional foretelling. With the United States now at war with Germany, he predicted that one classmate would grow rich manufacturing gunpowder, another would become famous for shooting down a Zeppelin, and others would serve as soldiers and Red Cross nurses.

✢

After graduation Hemingway wanted to join the army. The newspapers were full of stories of American boys preparing for battle. Hemingway devoured the recently published novel *The Dark Forest* by Hugh Walpole. The author had been turned down by the British Army because of his eyesight and instead joined the Russian Red Cross. Using his experience at the Russian front, Walpole created a poignant tale of a Red Cross volunteer who falls in love with a nurse in the course of his grisly battlefield work.

The book further convinced Hemingway that remaining behind in the United States was a mistake he would regret all of his life. But the military draft was solely calling up men over the age of twenty-one. The war might end before he reached that age. He could volunteer when he turned eighteen or even now if he gained permission of his parents. But despite the family veneration of its military history—both grandparents having fought in the Civil War—his father would hear nothing of this idea. He told his son that at age seventeen, he was too young to fight. So instead of going to war, Hemingway found himself in a car bouncing its way to northern Michigan.

3

JOHN DOS PASSOS'S SEA VOYAGE FROM NEW YORK TO BORDEAUX ON THE *Chicago* had been like a pleasure cruise despite elevated fears of submarine attacks now that the United States had declared war on Germany. He had whiled away the days lying on deck, his head resting on a life preserver with a book in hand, and he spent the evenings in song and drink. "Oh we're bound for the Hamburg show," the men sang. "And we'll all stick together, in fair or foul weather, for we're going to see the damn show through."

Dos Passos, who had been crossing the Atlantic ever since he was a young child, never enjoyed a passage as much as this one. "Being on board ship," he said, "headed for action at last, after all those frustrating years in what then seemed to me the airless hothouse of college life, changed my mood entirely." Each turn of the ship's screws brought him closer to the war. There had never before been a conflict like the one raging in Europe. If he wanted to be a writer, he had to be *there*.

He befriended another passenger who shared his sense of urgency. John Howard Lawson, a Williams College graduate and aspiring playwright with tousled hair and bright brown eyes, had joined the ambulance corps to escape the draft. Like Dos Passos, Lawson chided himself for his failure to live up to his beliefs. "I was opposed to the war," he said, "but my convictions were not strong enough to risk prison."

The presence of members of the American Expeditionary Forces on board reminded Dos Passos that war lay between him and his dreams of a literary future. One day he found himself within earshot of the two battle-hungry sons of former President Theodore Roosevelt.

"No sir, when this is over, the U.S. will be one of the greatest military nations in the world," said Theodore when Dos Passos made out what the men were talking about.

"The greatest," added his brother Archie.

"Then," continued Theodore, as the conversation drifted back out of hearing range, "we'll be all ready to—"

Dos Passos was apoplectic. In his cabin he penned an account of his eavesdropping to a Harvard friend, calling the Roosevelt boys "Princes of the Blood." The conversation among the presidential offspring was odious because of its truthfulness. In Dos Passos's view the war to which he was rushing was an abomination, not a crusade to make the world safe for democracy.

When the *Chicago* docked in Bordeaux the town's citizens turned out in large numbers to cheer on the Americans as they marched to the train station, and sidewalk cafés offered up drink and food. Dos Passos, one of the few among the Americans who spoke French, was enlisted to buy wine and crusty loaves of bread for the train ride to Paris. Through the window he watched as the French countryside unfolded before him. "Under the wan European sky the fields of ripening grain smoldered with poppies," he said. "Avenues of poplars led to hunched villages. Every village with its steeple and mossy tiles was a picture out of a book of old fairy tales."

+

On the evening of July 2, 1917, Dos Passos and a bevy of ambulance recruits climbed down from a train under the vaulted glass ceiling of Paris's Gare d'Orsay, a magnificent Beaux-Arts building directly across the Seine from the Louvre. The men piled their gear and themselves into horse-drawn taxis and headed out across the City of Light. The streets were cloaked in darkness to diminish the targets offered to German bombers crossing the nighttime sky. Only sparse moonlight illuminated their way in a stillness broken by the clopping of the horses' hooves on the wood-block pavement. Buildings Dos Passos had known as a child loomed in the faint light. Walking through the heavy dark curtain at the door of the hotel, hung to keep the light from spilling out onto the street, Dos Passos felt as if he were walking into a mystery melodrama.

The following morning Dos Passos, Lawson, and the other volunteers located the Norton-Harjes headquarters, which had served previously as the home of the American ambassador. They were sworn into service and dispatched to procure a uniform. Unlike in the military, ambulance volunteers had to purchase their own uniforms from a Parisian couturier on the fashionable rue de la Paix. The tailor fitted Dos Passos for an olive drab tunic made of worsted wool held closed by gray metal buttons and cinched with a wide brown leather belt. Jodhpurs, a soft trench cap, and knee-high laced boots completed the outfit.

That the war would have to wait while the tailor completed his work didn't trouble Dos Passos. Reunited with three Harvard classmates, among whom was his good friend the poet Robert Hillyer, he led the group around the city with credentials to prevent their arrest for being out of uniform. They strolled along the Seine by the Île de la Cité, admired Paris's gothic cathedrals and imperial palaces, refreshed themselves in cafés, inspected the bookstalls mounted along the quay walls, and were propositioned by the city's many prostitutes.

On moonlight nights Dos Passos and friends climbed up to Montmartre to watch the German bombing raids. The darkened city stretched out before them. First they heard the reverberations of antiaircraft guns, then came the wailing of sirens, followed by the humming of airplane engines. Soon a heavy growling sound rose from where the bombs landed. Then everything grew still again and the men descended back down into the city as fire engines hurried up and down streets.

On other nights Dos Passos and his Harvard friends attended the ballet or the opera or stopped in to see the scantily clad dancers at the Folies-Bergère. There might be a war on, but Paris's traditional pleasures remained open. "We had a lovely time wandering about the dark silent Paris," Dos Passos told Rummy, "quite forgetting the war and discipline and duty in our excitement at meeting."

Dos Passos's Paris revelry ended after two weeks when he and his fellow recruits were dispatched to a training camp that had been established on a marquis's hunting preserve north of Paris. They discovered upon reaching the spot that there were no ambulances to practice driving or to learn how to service the often-cantankerous engines. Rather, the men spent days marching about in useless drills. At long last a vehicle was obtained, and they gained a few days of practice before being sent back to Paris to await assignment to the front. Before leaving the encampment Dos Passos heard the distant sound of the artillery and hoped they would soon be booming in his ears.

✛

At the end of July, a month since departing from New York City, Dos Passos received his orders. Along with shipmate Lawson and two friends, including Hillyer, he was to join a section of ambulance drivers posted near Verdun northeast of Paris about sixty miles west of the front. On the train they learned about their destination.

The year before, Verdun had been the site of the war's greatest carnage. In fighting for control of a stretch of land less than four square miles in size, France and Germany had sent three hundred thousand men to their death and another four hundred thousand were wounded or crippled. The French were considered the victors, but it was unclear what they had won aside from a few thousand yards of blood-soaked soil littered with corpses.

As heavy rain descended, Dos Passos gained his first glimpse of the war zone when they approached their destination. The war's destruction reached for miles beyond the actual battlefield. Millions of shells had obliterated villages and turned fields and woods into barren landscapes. For miles, in every direction Dos Passos looked, stretched a wasteland riddled with craters and bisected by trenches in which men had lived and died for three years.

In all months except for a brief time in summer, the trenches were thick with mud that remained long after rainfalls. The wetness gave rise to "trench foot," an affliction in which a soldier's foot turned red or blue and became susceptible to gangrene. Despite frequent rain, nothing seemed to wash away the filth accumulated from the thousands of soldiers in close quarters, turning the trenches into a petri dish for disease, an incubator for lice, and, worst of all, a paradise for vermin of all kind, especially rats. The smell of putrefaction was inescapable. "We had on us the stench of dead bodies," a French soldier in Verdun wrote. "The bread we ate, the stagnant water we drank, everything we touched had a rotten smell, owing to the fact that the earth around us was literally stuffed with corpses."

The almost-constant barrage of shells and mortars took its toll even from soldiers who escaped physical injury from the detonations. The sound was diabolic and unceasing. And to the fear of all soldiers, the shells also delivered poison gas. Despite the prohibition by treaty on the use of poison gas, both sides in the war employed it. Only the month before, the Germans had started lobbing artillery shells with the newest chemical cocktail nicknamed "mustard gas." Its effects were delayed but deadly. After a dozen hours a soldier's body would begin to rot from inside and out, leaving him a mass of blisters, blinded, and fighting for breath. Sometimes the pain was so dreadful that nurses strapped their patients down. "I wish," wrote a nurse, "those people who write so glibly about this being a holy war and the orators who talk so much about going on no matter how long the war lasts and what it may mean, could see a case—to say nothing of ten cases—of mustard gas in its early stages."

✤

Driving through the tiny town of Érize-la-Petite, Dos Passos calculated the shelling had reduced half of the houses to piles of rubble. That night he and a companion walked in the damp night air on the final miles of the road leading to Verdun that had been nicknamed *Voie Sacrée* for its role as a critically important supply route. Dos Passos was disquieted. "This country behind the front has all the stillness of a charnel house," he said, "rather than the comfortable stillness of night."

Although close to the front, the ambulance men were still not called on to do much. With time on their hands, they continued their vacation-like existence of visiting churches, swimming in the Marne, and whiling away the hours in beer gardens while French cooks prepared suppers. Scribbling in his diary one night, Dos Passos listed their major preoccupations as searching for latrines, omelets and wine, and pleasant spots in the fields or woods to lie about and read.

One evening Dos Passos and two of his friends were invited to a local schoolteacher's house in Châlons. They sat around a marble table in a terraced garden filled with fragrant roses and balsam and looked down on the street. Their first sips of wine in the serene garden were interrupted by the rumbling of trucks, churning up a cloud of dust that rose and settled on the table and flowers. The soldiers in the truck were also shrouded in the white dust and looked to Dos Passos like corpses. "The poor young ones," said their hostess, "they know they are going to their deaths."

They tried to make polite conversation. For three years French infantrymen, given the name *poilus* (hairy), had been gathered up, trucked up roads like this one, and ordered to shoot at Germans. No end seemed in sight, and no spot seemed as deadly as Verdun. "The very name of which froze us with dread," wrote a French soldier in his diary. Bottles of Pinard, a foul-tasting wine supplied in abundance, anesthetized the men.

Dos Passos knew he was nearing his time to be at the trenches. The drivers were told to reposition their ambulances in preparation for a rumored Allied offensive. In the days remaining until the French launched their attack, Dos Passos and several other drivers loitered among the ruins of a villa in the small town of Récicourt. Although the house had been destroyed and the furnishings looted, the garden remained intact, full of fragrant roses and other blooming flowers. "I can't imagine a more charming place, though even here lingers a faint odor of poison gas," Dos Passos wrote in his diary. He felt inspired. "The great war novel," he wrote, "is forming gradually in my mind."

In the fragrant garden Dos Passos took his first stab at beginning the book. "War was the theme of the time," said Dos Passos. "I was in a passion to put down everything, immediately as it happened, exactly as I saw it." He asked his friend Hillyer to cowrite the novel. The two would-be authors walked into the village and found a shop that still possessed school supplies. After purchasing several *cahiers*, the little notebooks used by French schoolchildren to inscribe their lessons, the pair began to write.

They considered using Compton Mackenzie's *Sinister Street* as a model, a novel they had relished while at Harvard. But Dos Passos could not shake the more recent impressions he had from reading the gritty *Under Fire: The Story of a Squad* by Henri Barbusse, a Frenchman whose experiences in the trenches provided one of the first fictional portrayals of the war. Like Hemingway, Dos Passos had also been deeply impressed by Hugh Walpole's *Dark Forest*. He wanted to add his name to the list of Great War authors. For the novel he and Hillyer invented a young boy, whom they called Martin Howe, and began writing of his adventures in a world of unfeeling grownups. They took turns writing chapters and kept their work secret from others in their section, fearing they would be razzed for their literary pretentiousness.

But the writing of the novel came to a halt. On August 20 the anticipated offensive in Verdun got underway. Dos Passos and a Texan named James Parshall were assigned a Model T Ford from the fleet. When the troops saw ambulances gather they took it as an ominous sign. They presumed the vehicles were being positioned because they were about to be ordered to undertake an attack. "They must have thought us a collection of scavenger crows," said Dos Passos.

More nimble than the heavier Fiats, the Fords, with their four-cylinder water-cooled engine, could hit forty-five miles per hour on a good road. Not that they would get much of a chance to do that. Since the rain had returned, it was an enormous challenge to merely navigate the water-soaked, putty-colored roads. Pitted with shell holes, the roads were nicknamed "Dip of Death" or "Dead Man's Land." At night the ambulances ran with their headlights turned off, lest they became a target. To find their way through the darkness, Dos Passos or Parshall would either perch on the front fender or walk ahead with a white handkerchief draped from an epaulet.

Dos Passos and Parshall's ambulance joined a caravan of vehicles rushing back and forth from the front to ferry the hundreds of wounded men back for medical attention. It was like the children's game of dodgeball but on a deadly scale, as German shells descended on them. Their ambulance was punctured with holes from the shrapnel. The noise of the exploding shells provoked terror among the newcomers, who had been told to keep their mouths open to safeguard their eardrums. The men driving the ambulances quickly learned the rhythm of the cannons, each taking a different amount of time for reloading, and dashed from one location to another during the interludes.

In each trip back from the fighting Dos Passos's ambulance was loaded down with more wounded soldiers than it was meant to carry. Sometimes those soldiers with the more manageable injuries stood on the running boards or squeezed in on the front seat between Dos Passos and Parshall. "At every lurch, the wounded groaned horribly," said Dos Passos.

Then there was the gas. Thicker than air, it clung to the ground like fog. "The smell of death changed to the bitter-sweet smell of mustard gas," said Lawson, who was driving one of the ambulances nearby. On his first night at the front Dos Passos saw green-colored wraiths of gas curling like serpents above the blackened battlefield soil. He and his companion abandoned their ambulance, fortunately empty of wounded soldiers, and made a frantic dash to the entrance of a dugout.

Once inside, a soldier helped them strap their gas masks on. Over the course of the night Dos Passos switched out masks six times as the filters lost their effectiveness. "Couldn't see at all through masks," said the soldier who had come to their aid. "Dead horses and shell holes all around us and gas even came through our masks. As Dos and I poked our head out of the door, a Hun shell lifted a tree two feet in diameter from in front of the entrance and laid it over the dugout."

On some runs the remaining presence of gas was so strong that Dos Passos and Parshall got out of the ambulance every few miles to vomit in the roadside ditch. The horses pulling French 75mm field guns heaved and gasped, their eyes bulging and nostrils spurting blood. "I shall never forget," he wrote after one such run, "the frightened eyes of the horses, choking on gas, standing beside their overturned gun carriages, waiting for the shell that will finish them." That night Dos Passos wrote to Rummy that he could not imagine "a more hellish experience."

But he took to his tasks with energy, fearlessness, and indifference to danger. The men worked continuously, sometimes seventy hours with hardly any rest, hauling stretchers bearing the wounded in overburdened ambulances down nearly impassible roads, repairing engines, and manning sentry duty to prevent theft or, worse, sabotage of their vehicles. They caught what sleep they could on stretchers in deep, rat-infested dugouts, known as *abris*, sometimes only two hundred yards from the German trenches. It was a long way from the dorms of Choate and Harvard.

At rest Dos Passos joined other drivers sitting on boxes or perched on the hoods of their ambulances to watch the dogfights among the German and French planes dodging about in the sky like animals at play. In the night sky the planes and their lights seemed like shooting stars.

✦

The war Dos Passos had so wanted to witness now lay before him. What he and Lawson had imagined with schoolboy excitement on the voyage over was overtaken by the abiding horror of it all. "The world had become a different place," said Lawson, "and we had to register the change in the only way that was possible to us, by putting words on paper."

As the French celebrated the success of their offensive, which grabbed only a few miles of corpse-filled trenches, it was the ambulances that brought back the wounded *poilus*. The gruesomeness of what Dos Passos saw left him wordless. "I'm dying to write—but all my methods of doing things in the past merely disgust me now, all former methods are damned inadequate," he wrote in his diary. "Horror is so piled on horror that there can be no more." But he still made furtive efforts to write in his notebooks. "I want to be able to express later—all of this—all the tragedy and hideous excitement of it," he scribbled. "I must experience more of it and more—the gray crooked fingers of the dead, the dark look of dirty mangled bodies, their groans and joltings in the ambulances, the vast tomtom of the guns, the ripping tear shells make when they explode, the song of shells outgoing, like vast woodcocks—their contented whirr as near their mark." And on he went with his list possessed by a gambler's exhilaration.

"When one shell comes I want another, nearer, nearer," he wrote. "I want to throw the dice at every turn with the roisterer Death. . . . Tomorrow I shall live to the dregs or today I shall die." To endure what he witnessed, Dos Passos put on an emotional veneer like the mud that caked his clothes, boots, face, and hands. One day, not long after the offensive had ended, Dos Passos opened a can of sardines in a medical tent as doctors sawed off the leg of a soldier at a nearby operating table. "God knows," he said, "I was still morbidly sensitive to other people's pain, but I had learned to live in the world and stand it."

His anger and opposition to the war grew. The men, in his mind, were expendable pawns unwilling to resist their dispatch to war. Worse, he wrote to Rummy, the soldiers were "too unimaginative not to see which way they ought to turn their guns." It was not just the French who were victims, thought Dos Passos, but the German soldiers as well whom he carried in his ambulances. "None of the poor devils whose mangled dirty bodies I take to the hospital in my ambulance really give a damn about the aims of this ridiculous affair."

It was to Dos Passos's good fortune that censors did not see the letter. The French government was trying to repress as well as keep secret mutinies by infantrymen. Only a few hundred miles to the west Dos Passos's friends E. E. Cummings and William Slater Brown were locked up in an internment camp for their lack of verbal caution. Brown's intemperate letters home, unlike Dos Passos's, had fallen into the hands of the authorities. Dragged in with Brown for questioning, Cummings was on the verge of being cleared when an official asked whether he hated the Germans. "No," he replied, adding quickly, "I like the French very much." The reply sent him to join Brown in lockup, where the two awaited a hearing that could result in them being either freed or charged with treason.

✦

On the first of September the fighting ended for Dos Passos. His ambulance section was moved away from the front. Back in the Récicourt villa garden with time on his hands, Dos Passos reflected on what he had witnessed at the front. The French soldiers he talked to all realized the futility of the war and blamed greed, stubbornness, and the stupidity of the governments for the continued slaughter. "Oh but why talk?" Dos Passos lamented to Rummy. "It's so useless—There is one thing one learns in France today, the resignation of despair."

American troops could be seen everywhere now, growing in number every day. It was the death knell of the volunteer ambulance corps. It was one thing to have wounded French soldiers carted about by gentlemen volunteers, but it would certainly not do for American soldiers. At the end of August Richard Norton wired his brother in the United States that he was closing down his ambulance service. From now on the American Expeditionary Forces would be in charge.

Norton, in the company of Red Cross and army officials, arrived at Dos Passos's encampment to deliver the news. "As gentlemen volunteers you enlisted in this service," Norton said, "as gentlemen volunteers I bid you farewell." The choice given to the men was to enlist in the army or return to the United States when released from duty. Dos Passos gave no thought to joining the army and briefly considered fleeing to Spain.

Upon returning to Paris, Dos Passos learned of Cummings's imprison-
ment and tried to contact his friend. Knowing of Cummings's fate might
have tempered the speech in some men, but not in Dos Passos's case.
In a small, cold room on Rue Descartes near the Pantheon on the Left
Bank of Paris, he resumed work on his novel, the one he had begun with
Hillyer. Its contents were the literary summation of Dos Passos's wrath
against the military and the war. It would have driven French censors into
apoplexy had they seen it.

Desperate to remain in Europe but beyond the clutches of the military,
which was looking for stray Americans, Dos Passos decided to apply to
join a new American Red Cross section going to Italy. Competition was
stiff, but his experience won him a place.

Early one November morning, before much of Paris was awake, Dos
Passos and several dozen men loaded their belongings into a fleet of ambulances surrounding the Red Cross headquarters. In the fog the men
moving about in their bulky leather jackets appeared to a newspaper correspondent as "grotesque shadows in the midst." The journalist had come
to watch the caravan's departure for Italy, another of the city's seemingly
endless comings and goings to the warfront. For Dos Passos, he was trading one battlefield for another. He had been in the shadow of death at
Verdun, and now Italy's warfront awaited.

4

SITTING IN A PASSENGER CAR ON THE CHICAGO AND ALTON RAILROAD bound for Kansas City on October 15, 1917, Ernest Hemingway wondered whether the White Sox had won the final game in the World Series. A news and candy dealer coming through the car gave him the answer he hoped for. "White Sox, four to two," said the man as the train neared the Mississippi River. It was momentary bit of pleasure on a ride that was taking him miles from where he wanted to go. America had joined the war, and yet Hemingway still could not get his father's permission to enlist. All summer his grandfather had dutifully sent him copies of the *Chicago Tribune* full of reports on the thousands of young Americans who were heading east to war. Instead, he was on a train going in the opposite direction, bound for a cub reporter's job on the *Kansas City Star*.

Ernest's uncle Tyler Hemingway had secured the job for his nephew, using his connections as a prominent Kansas City businessman. For its part the newspaper was glad to get another body. The draft had decimated its staff of young men. When the train pulled into Kansas City Ernest's uncle was at Union Station. He drove his nephew home to his Victorian manor in a neighborhood with manicured lawns and shrubs much like Oak Park.

Not long after settling in, Hemingway caught up with one of his Michigan summer gang of friends who had also made an unsuccessful effort to court the green-eyed Katy Smith. He had a job working for a heating oil company in Kansas City, and the two made plans to find a place of their own. In trading the luxury of his uncle's home for a small, out-of-the-way apartment, Hemingway obtained the freedom he craved. Far from his father and no longer under the watch of his uncle, Hemingway was now truly on his own.

Entering the three-story *Kansas City Star* building for his first day of work, Hemingway stepped into a palace of words. In a cavernous expanse crammed with desks, copyboys dashed about, phones rang, typewriters clattered, and, above it all, editors yelled. Like orchestral conductors, their job was to channel the work of the disparate players into a single score that came off the press every afternoon. For an aspiring writer this was paradise.

A newspaper imbued writing with a sense of urgency and importance. Words crafted in the morning were in print by day's end. A reporter riding a bus home could watch commuters actually reading his work. Writer's block was never a permissible condition. The printing press waited for no one. A breaking news story not on an editor's desk by deadline never appeared.

Newsrooms were also a place where one could find experienced writers willing to advise the inexperienced. The *Kansas City Star* was no different. One of its rewrite men was already legendary while still only twenty-six years old. "He could carry four stories in his head and go to the telephone and take a fifth and then write all five at full speed to catch an edition," an awestruck Hemingway said.

The paper's assistant city editor gave Hemingway his desk, his assignments, and his introduction to the *Kansas City Star* literary catechism. Contained in a style sheet developed by the newspaper's late founder William Rockhill Nelson, it listed 110 tenets that were to be obeyed like religious commandments in the newsroom.

Printed in small type in three columns on a single side of paper, the instructions began with "Use short sentences. Use short first paragraphs. Use vigorous English." From there it covered a wealth of topics from splitting infinitives (frowned upon), to careless use of words such as *also* or *only* (they can give unintended meanings to a sentence), to eliminating superfluous words and adjectives (unneeded), and ending with an injunction against using *A woman of the name of Mary Jones*, which implied disrespect: "Never use it even referring to street walkers."

"They were the best rules I ever learned for the business of writing," Hemingway recalled years later.

✛

Kansas City was a booming metropolis of three hundred thousand that was shaking off its frontier town roots. It offered a feast of violent crime, unconcealed bawdiness, and human drama for an ambitious reporter. At first Hemingway was assigned to the quiet Federal Building beat. It was safe but boring. After a month he persuaded his boss to assign him to cover the police station, hospital, and the train depot. Now Hemingway had the fodder a city reporter craved. In the hospital, for instance, he could hear firsthand accounts from the victims of crime he had learned about at the police station. On some nights he even rode in ambulances.

Hemingway loved every part of the work. He excitedly reported to his father that he had a desk and a *typewriter*. "Everything we write is on the Typewriter," Hemingway scribbled on the back of a police department bulletin. He couldn't be pulled away from the paper. On some nights, when it was too late to catch a bus home, he would make his bed in a bathtub at an office used by reporters in the city's main hotel. On nights he was home he would keep his roommate up with tales of his work.

At first Hemingway's reporting comprised short, poignant items. It was the kind of material a newspaper counted upon to fill the holes around the main news of the day. After a while he graduated to longer articles, demonstrating a knack for selecting telling details and using quotations that revealed character all told in an unadorned matter-of-fact style.

In January 1918 Hemingway put together into an article his observations of his nights at the city hospital's indigent care ward. He began with a description of an ambulance attendant pushing a stretcher down the corridor of the General Hospital. The patient was identified by a receipt he had in his pocket for a $10 payment toward a house in a Nebraska town. "The surgeon opened the swollen eyelids," Hemingway wrote. "The eyes were turned to the left. 'A fracture on the left side of the skull,' he said to the attendants who stood about the table. 'Well, George, you're not going to finish paying for that home of yours.'"

Others patients, such as a man who had been cut by a razor in a fight or a robber shot by a store clerk, survived. "And so the work goes on," wrote Hemingway. "For one man it means a clean bed and prescriptions with whisky in it, possible, and for another, it is a place in the potters' field."

Hemingway's stories were usually not front-page material. But a few weeks prior to his hospital tale he clipped a long front-page account of how a tax agent was mistakenly shot by detectives in a revolver battle. He sent it to his sister, passing it off as his own work. His father Clarence scribbled at the top of the clipping, "Ernest's work entire column." Like the dead quail for which he took credit when hunting with his father, Ernest was willing to let his father believe something not true.

+

On most days the front page of the *Star* was consumed by news of the war, much of it with the aim of supporting America's entry into the conflict. A Kansas City minister, for instance, penned a number of articles for the *Star* describing the fighting and the work of British Red Cross volunteers he saw on a visit to the Italian front. It was, according to the man, the "most romantic of the battle fronts. Here war retains something of its old glamour."

Stories such as those by the minister heightened Hemingway's desire to go overseas and soon. He was now eighteen years old. No longer needing his parents' permission, he spoke more freely about joining the military. Perhaps he could return to Michigan for one more summer, he told them, but he couldn't stay away from the war any longer than that. "Believe me," he wrote to his sister, "I will go not because of any love of gold braid glory etc. but because I couldn't face any body after the war and not have been in it."

At his desk one day Hemingway tapped furiously at his typewriter, pausing periodically to unjam the typebars. When he reached the end of his article he pulled the paper out of the roller and called for a copy boy to take his story to the city desk. "When I get a little excited this damn type mill goes haywire on me," Hemingway told the new man at the adjacent desk.

"Your thoughts are faster than your fingers," replied the man.

"Something like that," said Hemingway, rising and proffering his hand to the new reporter. But Hemingway knew who he was. His name was Theodore B. Brumback and his homecoming had been heralded on the front page of the paper. The twenty-two-year-old had gone overseas in July, worked for the Norton-Harjes Ambulance Corps, and had been dismissed, along with Dos Passos, when the service was disbanded in September.

As he told stories of his time with the ambulance corps, Brumback fired up Hemingway. Since coming to Kansas City Hemingway had told friends and family that he had failed at his various attempts to enlist in the military, blaming his weak left eye. The army may well have turned him away but in other instances was willing to take men with poor vision, including nearsighted Harry Truman. But Hemingway managed to occasionally wear a uniform by enlisting in the Missouri National Guard. It did not, however, get him to the war. Brumback's plan could.

✛

The Red Cross was in need of men in Italy, where Dos Passos and other veterans of the Norton-Harjes Ambulance Corps now worked. On February 22, 1918, the *Star* published a call for volunteers specifically seeking four drivers and one canteen worker. The posting was appealing to Hemingway especially because of Hugh Walpole's novel he had read that summer, which told the story of a Red Cross volunteer's battlefield life and love affair with a nurse. Hemingway and Brumback immediately mailed applications to the Red Cross office in St. Louis. Brumback had a glass eye from an accident in college, but it had not kept him from service as an ambulance driver. So both men assumed their poor eyesight would not be an issue.

But the recruiter replied he had been told to call off his efforts to find ambulance drivers. He promised, however, to keep their applications on file. Hemingway's six months with the paper came to an end, and he returned to Oak Park. In early May, when Hemingway was with his family, a telegram arrived from the St. Louis Red Cross office. It told him to resubmit his application promptly—there were now openings.

Hemingway grabbed a train and caught up with Brumback in New York City. The Red Cross provided the two recruits with hotel rooms in

Greenwich Village and sent them off for physical exams. The oculist who saw Hemingway gave him a passing mark but told him to get glasses. They were also fitted with US Army officer's uniforms, to which Hemingway added a pair of $30 cordovan leather boots. "Our uniforms are regular United States Army Officers' and look like a million dollars," Hemingway wrote his family. "Privates and non coms must salute us smartly."

On May 19 Hemingway marched with thousands of nurses and members of Red Cross auxiliary units down Fifth Avenue to the beat of marching bands from church, military letter carrier organizations, and even members of the New York Institution for Deaf and Mute Band. For a time they were led by President Woodrow Wilson. Cheers rose from the crowd when 150 nurses dressed in white and wearing red scarves formed into a human red cross. For more than six hours the men and women flowed down the avenue. The president took his leave halfway through but asked his driver to take the car by the remaining portions of the parade so they could see him. Hemingway recounted his participation in the parade to his parents, claiming his group had been the star attraction reviewed by President Wilson.

The truth-stretching account of his participation in the parade made his mother and father proud, but not the fib that followed closely on its heels. For some reason Hemingway thought it funny to write a letter home that he was getting married, causing his mother to reach for the smelling salts. It required a telegram explaining that it had been a joke, followed by a contrite series of letters to restore familial calm.

✠

A few days after the parade Hemingway and his companion, Brumback, boarded the *Chicago*, the same French ship that had ferried Dos Passos to war the previous year. Under the cover of night the vessel carrying about seventy-five other Red Cross recruits slipped out of New York City harbor with its running lights off because of a reported U-boat sighting. The crossing, however, turned out to be uneventful, aside from some rough weather. As the ship approached France, lookouts spotted a small raft bobbing in the water. The ship changed course, fearing it was a German submarine trap. Hemingway, eager for his first taste of battle, felt cheated by the evasive maneuvers.

Following Dos Passos's path of eleven months earlier, they made landfall in Bordeaux. The men spent a bacchanalian night drinking French red wine before catching the train for Paris, where the war was taking a toll on the city. Since March the Germans had been using a new long-range gun that peppered explosive shells on Paris from seventy-five miles away. The guns were highly inaccurate, but nonetheless they brought the war into the city. One of the shells landed on a church during Good Friday services and killed one hundred parishioners.

As Hemingway and the men exited from the train station German shelling was underway.

"Come on, Ted," Hemingway said. "We're going to see something."

Jamming themselves and their luggage into a small, two-cylinder taxi, Hemingway told Brumback to use his French to get the driver to take them to the parts of the city that were being shelled. Unlike Dos Passos, who had witnessed bombing raids on Paris the year before from the safety of a hilltop, Hemingway wanted to drive into the line of fire.

"We'll get a story for *The Star*," Hemingway said, "that'll make their eyes pop back in Kansas City."

"There's no sense in deliberately exposing ourselves to danger," Brumback said. "How would this look in the *Star*: Two Kansas Citizens were killed today while sightseeing in Paris?"

Despite Brumback's protestations and the driver's reluctance, the latter problem cured by a large increase in the fare, the men set off in search of falling shells. After an unproductive hour of chase, the men arrived at L'église de la Madeleine, only a mile from the railroad station where they started. At first the wailing noise they heard from above was like that of an approaching train. "It sounded as if it were going to land right in the taxi with us," said Brumback. The shell passed them and struck the facade of the church, decapitating the head of a large recessed statue of St. Luke.

The close call with the shell did not diminish Hemingway's impatience to see action. "I wish they'd hurry up and ship us off to the front," he said. He got his wish.

✛

On June 6, 1918, Hemingway and his fellow ambulance drivers boarded the Paris-Lyon-Mediterranean Express bound for Milan. In boxcars, with their legs dangling through the open doorways, the men watched as the beautiful scenery unscarred by war passed by. When the train pulled into Milan they learned that in the outskirts of the city the storage site of a Swiss munitions factory had just exploded. Hemingway and a few others from the corps were dispatched to render aid. Thirty-five people had been killed, many of whom were women.

The men fanned out to collect the bodies and search for human remains. The teenaged Hemingway, who until this moment in his life had only seen corpses in the manner of birds and small animals he shot in Michigan, faced carnage like that from a Francisco de Goya depiction of war. Arms, legs, backs, torsos, heads, and bits of hair clung to the barbed-wire fence surrounding the place. Hemingway and Milford Baker, another Red Cross volunteer, grabbed a stretcher and made their way to the wall of human fragments. The first thing the two men saw was the headless and legless body of a woman whose intestines lay exposed. "Hemmie and I nearly passed out cold," said Baker, "but gritted our teeth and laid the thing on the stretcher."

When they got back to Milan in the late evening other Red Cross men immediately besieged them. Like adolescent males basking in the glow of their lost virginity, Baker and Hemingway savored the moment. They were the envy of the group. "Having a wonderful time!!!" Hemingway scribbled on a postcard to his friends at the Kansas City Star. "Had my first baptism of fire my first day here, when an entire munitions plant exploded. . . . I go to the front tomorrow. Oh, Boy!!! I'm glad I'm in it."

The following day Hemingway received his orders. He was being assigned to the American Red Cross Section Four in Schio, a small town in the foothills of the Dolomites, a mountain range about 150 miles northeast of Milan. Once again he boarded a train in the company of Baker and fourteen others. In Vicenza, ambulances carried them the rest of the way.

They drove through rolling farmland and into the cobblestoned street of Schio. Passing a square with a sculpture of the General Giuseppe Garibaldi, they came to a second square with the city's cathedral and the Albergo due Spadi restaurant. The driver said it was the best place to eat. At last they reached the Red Cross facility, an abandoned factory building that the town's wool-making business had used before the war. Its garage, with a paved courtyard, was perfect for maintaining the ambulances.

Hemingway found a bed on the second floor among the cots that had been set up where wool had once been stored.

✛

In Schio Hemingway was assigned one of the battleship-gray Fiat ambulances with a red cross on the roof to deter aerial attacks. Several times he navigated the ponderous vehicle up a steep winding road so narrowed by rows of barbed wire that the ambulances were scarred with scratches. At the end of the road he came to the backside of the Italian army battling Austro-Hungarian troops. At first aid stations he would either pick up six wounded soldiers in stretchers or a dozen men with lighter wounds capable of sitting upright for the return trip to the hospital in Schio. In the evening Hemingway joined his comrades at long refectory tables where Italian waiters served pasta, rabbit stew, fried eggs, dark bread, and pots of apricot jam along with large quantities of wine.

Hemingway had only been at work for a few days in June 1918 when a pair of drivers from the other section, both Harvard men, sat down by his side in the mess hall and introduced themselves. The taller of the two said his name was John Dos Passos.

5

THE UNTRUSTWORTHY FIAT AMBULANCE ASSIGNED TO DOS PASSOS AND his partner, Harvard-educated Englishman Sydney van Kleeck Fairbanks, had broken down delivering patients to Schio. The Italian-made vehicles were so notoriously unreliable that Dos Passos had earlier composed a refrain in a poem to them while awaiting repairs in Milan.

> Fiat 4, Fiat 4,
> Oh mecanician of Milano
> When will she roll, my Fiat 4
> Piano, signore, va piano.

Now, while once again awaiting the mechanics to restore life to their ambulance, Dos Passos and Fairbanks had gone to get a bite to eat in the mess hall and come across Ernest Hemingway. Amidst the clatter of plates and the jocular bantering, the older, more experienced Dos Passos sat for a spell and chatted with the new recruit. The two Chicago natives found they had a lot in common, and their steady banter made Fairbanks feel left out. Dos Passos was struck by Hemingway's handsome looks and seemingly boundless energy. But the meal ended, as work had to resume. The Fiat was running again, and Dos Passos took his leave. Soon both men forgot the other's name, and the moment took up residence in the dimmest portions of their memories until years later.

✛

Six months earlier in November 1917, when Dos Passos had joined the Italy-bound ambulance convoy, his spirits had been high. He had been once again in the company of friends. Lawson, the aspiring playwright he had met on the boat passage from New York, was among the drivers, as well as a few of Dos Passos's Harvard classmates. From Paris they made their way in their ambulances like tourists up the Loire Valley through the wintery ashen-gray forests and across the barren wine country of Macon, down the Soâne River and eventually into the warmth and sunlight of Midi. Along the way they encountered castles, turreted churches, Roman arches, and other irresistible distractions.

On the road the men never lacked for entertainment. In Marseille, where they stopped to repair their trucks, Dos Passos went for dinner with one of his fellow drivers to a dockside restaurant where the waitresses demonstrated unusual skills in retrieving the coins left on the corner of the table as tips. To the pleasure of the male patrons, the women lifted their skirts and grasped the coins with the outer lips of their vulvae. "Waitresses, bar maids picking up pennies in their cunts!" Dos Passos wrote that night in his diary. "Bah one has seen it every day of one's life."

Diary bravado aside, Dos Passos remained reluctant to join Lawson and his other companions in their pursuit of sex. "The people I'm with want to go whoring. I wish I did," Dos Passos wrote several nights later in his diary. "Why people think it is worth the trouble I can't imagine." Not that Dos Passos was a virgin—Paris had resolved that issue. Yet for him sex without love or attraction was unappealing, a sentiment perhaps tied to his bastard origins, a stigma in his era. On this trip Dos Passos reread passages of Petronius's *Satyricon*, in which the narrator's male lover is continuously enticed away by others. "It brings out the tragedy of lust," Dos Passos wrote.

As they resumed their drive, the ambulances, particularly the Fiats, continued to keep the men busy with frequent mechanical troubles, and it took until December for the caravan to cross into Italy. The arrival of fifty new Ford ambulances permitted the group to abandon some of their most ill-tempered vehicles. They were a gift of the American Poet Ambulance fund in New York, which had raised sufficient funds for yet another hundred such vehicles.

The writer and diplomat Robert Underwood Johnson had launched the organization. He enlisted the aid of forty-three poets and writers to solicit funds. The committee counted among its ranks the remarkable novelist who wrote under the name Mrs. Schuyler van Rensselaer; William Dudley Foulke, a noted critic of the Ku Klux Klan and an early president of the American Woman Suffrage Association; and Richard Francis Burton, who when not penning poems, explored the far reaches of the earth, bringing back accounts of the sexual lives of its inhabitants as well as his measurements of the male sexual organs he encountered. The organization embossed its stationery with an engraving of a motor ambulance being pulled by Pegasus and a line from Robert Browning: "Open my heart and you will see / Graved inside of it, 'Italy.'"

In the courtyard of an aging Milan palace, festooned with crossed Italian and American flags, the new and old ambulances were parked in a horseshoe pattern facing a podium where military officials in full regalia welcomed the men and their machines. Dos Passos stood at attention for review. Unlike his service with the Norton-Harjes Ambulance Corps in France, the drivers here were to be soldiers in a propaganda war. The ambulances weren't merely intended to save lives of Italian soldiers but to signal to the nation that American troops were on their way.

The compliant Italian press praised in breathless prose the arrival of the drivers. The drivers are a link between the armies of Italy and America, began one newspaper account. "They come as a message of sympathy from the American people who have gladly and readily assumed their share of the world's burden in caring for the wounded, relieving the sick and suffering, cheering the lonely wives and children and in ministering to the thousands of wants to which distressed humanity is heir."

On New Year's Eve 1918 Dos Passos overheard remarks of two drunken officers that rang true. That night Major Guy Lowell, the man in charge of Red Cross operations in Italy, and his companion spoke openly that the ambulance crews were here to convince the Italians that America's entry into the war would turn the tide of the conflict. "God, it made you want to vomit to hear it," Dos Passos wrote in his diary. "So we are here to help cajole the poor devils of Italians into fighting—they don't know what, they don't care why." The virulent loathing of war from his time in Verdun came back. "Bitter hate is the only protection one has against the cozening influences in a world rampant with colossal asininity," he wrote.

✦

By late January 1918 Dos Passos had taken up his duties in Bassano del Grappa, fifty miles to the northwest of Venice. It was close enough to the fighting to be shelled but was a calm spot in comparison to the French warfront where Dos Passos had worked the previous summer. The work was also vastly different. Instead of suffering from bullet and shrapnel wounds, most of the men they brought back from the trenches had frost-bite or dysentery. The Italian soldiers kept their heads down while the government procured a fresh supply of armaments from America. It was far removed from the life-and-death ambulance runs of Verdun.

Boredom descended. Garrisoned in a drafty villa with gasoline stoves hardly capable of heating water much less the cavernous rooms, Dos Passos pulled a blanket around himself and worked on the manuscript he had started in France with his friend Hillyer. But when he read an excerpt to Lawson and another aspiring writer, they were unimpressed. "Their sum of criticism was that things are too jerky, not elaborated enough and that too much is left unsaid, so that the unfortunate reader wallows desperately in a slough of constant misunderstandings," Dos Passos wrote in his diary. "I rather agree with them that it isn't done successful."

Dos Passos figured he could improve the writing, but of greater concern to him was that the manuscript had not yet reached the point when his protagonist experienced the war. No matter how hard he tried since arriving at the French front, nothing of what he wrote about the war satisfied him. "God! I have a brain like a peanut," Dos Passos angrily penned in his diary. He knew the past year had stripped him of what he deemed his sophomoric sentimentalism. "I suppose I must thank the war for some of it," he confessed in his diary. "In fact I'm a much heartier son of a bitch than I used to be, much readier to slap my cock against the rocks of fact."

Frustrated, bored, and despondent, he stewed. Matters were made even bleaker by his inability to learn anything about the fate of Cummings and Brown, who had been imprisoned by the French for their seditious views. "I sympathize with him so thoroughly," Dos Passos wrote Cummings's mother, "and my letters being anything but prudent, that I expected I'd be in the same boat but the censor evidently didn't notice me."

Dos Passos knew censors sifted through all the mail. A driver in his section had already been threatened with a court martial because his correspondence had allegedly divulged military information and had been critical of the Allies. It was also of no help to the man's case that his name was Heine Krieger. He escaped punishment but was forced to resign.

The United States was at war not only with the Central Powers but also against words. The US Espionage Act permitted sending citizens to prison for promoting the success of the nation's enemies and for obstructing by speech or writing the enlistment of soldiers or encouraging disloyalty. The Sedition Act provided for fines and prison terms to anyone who chose to "utter, print, write, or publish any disloyal, profane, scurrilous, or abusive language about the form of government of the United States." Using its new powers, the government arrested and prosecuted more than fifteen hundred of its citizens, most famously imprisoning Eugene Debs after he made a speech in which he urged resistance to the military draft.

Nonetheless, Dos Passos continued to fill his correspondence with an invective stream of attacks on the war, politicians, capitalists, and his superiors. It was one thing to pour anger into the manuscript he kept with him but a more dangerous matter to do so in a letter that others might read.

A censor intercepted one of Dos Passos's letters. Written in French, the letter was addressed to a Spanish friend. Dos Passos told his friend that it was up to others in countries like Spain, which had remained out of the war, to make revolution, even violently, in order to safeguard humanity. "For all the things of the mind, for art, and for everything that is needed in the world," he wrote, "war—I mean modern war—is death."

"From a distance the war must seem a little theoretical, but here, or anywhere on the front, I assure you it is a wholly different matter," he continued. "It is boredom, slavery to all the military stupidities, the most fascinating misery. . . . It is nothing but an enormous, tragic digression in the lives of these people."

A translated copy of the letter was put on the desk of Captain Robert W. Bates, who was in charge of the ambulances and rolling kitchens. A native Californian, Bates had already served an earlier tour of duty with ambulances in France and, as a result, was given considerable authority over the men. He had already warned the men under his command to temper remarks sent home. "Every line of our letters is read and the Italians are very sensitive," he told his family. "That is why you will notice that if I happen to mention them in my letters it is always in terms of admiration."

Bates read Dos Passos's letter and contacted his superior Major Guy Lowell, one of the drunken men whose talk of drivers being used as propaganda had so enraged Dos Passos on New Year's Eve. Bates urged Lowell to dishonorably discharge the author of the offensive screed. In Bates's view Dos Passos was endangering relations between the United States and Italy by ignoring warnings and the example made of Heine. "It is about time we had another object lesson," he told his superior. "I have no sympathy for him."

"The hounds are on the scent," Dos Passos scribbled in his diary. His six-month term of service was coming to a close in May 1918, and this created a problem for Captain Bates in charge of the ambulance crews. Despite his wish to rid himself of Dos Passos, he did not want to lose the services of veteran drivers at this crucial moment. The new recruits, whose ranks included Hemingway, had still not reached the front and were untrained. "We were in a precarious position," Bates wrote in his journal. "We asked the old men to stay on for a few days until they could be replaced, and most of them agreed to do so." Bates's plan of teaching Dos Passos an "object lesson" had to be postponed. In extending the service of the volunteers into June, he made it possible for Hemingway and Dos Passos to break bread together in the midst of the war.

✦

Dos Passos was not alone in facing Bates's accusation of disloyalty. When he and several friends went to Red Cross Headquarters in Rome to learn about other postings that might be open, they were given a cold shoulder. "We are in Rome pending all sorts of things under the ridiculous accusations of being pro-German," Dos Passos wrote to a friend in the United States. "The whole affair is wonderfully absurd and rather diverting. But it shows the canker is growing." Bates may have failed to punish Dos Passos while under his command, but he made sure the man could not entirely escape consequences for his disloyalty. Instead of advising Dos Passos to look for more work with the Red Cross, Major Lowell in Rome told him he should return to the United States. There was, he hinted, a black mark on his record.

"What for?" asked Dos Passos. Lowell said nothing. In the ensuing silence Dos Passos realized he was being accused of disloyalty. He was entering the shadowy world of a loyalty inquisition that had kept his friend E. E. Cummings behind bars for months. He told the major he had obeyed Red Cross regulations, but as an American he had the right to his own ideas. Lowell muttered something inaudible about letters.

"He seemed," said Dos Passos, "embarrassed to have to tell me he wasn't at liberty to explain anything further." Dos Passos conceded he might have been injudicious in his letters to friends or to a Spanish correspondent as well as in his letters in support of Cummings and Brown. Lowell viewed the admissions as compounding the offense.

For a while Dos Passos remained in the dark as to what exactly Lowell and the Red Cross had on him. His friend Lawson, who had come to Rome with Dos Passos, escaped attention from the censor and landed a job in the publicity office. There he found the incriminating file and shared its contents with Dos Passos. Bates's evidence of Dos Passos's disloyalty and the recommendation for his dismissal would now hound him anytime he sought employment with the Red Cross.

Dos Passos also learned that Bates wasn't his only problem. A more serious one was brewing back home. Having been in Europe for the past nine months, he had unknowingly failed to respond to a draft board order to show up for a physical in 1917. As a result his name had been placed on a delinquent list, and he was ordered to report to the New York adjutant general. His failure to have met with the adjutant placed him in the position of being charged with dodging the draft, even though he had been at the war's two western fronts the entire time.

The only place, save returning to New York, where he could work to repair his standing with the Red Cross and rectify the misunderstanding with the draft board was in Paris. On June 20, 1918, he left for Paris, where he immediately went to the American Red Cross headquarters and those of the American Expeditionary Forces to take up his case. But he knew the bureaucrats in both buildings would move slowly, so he resumed work on his manuscript in a room he rented above the restaurant Rendezvous des Mariners on the Île Saint-Louis.

Dos Passos had given the work the awkward title *The Walls of Jericho* or *Seven Times Round the Walls of Jericho*, a reference to the Old Testament where Joshua brought the walls of the city down with his trumpet. For all his labors Dos Passos had produced a weighty manuscript in which his protagonist, Martin Howe, had done little more than grow up. It was an overture that was too long, too cumbersome, and too slow. Frustrated, he turned to drawing, using his artistic talents to sketch along the Seine. He was managing, as he reported to Rummy locked away in boarding school, "to have an awfully good time in a quiet mournful way."

Being back in Paris also meant for Dos Passos spending time with Kate Drain, a comely twenty-four-year-old nurse's aide whom he had briefly seen in Paris before leaving for Italy in November. They had much in common. She too had a wealthy lawyer as a father and had been drawn to Europe to help wounded soldiers. Now they spent hours together in her place overlooking the famous Avenue des Champs-Élysées. On many nights friends packed into the tiny flat as Dos Passos, sitting on the floor, nibbled Camembert and read from his manuscript. For Dos Passos, despite his uncertainty about what came next, his blacklisting in the Red Cross files in Rome, and the dangers presented by an angry draft board back home, Paris retained its charms.

6

BACK IN THE HILLS OF NORTHERN ITALY, FOLLOWING DOS PASSOS'S DE-
parture, Ernest Hemingway came face-to-face with war. If anybody had
told him when he read the class prophecy a year earlier, he wrote to a high
school classmate, that he "would be sitting out in front of a dug out in a
nice trench 40 yards from the Piave River and 40 yards from the Austrian
lines listening to the little ones whimper way up in the air and the big
ones go scheeeeeeeeek Boom and every once in a while a machine gun
goes tick a tack a tock I would have said 'Take another sip.' That is some
complicated sentence but it all goes to show what a bum prophet I was."

Despite his proximity to the fighting, Hemingway found work as a
driver dull. Except for one hairpin turn on the dirt road leading to the
front, the infrequent trips to fetch soldiers in need of medical care were
boring. "There is nothing here but scenery and too damn much of that,"
he told his Kansas City companion Brumback. "I'm going to get out of
this ambulance section and see if I can't find out where the war is."

When Captain James Gamble, the field inspector of the American
Red Cross canteen service for the Italian front, issued a call for volunteers, Hemingway thought it was just what he had been looking for. The
canteen service provided cigarettes, chocolates, and coffee to the Italian
troops on the front and manned hospitality posts where the soldiers could
listen to music, drink coffee, smoke, and write letters. But recently the
Italian forces had surged forward, and there had not been time to open

new canteens in the newly gained territory. Gamble asked for volunteers to bicycle to the front trenches with panniers full of chocolates and cigarettes. Hemingway immediately requested the assignment.

Hemingway knew the job was not without risk. The Italian soldiers to whom he would be assigned were located in the frontline trenches, frequently under attack. In the short time since Hemingway had been in Italy an Austrian shell had killed volunteer Richard McKey while provisioning the troops in Fossalta. His death was the first for the Red Cross volunteers, and much had been made of it.

Each morning and afternoon Hemingway peddled his way to the front line, bringing with him his helmet, which he called his "tin lid," and a gas mask. His limited vocabulary of Italian provided merriment to the war-weary soldiers. Appreciative of Hemingway's efforts, the men dubbed him *giovane Americano*, young American. Unlike when he had been behind the steering wheel of an ambulance, Hemingway now stood side by side with soldiers in the trenches.

In the moonless sweltering darkness of the night on July 8 Hemingway biked along the bank of the Piave River. He leaned his bicycle up against a command post wall, gathered up his supply of chocolates and cigarettes from the bike's basket, and stepped down into the trenches that ran in a serpentine path along the battlefield. As Hemingway distributed his bounty to the soldiers, he could make out the sound of trench mortar fire coming from the enemy's line.

Heard from a distance, mortars made a muffled plopping sound when the propelling charge ignited upon hitting the bottom of the launch tubes. "It is best likened to the 'clap' of a pigeon-trap," said one soldier, comparing it to the launch of the clay targets used in sport shooting. Filled with explosives and metal shards, mortars traveled in a high arc so they descended vertically into the trenches, whose walls channeled the detonation into a deadly affair. The launch sound, followed by silence, portended an inescapable death or maiming to those soldiers at the bottom end of a mortar's slow, lofting arc.

Hemingway saw the flash first and then heard the roar that followed. The heat was intense, and the ground seethed upward, wood beams splintered, and the men were tossed about like rag dolls. The detonation killed the Italian soldier who had been standing between Hemingway and the mortar. Another soldier's legs had been blown off. Hemingway lay in the dirt unconscious. The war he so wanted to witness had found him.

+

Like the injured Hemingway covered in dirt and debris, the story of what happened to him was soon buried in contradictory accounts and, with time, overlaid with exaggerations. Six days later Hemingway provided its first telling when Brumback came to see him at the Ospedale Croce Rossa Americana in Milan where he had been brought after several days in a first aid station close to the front.

The hospital occupied a building that had previously served as a boarding house. The top floor housed the patients in airy rooms, and the nurses resided on the floor below which contained a library whose phonograph and piano made it a frequent gathering place for patients and nurses. The nurses greatly outnumbered the patients, who mostly suffered from malaria or influenza. When Hemingway arrived, only two men were being treated for war wounds.

On July 14 Brumback sat at Hemingway's bedside. Splinters still in Hemingway's hands made it hard for him to write, so his friend listened attentively in order to compose a letter to Hemingway's parents. The only news of their son to reach them so far was a single telegram from the Red Cross tersely reporting that a trench mortar had hit Ernest.

Hemingway recounted to Brumback the night when the mortar exploded. After regaining consciousness, Hemingway told his colleague from the Kansas City paper that he found a soldier still alive but badly injured. Standing on legs riddled with shrapnel, Hemingway claimed he lifted the man onto his back and carried him to a first aid station. "He says," Brumback wrote, "he does not remember how he got there nor that he had carried a man until the next day when an Italian officer told him all about it and said it had been voted to give him a valor medal for the act."

Brumback sought to comfort Hemingway's parents by telling them their son was recovering rapidly and predicting he would be out of the hospital in two weeks. No bones were broken, and his joints were unharmed. "Although some two hundred pieces of shell were lodged in him none of them are above the hip joints," Brumback wrote. The most serious task for the doctors was removing bullets lodged in his knees and in right foot, but they were confident they would soon extract them along with the shrapnel that had already been removed. "We have," said Brumback, "made up a collection of shell fragments and bullets that were taken out of Ernie's leg which will be made up into rings."

Shrapnel was a serious matter for doctors. It had killed six out of ten men who had died up to this point in the war. Hemingway was only alive because an Italian soldier had died absorbing the worst of the blast and shrapnel.* But he still had cause to worry. The hundreds of incisions made by small bits of shrapnel in his legs could become infected. At best, in a pre-antibiotics age, lacerations were doused with carbolic solutions or smeared with a paste of bismuth iodoform paraffin. Frequently doctors cut away the flesh surrounding a wound and sealed the area with sterilized gauze. Amputation was an all-too-common procedure. Lying in bed, his legs held rigidly, Hemingway didn't know whether he would keep them.

While Brumback's letter made its way by post to the Hemingways in Oak Park, their son composed a follow-up telegraph to the one the Red Cross had already dispatched to his family. "Wounded in legs by trench mortar; not serious," he wired, "will receive valor medal; will walk in about ten days."

Two weeks after sustaining his injuries Hemingway could hold a pen. He put it to paper and composed a letter to his parents detailing his condition along with a cartoonish sketch. He said he hoped his cable had not unduly worried them, but Captain Bates thought it best they hear from him about what happened rather than from the newspapers. "You see I'm the first American wounded in Italy and I suppose the papers say something about it," he announced, ignoring McKey's death the previous month.

Hemingway did not recount the details of what had happened, letting Brumback's account stand, but he told them he had sustained 227

---

* Remarkably the identity of the Italian soldier, whose death made possible the life of one of the century's most important writers, remains unknown. His name—or even mention of his death—is not recorded on the monument marking the site in Italy where Hemingway was wounded. Readers interested in this question should consult the Postscript on page 253.

lacerations his legs. Most of the shrapnel, large and small, had been re-moved, and the surgeons were at work removing the remaining bullet tucked under his left kneecap, Hemingway reported. "By the time you get this letter the surgeon will have operated and it will be all healed."

In a second letter to his parents Hemingway provided the first account in his own hand of what had happened. The shrapnel hitting his legs had not hurt except he had felt the odd sensation of standing in rubber boots full of hot water, he said. When he rose to his feet the machine gun bullets that struck his legs felt like icy snowballs and knocked him back down. "But I got up again and got my wounded into the dugout," he said. "The Italian I had with me had bled all over my coat and my pants looked like somebody had made currant jelly in them and then punched holes to let the pulp out."

The Italian captain and soldiers, into whose shelter Hemingway fell with the man he carried, were convinced that their *giovane Americano* was mortally wounded. "They thought I was shot through the chest on ac-count of my bloody coat." Removing his garments, they discovered his injuries were limited to his legs. Men with a stretcher arrived to take him and the injured man to a first aid station. It was a two-mile walk down a road so dotted with craters that it was impassible at spots. When shelling resumed, the men had to dash for cover.

Once in the first aid station, Hemingway told his family, he had insisted the more seriously injured soldiers be given priority for the awaiting am-bulances. When his turn came he was transported to medics who admin-istered a tetanus shot and a dose of morphine, shaved his legs, removed twenty-eight bits of shrapnel, bandaged him up, and prepared him for transport to the new hospital in Milan.

Hemingway's family mailed him copies of the two newspapers pub-lished in Oak Park. "It's the next best thing to getting killed and reading your own obituaries," he said after seeing the accounts. Even in Milan his wounds had transformed the chocolate and cigarette dispenser into a hero. One day Hemingway was carried out of the hospital onto the plaza in front of the hospital, his legs strapped to a board. With six Ital-ian officers by his side, he reviewed the troops. "The crowds cheered for about ten solid minutes and I had to take off my cap and bow about fifty times," Hemingway wrote his parents. "They threw flowers all over me and everybody wanted to shake my hand and the girls all wanted my name so they could write to me." He was, he said, "known to the crowd as the American Hero of the Piave."

If war offered a macabre lottery, Hemingway held a winning ticket. He had experienced the exhilaration of surviving an encounter with death, leaving him with wounds that portended no mortal risk. Like Stephen Crane's Henry Fielding, Hemingway had accidentally earned his red badge of courage. The wounds would heal, but their benefits would remain forever. Instead of merely witnessing battle, he now possessed valued scars of combat, earning him the admiration of his comrades-in-arms, family, friends, and women.

All that remained for him to do now was convalesce in comfort far from the front in a place that resembled more a resort than a war hospital. "Here," noted Brumback, "he is being showered with attention by American nurses."

+

At the end of the day on July 21 twenty-six-year-old Agnes von Kurowsky was having a hard time getting to sleep in the nurses' quarter on the floor below Hemingway. She took out the Italian-made clothbound diary she had begun using since the eve of her departure the month before from the United States for service in the Red Cross. She briefly recorded the day's events, focusing in particular on the strikingly handsome teenager who had caught her eye. "Mr. Hemingway's birthday," she wrote in her fine handwriting, "so we all dressed up, and had Gelati on the balcony and played the Victrola."

Five feet eight inches tall, lissome, and shapely, Kurowsky possessed transfixing blue-gray eyes, chestnut brown hair, and a smile so broad that its corners pressed up against her apple cheeks. Her independent spirit, vivacity, and forwardness led the men whom she met to regard her as coquettish. Since arriving she had been incessantly wooed by an Italian captain.

Kurowsky knew of her effect on men. In fact, she, along with several of her nursing school classmates, engaged a Milanese tailor shortly after arriving at the hospital to give their matronly uniforms a more closely fitted and stylish look, disposing of their mottled gingham cloth dresses as well as their aprons. Not surprisingly, Kurowsky became a favorite of the wounded men in the ward. "Easily the most scintillating of the nurses," recalled one patient who fell under her spell. "Fresh and pert and lovely in her long-skirted white uniform, moving lithely about her tasks, wasting no time yet never seeming to hurry, she radiated zest and energy."

From Hemingway's white iron bed it was if the pages of Hugh Walpole's *Dark Forest* that he had devoured the summer before had come alive, except now the beautiful Russian Red Cross nurse Marie Ivanova of the novel was an American Red Cross nurse named Agnes Hannah von Kurowsky.

7

AS ERNEST HEMINGWAY RECUPERATED IN MILAN FROM HIS WOUNDS UN-
der the ministrations of Nurse Kurowsky, John Dos Passos was at his
wit's end in Paris. Nothing he did improved the prospects of reconcili-
ation with the Red Cross nor got him out of trouble with the army. His
dispute with the Red Cross, frustrating as it was, prevented him only from
getting another posting. Conversely, his failure to respond to a draft notice could send him to prison. The American military authorities in Paris
ordered him to return to the United States and report to his draft board.
They warned that if he tried to leave for Spain or another neutral country,
which harbored draft dodgers, he would be arrested. In fact, American
officials further threatened to have the French government deport him,
which could bar him from France for the remainder of his life.

Remaining in Paris was futile. Dos Passos signaled his surrender. "My
bitching, my twilight, my *soucis* proceeds," he wrote to Lawson, whose
fortunate success landing a Red Cross job kept him securely in Rome.
"Nothing was of avail and followed by a *cortége* of curses I am going to
America." He booked passage home for early August 1918.

As his departure neared, Dos Passos put his medical experience to
work one last time. He responded to a call for volunteers at the Red Cross
Military Hospital Number 2. It was overwhelmed with casualties coming in from the Battle of Château-Thierry fifty-five miles away. There
American soldiers had successfully held back a German attack, perhaps

saving Paris. Ambulances crammed with wounded soldiers poured into the Paris hospital.

The operating room ran continuously for six days, with as many as 120 patients lined up in the halls awaiting surgery. Back at work for the military and medical organizations that had rejected him, Dos Passos hauled buckets crammed full of amputated legs, arms, and hands from the operating room. "Who could hold to dogmatic opinions in the face of these pathetic remnants of shattered humanity," Dos Passos said. "The world, somehow, never seemed quite so divided into black and white to me after that night."

Several days later Dos Passos boarded the SS *Espagne*, the same French-owned liner that two years earlier had taken him to Spain when his father persuaded him to delay joining an ambulance corps. Dos Passos traveled in style. Using money from the sale of his mother's house in Washington that he had inherited with his father's death, he slept in a first-class cabin and joined the well-heeled passengers for dinners and entertainment. "Since I had changed to civilian clothes none of the passengers suspected I was a pacifist ambulance driver in disgrace," he said.

When the ship cleared the Gironde estuary Dos Passos took out a new yellow notebook. On its flyleaf he scribbled what words he could remember from the chorus of a ballad he and his friends had sung while hiking about Italy on leave. It went something like: "Oh Sinbad was in bad / In Tokyo and Rome / In bad in Trinidad / And twice as bad at home." From the simple act of recording the ditty on paper to making notes reconstructing the gruesome scenes of the death and destruction he had witnessed, Dos Passos wrote out of a sense of urgency. "I sat in my cabin and wrote and wrote," he said. "To get my feelings off my chest, to tell my side of the story I picked Martin Howe out of the unfinished novel and put him through everything I had seen and heard that summer on the *Voie Sacrée*."

Unlike in the manuscript pages he had left in Paris, a rather clumsy and predictable writer's first attempt at a novel, this was different. Dos Passos decided it was time for his literary alter ego to come face-to-face with the war. As the *Espagne* plowed through the Atlantic waters, he began by portraying nineteen-year-old Martin Howe's sendoff from America like the one he had experienced when he boarded the *Chicago* the previous year, complete with dockside Hawaiian music. It had been for Dos Passos an ebullient moment, and so it was for Howe.

He had never been so happy in his life. The future is nothing to him, the past is nothing to him . . . Now a leaf seems to have been turned a new white page spread before him, clean and unwritten one. At last things have come to pass.

✛

Confining himself to his cabin and scribbling furiously on the pages of the yellow notebook, Dos Passos found the words he had searched for since Verdun the summer before. His main character's confrontation with war—not his comfortable coming of age—would be the subject of the book. To accomplish this, Dos Passos devised a story that put Howe on the same path he had taken to the front, including time on the streets of Paris.

Dos Passos reconstructed the moment in a Paris café when he saw a soldier wearing a dark metal prosthesis where his nose had been blown off. To set up the scene he wrote the first in a number of starkly contrasting images that he would use to illustrate the war's destruction. Howe sits in a café at sunset. Before him is the green foliage of the Jardin du Luxembourg, mauve-colored houses, kiosks with bright advertisements, and a pool of jade-colored water. Then Howe spots the wounded soldier. Just as the sight had jolted Dos Passos, he portrayed Howe in shock, wandering the unlighted streets of Paris while hearing the echoes of laughter and conversations.

But wherever he looked in the comradely faces of young men, in the beckoning eyes of women he saw the brown hurt eyes of the soldier, and the triangular black patch where the nose should have been.

After Paris Dos Passos moved Howe to the front. Again he drew from memory and notes the sight of the crumbling and burnt-out buildings punctuated by the occasional untouched structure, standing like survivors from the wreckage of a storm. Howe is in awe of one such building, an intact abbey dating back to the Middle Ages. But despite its survival over the centuries, bombs soon reduce it rubble as well. To Dos Passos the war destroyed everything of value.

Howe sits as the author had at the schoolmaster's table when trucks rumbled by, loaded down with soldiers donning gas masks, and ambulances ran down dark and muddy roads while dodging falling mortars. The barren landscape of the front lies ahead.

Dawn in a wilderness of jagged stumps and ploughed earth against the yellow sky, the yellow glare of guns that squat like toads in a tangle of wire and piles of brass shell-cases and split wooden boxes. Long rutted roads littered with shell-cases stretching through the wrecked woods in the yellow light; strung alongside of them, tangled masses of telephone wires. Torn camouflage fluttering greenish-grey against the ardent yellow sky, and twining among the fantastic black leafless trees, the greenish wraiths of gas. Along the roads camions overturned, dead mules tangled in their traces beside shattered caissons, huddled bodies in long blue coats half buried in the mud of the ditches.

The hours, days, and weeks of ambulance runs to and from the front came to life again as the shipboard Dos Passos wrote on. He puts Howe into an ambulance rushing down a dark road as the reverberations of shells rattle the walls of the ambulance and his wounded soldier's breathing turns into gurgling sounds. In the darkness the smell of blood fills Howe's nostrils.

Martin, his every muscle taut with the agony of the man's pain, is on his knees, pressing his chest on the man's chest, trying with an arm stretched along the man's leg to keep him from bounding in the broken stretcher.

"Needn't have troubled to have brought him," said the hospital orderly, as blood dripped fast from the stretcher, black in the light of the lantern. "He's pretty near dead now. He won't last long."

The *Espagne* drew close to the New York City harbor, and Dos Passos put aside work on the manuscript. As the ship slipped through the Narrows, he passed the remaining hours working on a poem called "Figaro Sings in the Steerage." It was like a final literary indulgence before facing the angry members of the draft board.

✛

Back in Milan Hemingway was taking his first steps since the night he was wounded. His injured left leg now bent normally, and the cast on his right leg, from which doctors had removed the bullet, was off. "I now get around my room and this floor of the hospital on crutches," he wrote to his mother. "Also, Mom I'm in love again."

The confession was not a teenager's delusion brought on by the ministrations of a pretty nurse; the feelings were reciprocated. Twenty-six-year-
old Agnes von Kurowsky was falling for her handsome nineteen-year-old
patient on crutches. She noticed his interest in her in late August, a month
after she had begun caring for him. "Ernest Hemingway has a case on
me, or thinks he has," she wrote in her diary at the end of August. "He is
a dear boy and so cute about it." But it was not long before she began to
confess her own tentative fondness for him. "He is adorable and we are
very congenial in every way," she wrote. "I'm getting so confused in my
heart and mind I don't know how I'll end up."

It became clearer two days later when the pair left the hospital on a
date. They went to Du Nord restaurant for a quiet meal accompanied by
a bottle of Asti Spumante that loosened tongues. By the next week one of
Kurowsky's yellow hairpins was found under Hemingway's pillow. "One
couldn't help noticing that Ernie received an extra share of her attention," recalled a patient in the room next to Hemingway's. "There was a
tacit acceptance, a subtle understanding, by nurses and patients alike, of
the special relationship that was developing between them."

Milan was a long way from home for Hemingway and Kurowsky. The
proximity of war and the patient's wounds, both reminders of life's fra-
gility, along with the boredom of recovery intensified their exhilaration
at carrying out their surreptitious trysts. In the evenings they sat together
on the balcony holding hands and watching the swallows dart in and out
of the building's eaves. In the day, when her duties permitted, Kurowsky
and Hemingway turned the city into their playground. In open carriages
they toured the massive Duomo di Milano, Milan's cathedral that took
six centuries to build; paused for pastries and espresso at the Caffè Cova,
the century-old haunt of writers, artists, musicians, and journalists; and
cheered on the horses at the racetrack of San Siro.

Kurowsky became "Ag" and he the "Kid," although she soon also adopted "Mrs. Kid" as one of her monikers. One night she gave her class ring
to Hemingway and excitedly noted in her diary the pleasure he took from
the gesture. The soon-inseparable pair disengaged briefly in September
when Hemingway used a pass for a week's convalesce at the resort Hotel
des Iles Borromees on the shores of Lake Maggiore in northern Italy.

On the night after Hemingway's departure Kurowsky stood in his empty room. "Talk about chairs that whisper!" she wrote to him. "That whole room haunted me so I could not stay in it."

"Don't forget to come back to me, Boy O.M. [of mine]—cause I miss you most awfully," she closed, signing her letter "Yours till the War Ends."

✛

Kurowsky was in the corridor of the fourth floor a week later when Hemingway emerged from the elevator holding out his arms. He was clad in a new olive-gray tunic he had procured from one of Milan's best military tailors. As promised, he had returned. But now she told him it was her turn to leave. She had to go to Florence, where cases of influenza were mounting. The night before her departure they met in the hospital's library to exchange words of reassurance, and when the time came for Kurowsky to catch her train, he accompanied her to the station. On the train Agnes spotted a couple that made her think of Hemingway. "I kept wishing I had you alongside of me, so I could put my head on that nice place—you know—the hollow place for my face—and go to sleep with your arm around me."

Two hundred miles apart, the lovers' pens were left to sustain the romance. One night Kurowsky was alone with a patient. It was so quiet that she compared the noise her pen made moving across the paper to that of an Italian twin-engine bomber plane. "Gosh—if you were only here," she wrote. "I'd dash in and wake you up about now and you'd smile at me and hold out your brawny arms."

On long nights she kept his letters in the pocket of her apron and took them out to read. "I love you more and more," she said after savoring his letters. "So kiss me good-night." The intensity of words between the two never faltered. "I know very well you are going to live to a ripe old age," she wrote, "and no little war is going to separate us, so I'm not going to be cowardly about it any more—at least not to you."

The letters flowed unceasingly between the two. So when Hemingway occasionally failed to get a letter off, Kurowsky rebuked him for making her feel lost and alone. As he had done in person and now on paper, Hemingway deluged Kurowsky with torrents of affection. "I am but human," she wrote back to him, "and when you say these things I love it, and can't help but believe you." Reading his letters over and over, sometimes she confessed that she worried he would cease to love her.

His replies never disappointed. For each confession she made of her love, he responded in kind. The effect stirred Kurowsky's heart. "I've never pined for anybody before in my life," she wrote. In the books she read, Kurowsky found stories like their love affair. "I never imagined anyone would be so dear and necessary to me."

In November Kurowsky got word she would be returning to Milan. In her absence Hemingway had left the hospital and procured a ride to where his old ambulance corps was stationed. The Italian artillery was pounding the Austrians, whose days as a fighting force now seemed numbered. His unapproved departure from the care of doctors came to a quick end when he contracted jaundice. He rushed back to the hospital and again took to his bed, his eyes the color of mustard and skin tinted yellow.

As he recovered, Hemingway considered parlaying his brief time as a cub reporter into a job with the Red Cross publicity office in Rome where Dos Passos's friend Lawson was working. That way he could stay in Italy and be near Kurowsky. "I guess you don't trust me much," she wrote upon hearing the news, "as you are unwilling to place the old Atlantic between us, and I can't very well blame you, seeing what I did to the doctor," referring to a suitor she had left behind in the United States when she joined the Red Cross.

"Oh dear," Kurowsky wrote as the date of her return to Milan neared, "I'm pinin' so for you. Will you be strong enough to hug me, Ernie, when I come back? You'd better be." Comparing his eloquent missives with her letters, Kurowsky apologized for her perceived inadequacy in expressing her ardor. "Anyhow," she said, "I love you more and more." War news intensified the happiness they felt at the prospect of soon being together again. Italian military victories so damaged the Austro-Hungarian Army that its commanders capitulated. On November 3 the guns were silenced on this portion of the front after the signing of an armistice.

By Monday evening November 11, when Kurowsky's train pulled into Milan, peace had come to all of Europe. Hemingway's war service had comprised a handful of days near the front and almost four months in a Milan hospital. The pair of lovers savored the end of hostilities and made plans for their marriage, possibly in the spring. "I sometimes wish we could marry over here," Kurowsky told him, "but, since that is so foolish I must try and not think of it."

Swearing her to secrecy, Hemingway told his sister Marcelline about Kurowsky. "So when I say I'm in love with Ag it doesn't mean I have a case on her," he said. "It means that I love her." To persuade his older sister that it was not a passing fancy, he reminded her of the photographs taken of him before he left home. "Well," he wrote, "showing them to Ag the other day she didn't recognize me in them. So that shows I've changed some."

✛

In the quiet of the hospital, made lonelier by Kurowsky's absence, Hemingway took out several sheets of Red Cross stationery. But instead of scribbling his almost-daily love letter to Agnes, he started work on a short story. For the first time Hemingway turned the world of his life into fiction. His previous efforts in high school had been the fanciful product of a teenager's imagination. His wounds provided the grist of the manly adulthood he sought and gave him license as he took up his pen.

In a hospital bed and room like his he placed an American soldier named Nick Grainger. But unlike himself, Hemingway's character has lost both legs and an arm. Through the open windows Grainger hears the cries of "Viva la Pace, Viva Wilson!" rising from the crowded and jubilant street below in celebration of the war's end. Grainger fingers the medals he has been given and rereads the accompanying citation.

Wounded twice by the machine guns of the enemy, he continued to advance at the head of his platoon with the greatest coolness and valor until struck in the legs by the shell of trench mortar.

On Grainger's beside table, next to the leather boxes in which the medals came, is a bottle of mercury chloride, a highly poisonous antiseptic frequently used topically to treat syphilis. While the nurse is out of eyeshot Grainger stashes the bottle in his bed. When she returns, the absence of the antiseptic puzzles her, but she accepts Grainger's suggestion that another nurse had taken it. Alone again in the solitude of his room, Hemingway has Grainger reflect on his condition.

I had a rendezvous with Death—But Death broke the date and now it's all over. God double-crossed me.

Hemingway leaves the highly toxic bottle of mercury chloride on the table, suggesting a solution. It wasn't that Hemingway thought to do the same; rather, after escaping death on a battlefield he had given thought to death in a manner that most nineteen-year-olds rarely do. "Dying is a very simple thing," he wrote to his family the month before writing his story. "I've looked at death, and really I know."

✦

As Christmas 1918 neared, Hemingway and Kurowsky were apart again as she had been transferred to another hospital. But they were set on a plan. Hemingway would return to the United States at the beginning of the New Year, and Kurowsky would follow a few months later when released from duty. Hemingway wrote Bill Smith, the brother of Katy, the woman who had entranced him the summer before in Michigan, asking him to be ready to serve as best man in the spring. "Why man I've only got about 50 more years to live," he told Smith, "and I don't want to waste any of them and every minute that I'm away from that Kid is wasted."

The Great War was over, and Hemingway had not missed it. On the contrary, it had brought him fame and the love of a woman. And like the remaining bits of shrapnel in his legs, he was certain he would be taking both back with him. But back in Italy, at her new post in Treviso, the seven-year-older Kurowsky began to have second thoughts now that Kid was no longer by her side. "It makes me shiver to think of your going home without me," she wrote. "What if our hearts should change? And we should lose this beautiful world of us?" The question was lost on Hemingway. Certain of their future together, on January 4, 1919, he boarded the *Giuseppe Verdi* in Genoa bound for home.

8

ON THE MORNING OF JANUARY 21, 1919, THE 503-FOOT-LONG *GIUSEPPE Verdi* glided slowly past the Statue of Liberty in Upper New York Bay. Tugboats brought it to rest at its dock in Jersey City across the Hudson River from Manhattan. Reporters from the *New York Evening World* and *The Sun*, two storied newspapers with pedigrees from the age of Yellow Journalism, waited impatiently. The ship's passenger manifest, listing aviators and Red Cross volunteers, promised a treasure trove of war stories.

When it came time for the forty-two nurses and ambulance drivers to descend the gangplank, there was no question which person had what the journalists sought. Limping his way toward them with a cane, draped in an officer's cape lined with red satin and sporting a Bersaglieri hat, complete with cock's feathers, was Ernest Hemingway, looking every part the hero.

The nineteen-year-old—claiming to be twenty-one—obliged the journalists by recounting the events that led to the two medals of valor pinned to his chest. What went into print—whether by his fault or that of the reporters—added new dimensions to the tale. The *Evening World* reported that an Austrian spotlight had removed the protection of darkness, and a well-aimed shell wounded Hemingway 227 times as he carried an injured Italian soldier to safety. The *Sun* offered readers its own inaccurate version of events. But in its account Hemingway was being carried on a stretcher when a hail of machine gun bullets rained down, wounding him in the shoulder and right leg.

The reporters got their story. The editors at the *Evening World* were happy and chose to run the story twice, the second time with a photograph of the young war hero. For Hemingway the correctness of the facts mattered little as he himself doled out varying versions of his injuries. But he could not have hoped for better copy. He was, according to the *Sun*, returning with "probably more scars than any other man, in or out of uniform, who defied the shrapnel of the Central Powers." A year before he had been writing news for a newspaper, now Hemingway was the news.

Off the ship Hemingway met up with William D. Horne, a Chicagoan with whom he had become friends while in the Red Cross in Italy. The men, sometimes in the company of Horne's dark-haired girlfriend, who couldn't keep her eyes off Hemingway, dined and drank their way across Manhattan. After three days Horne finally took Hemingway to Grand Central Terminal and put him on the *Chicago Limited* for the last twenty-four-hour-long leg of his journey home.

On a cold, snowy January Saturday afternoon, Hemingway was back at Chicago's La Salle Street Station, nine months after having boarded a train for New York and the war. His mother chose to wait for him at the Oak Park house, but his father and sister Marcelline were there to greet him.

"Here, boy!—Here, lean on me!" his father said as they began down the steps of the station toward the car.

"Now, Dad," replied Ernest, "I've managed alright by myself all the way from Milano, I think I can make it okay now. You and Marce go ahead to the car. I'll follow down the steps on my own pace. I'm pretty good with this old stick."

That night the Hemingway home glowed with every light in the house turned on. In the dining room hot chocolate with marshmallows was served as Ernest stood about being kissed and backslapped. Ernest's four-year-old brother, Leicester, was hoisted on his shoulders, "It was pretty glorious stuff being kid brother to the guy who had personally helped make the world safe for democracy," recalled Leicester. "And I was not the only one who saw him in that light."

✛

In comparison to Hemingway, Dos Passos's homecoming the previous August had been unnoticed. No welcoming party. The only ones who wanted to see him were the angry members of the draft board whose patience was nearing its end as they continued to wait for an explanation as to why Dos Passos had failed to report to them during the past year.

After debarking from the *Espagne* in New York City he had taken the train to Bay Head, a New Jersey seaside community where his cousins owned several beach cottages and were always willing to lend him one. Finding a spot in the aging hull of a boat beached in the shade of the town's boardwalk, Dos Passos set about finishing the manuscript he carried with him from Italy and so assiduously worked on while sailing to the United States.

He needed only to bring it to a conclusion, and to do that he drew directly from his notebook as well as his letters to launch his main character, Martin Howe, into a peroration about the war. Howe's battlefield discovery is that he has been enslaved. From the flag-lined streets upon which he and other young men walked off to war to the newspapers that egged them on, everything had conspired to make him a cog in a machine of war.

Oh, the lies, the lies, the lies, the lies that life is smothered in! We must strike once more for freedom, for the sake of the dignity of man. Hopelessly, cynically, ruthlessly we must rise and show at least that we are not taken in; that we are slaves but not willing slaves. Oh, they have deceived us so many times. We have been such dupes, we have been such dupes!

As the end neared, Dos Passos placed Howe on his knees beside a stretcher on which a soldier with white bandages clotted with dark blood rests. Desperate to make conversation with the wounded man, Howe asks about others in the unit. With each man's name, the soldier replies, "dead."

"Why ask?' came the faint rustling voice peevishly. "Everybody's dead. You're dead, aren't you?"

"No, I'm alive, and you. A little courage. . . . We must be cheerful."

"It's not for long. Tomorrow, the next day . . . "

The blue eyelids slip back over the crazy burning eyes and the face takes on again the waxen look of death.

✢

The manuscript done, Dos Passos set about clearing his name. His aunt enlisted the help of a Washingtonian lawyer who had worked in the Judge Advocate Corps. Matters were smoothed over with Red Cross officials. Dos Passos next went for his long-awaited appearance before the draft board.

Again, thanks to the intercession of his aunt's high-placed friend, the board agreed to forgive Dos Passos's transgressions if he reported promptly to Camp Crane in Allentown, Pennsylvania, to begin training for the Army Medical Corps. The draft board official who completed the paperwork vigorously shook Dos Passos's hand and spoke lyrically to him about war and the possibility that one could be killed at any moment. The socialist pacifist had been invited to enter the belly of the beast.

Camp Crane turned out to be a collection of livestock exhibition halls on a county fairground that had been commandeered for military training. The soldiers nicknamed the place "Syphilis Valley." "Glances meeting comprehending," Dos Passos wrote in his diary one night after watching the men and women milling around at a band concert, "and behind the glances the invariable picture of skirts lifted and clothes undone—of white legs and hair between them and the necessity of junction of body strain to body. The band played on."

Most of the men, Dos Passos decided, regarded the opposite sex more "as a piece of tail than of a woman." Writing to Rummy, who had just turned eighteen, Dos Passos explained that men thought this way because of the conventions of society required that sex be licensed through marriage. "The result is that people degraded their every habits to a sexual stupidity hardly shared by animals."

The army training camp was an entirely different experience from the ambulance corps. Then Dos Passos had been with the offspring of wealthy families—well educated, worldly, and motivated by idealism. Now he bunked with Americans of all sorts mostly dragged in by the draft who had no interest in politics, art, or travel. These were fellow countrymen Dos Passos had never before met. "You wanted to be in America," he wrote in his diary, "well, here you are—drowned in it."

On his first day Dos Passos was assigned to work with a sergeant and his assistant in a large hot room shuffling paperwork. Boredom set in. "I just looked at my watch, expecting it to be say five o'clock—It is just ten past two!" Paperwork turned into barrack sweeping, which turned into window washing. The task, he told Rummy "has the philosophical concept of eternity: for to washing of the windows there is no end."

Yet Camp Crane was also a treasure trove to a writer. He had a new war novel brewing, and its characters surrounded him. At night he recorded his observations, notes, and reconstructed conversations in his journal. He decided to call the new book *The Sack of Corinth*, after the Roman victory that ended Greece's autonomy and marked the beginning of Rome's domination.

In November, wearing the stripes of acting quartermaster sergeant, Dos Passos led his men to the New Jersey docks to be shipped out to Europe. After some delay the men boarded the *Cedric*. They were heading overseas but no longer to war. The armistice had taken effect the day before. Their military use would be as a safeguard for France until Germany accepted the terms of a peace treaty. After a stop in England the men were deployed to a camp south of Paris, and military boredom descended once again. Passes were freely distributed, and Dos Passos used every opportunity to spend time in French towns such as Strasbourg, where he came across a dive with songs blaring from a music box. "The wildest little café ever discovered," he wrote to Rummy from one of its tables. Finished with his letter, he stepped out into the cold January evening, a noticeable figure in his US Army uniform on the streets of the recently reconquered city. The war might be over, but Dos Passos was not yet free.

In March Dos Passos won one of the scholarships set aside for members of the American Expeditionary Forces to attend the Sorbonne in Paris. The guns of war had been silenced. The heady atmosphere in Paris from the ongoing Treaty of Versailles negotiations, the company of old friends, and the charms of a beautiful French pianist who played for him when he came for tea all inspired Dos Passos. The city was his muse. The academic requirements at Sorbonne for the military students were almost nonexistent, and Dos Passos rarely attended class. Instead, day and night he typed away in a small room near the Pantheon. On some evenings he read his work aloud to friends. "There is, alas, so remarkably little time in twenty-four hours. Why don't days have forty-eight?" he wrote Rummy.

In Oak Park Hemingway also returned to school. In his case it was to address a Friday assembly at his high school. For props he brought with him an Austrian helmet, a revolver, and his bloodstained, torn uniform. By now his much-repeated account included some new elements, adding to the drama. On this March day Hemingway told the spellbound students that one man lay wounded near him, calling out for his mother. He said he told him to shut up. Describing his own pain, Hemingway said he threw away his revolver. "The temptation to finish the job was so acute." The pain had certainly been real, the revolver not—the Red Cross had not issued revolvers to its men.

At home it was clear to family members that Ernest was still recovering from his near-death experience. At night he could not sleep with the lights off. His sister Ursula would doze on the stairs leading to his third-floor bedroom until her brother came in at night, fearful that he might have been drinking alone. Then, perhaps after a drink together in the house, the two would retire to his room where she slept by his side so he would not wake alone.

Returning to the house one day Hemingway found an envelope with an Italian postmark sitting on the front hall marble-topped table. As was his custom, he grabbed the letter and retreated to his third-floor room. "Ernie, dear boy," began Agnes von Kurowsky's letter. The change from "Dear Kid" was jarring. "I am writing this late at night after a long think by myself, and I am afraid it is going to hurt you, but, I'm sure it won't harm you permanently," she continued. The love they had professed for each other, at least hers for him, had not been a real love affair. "Now, after a couple of months away from you, I know that I am still very fond of you, but, it is more as a mother than as a sweetheart." Kurowsky claimed she had tried to temper the ardor of their relationship before he left, but he had not listened and she had not wanted to hurt him. "Now, I only have the courage because I'm far away." As Hemingway read on, worse news followed. Agnes told him she was marrying another man.

After reading the letter Hemingway vomited and took to his bed. The family had no idea the cause of his ill health until his sister Marcelline came to his room. At first Ernest thrust the letter toward her. "Read it," he said. "No, I'll tell you." Lying on his bed with his back to her, Ernest told her the news.

The Dear John letter was not entirely surprising. Since his return to the United States Kurowsky's letters had grown increasingly cool. But suspicion or anticipation did nothing to lessen the heartbreak. "All I wanted was Ag and happiness," Hemingway wrote that day to Horne, who had put him on the train in New York. "And now the bottom has dropped out of the whole world and I'm writing this with a dry mouth and a lump in the old throat and Bill I wish you were here to talk to."

"Aw Bill I can't write about it. 'Cause I do love her so damned much."

During the following weeks Hemingway hid in the family's boarded-up Upper Michigan summer home or went into Chicago, where he lost himself in long evenings in bars with new Italian American friends. He was moody and restless. A month later the pain from the hurt began at last to recede. "The first time you are jilted though is supposed to be the hardest," Hemingway told James Gamble, who had been the captain of the canteen unit in Italy. "At any rate I'm now free to do whatever I want. Go wherever I want and have all the time in the world to develop into some kind of writer."

+

Almost every day now Hemingway was writing short stories. He had $1,400 coming in from insurance payments for his wounds. The sum could easily support him for more than a year, so he had no pressing need to find a job. Instead, he spent the spring of 1919 tied to a typewriter in his room that reeked of Russian cigarettes, the taste for which he had picked up while overseas.

But although the stories were more sophisticated than his efforts in high school of a few years earlier, they were crippled by his inclination to mimic the pulp fiction favored by magazines. For instance, in "The Woppian Way" he told a Horatio Alger tale of a prizefighter nicknamed Pickles McCarty who joins a band of elite Italian storm troops and slaughters Austrians in hand-to-hand combat in the Italian mountains where Hemingway had been wounded. His narrator, a journalist who slipped behind the lines of combat in hopes of meeting an Italian war hero, echoes

Hemingway's thoughts in his Milan hospital bed because he had failed to die in battle.

In another story he returned to the war. In this one his narrator enters a Chicago bar where he encounters a pair of French and Italian mercenaries. Adopting the story-within-a-story technique, frequently used by Ring Lardner, whom Hemingway had imitated in school, "The Mercenaries" recounts a duel over a red-lipped signora with eyes like inkwells and skin like ivory.

The melodramatic tales were intertwined with war and romance, just as Italy had been for Hemingway. The war had been an adventure, not a futile monstrosity. Unlike Dos Passos, Hemingway had no interest in pondering its causes, worrying about its conduct, or even being bothered by the banality of military life. Dos Passos wanted to write about war to end it. In Hemingway's mind, war was inevitable and a man was measured by it, as he had been. Literature could capture the experience, not change it.

In Oak Park, pounding out his stories on his typewriter, he soaked in a kind of rapturous nostalgia and sought to convert his wartime service into rapid literary success and cash. But his first two stabs at turning his wartime experience and wounds into literature amounted to failed bits of pulp fiction, especially in the eyes of editors at the *Saturday Evening Post* and *Redbook*, who promptly rejected them.

Nonetheless, Hemingway persevered and moved his writing to Michigan for the summer. The gang was there, including Katy Smith. Her most current suitor had gone home. Hemingway readily tried to take his place. He was not put off by the four-year age difference between them. Quite to the contrary. Kurowsky, after all, had been older than he.

Hemingway and Smith played out the waning days of summer. They drank their fill of bootlegger's liquor supplied by a candy store and drove about in her brother's Buick. On one outing Hemingway stopped the car in front of a Catholic church, and the two went in. He lit a candle. "I prayed for all the things I want and won't ever get and we came out in a very fine mood," Hemingway told his sister, suggestively adding "and very shortly after to reward me the Lord sent me Adventure with a touch of Romance." Then, in the rain, he drove back with Smith asleep in the seat by his side.

9

IN THE WANING SUMMER DAYS OF 1919 DOS PASSOS AND A HARVARD classmate were rambling across the tumbling hills and craggy rock ridges of northern Spain under the baking Iberian sun. Above the Bay of Biscay on the northern coast of Spain they delighted in the Basque landscape of green sloping pastures and gray towering mountains, made taller by their proximity to the sea. The pair lunched on tiny eels in a seaside restaurant, drank hard cider and wine that was cheap and plentiful, bathed in the ocean, and shared campfires with shepherds.

Dos Passos was back in Spain for the first time since his father's death. It was a land that had charmed him since his first visit as a teenager and whose art and culture he had studied at Harvard. His return was, as Dos Passos told a friend, one of the finest months of his life.

It had been only a few weeks since Dos Passos had been wearing a US Army uniform at a work camp in Gièvres in central France where the men moved scrap iron from place to place for no apparent purpose. Despite the war's end nine months earlier, the paperwork for his release had been mysteriously delayed somewhere in the bureaucracy. He became so desperate that he left the camp secretly, taking three separate trains to Tours, where a sympathetic sergeant at the American Expeditionary Forces headquarters located the missing file. Dos Passos then rushed back to camp in time for roll call and presented his documents to a disbelieving commander.

Returning to Tours a free man, he purchased a shirt, tie, and socks—what he called "emblems of freedom"—and a brown felt hat. "So equipped I went to a public bath, stripped off my ancient smelly galley-slaves' garments; dressed in a borrowed civilian suit and strode out into the world," he reported to Rummy. "I am a free man."

Following his perambulation Dos Passos went to London to pursue a freelance reporting job and knock on doors of book publishers. The editors at the *Daily Herald*, a four-year-old labor newspaper, offered him the post as their stringer in Madrid, and the editors at Allen & Unwin, a distinguished book-publishing firm, said they would take a look at his manuscript about the war. Armed with work and a potential book deal, Dos Passos crossed back over the channel and headed back to Spain.

Dos Passos wanted to use every moment of his acquired freedom to write a novel that was more daring and direct than the short autobiographical work he had left on an editor's desk at Allen & Unwin. This time he would seek to portray both the barbarity of war and spirit-crushing oppression of military life. "The story's all ready to be written," he wrote Rummy when he settled into a room in Granada, "but it won't come."

If he couldn't write to his satisfaction after months of not writing, at least he had the plot and characters all worked out. "The feeling of revolt against army affairs has long crystalized itself into the stories of three people," he told Rummy. "There is going to be rather a lot of murder and sudden death in it, I fear. I am rather excited about it, and it is just agony being unable to put it on paper."

✛

Slowing Dos Passos's book writing was his obligation to his newspaper employer. He wasted a month in Portugal pursuing his editor's mistaken impression that a revolution was brewing there. Upon his return to Spain he fell ill with rheumatic fever, which swells and creates pain in joints, brings on fatigue, and may damage one's heart. While spending several weeks recuperating in bed, one bit of good news came his way. Allen & Unwin had agreed to publish *One Man's Initiation: 1917*, the name now affixed to his novel. However, doubting its sales potential, the firm expected the author to provide a $300 subsidy. Tapping inheritance funds under his aunt's care, Dos Passos succumbed to the indignity and came up with the money. "It's fairly rotten and I know nobody will read it," he wrote a friend. But, he figured, having a book to his name would help him get others published.

Recovered from his illness and now in Madrid, Dos Passos finally got to work in earnest in December. At a desk in the ornate Ateneo de Madrid, a nineteenth-century private library, he was determined to stay put until he had a complete manuscript.

In his previous attempt to write about the war his main character, the American ambulance driver Martin Howe, had remained an observer. Now that Dos Passos had actually experienced life from inside the army, he decided to expand the scope by creating three characters who participate in combat and are crushed by the brutality of military life. The first two—Daniel Fuselli, a clerk from an optician's office in San Francisco, and Chrisfield, a farmer's son from Indiana—came straight from the copious notes he had taken while at Camp Crane. The third figure—John Andrews, a Harvard-educated musician from the East—Dos Passos plucked from the *Seven Times Round the Walls of Jericho* manuscript that he and Robert Hillyer had started while at the French warfront.

Dos Passos gives Private First Class Fuselli the same trials and tribulations he himself had gone through with the New York draft board official who wished he could feel the danger of death in war. Fuselli accepts the parting remark unconcernedly. His only sense of the war at this point are the propaganda films in which US soldiers pursue terrified Germans across farm fields, saving Belgian milkmaids from sexual assaults. To Fuselli, the army offers a chance at advancement, and he is willing to do almost anything to please his superiors until one day he realizes that he is merely an expendable cog.

The second member of Dos Passos's group fares no better. Chrisfield is high strung and hotheaded. Dos Passos uses him to provide the first exposure to the Great War in the novel. Alone in the woods near the front, adrenaline coursing through his veins, his fingers itching to pull the trigger on his rifle, Chrisfield comes across the body of a German soldier lying among the leaves.

He kicked the German. He could feel the ribs against his toes through the leather of his boots. He kicked again and again with all his might. The German rolled over heavily. He had no face. Chrisfield felt the hatred suddenly ebb out of him.

Where the face had been was a spongy mass of purple and yellow and red, half of which stuck to the russet leaves when the body rolled over. Large flies with bright shiny green bodies circled about it. In a brown clay-grimed hand was a revolver.

Chrisfield felt his spine go cold; the German had shot himself.

For his third figure, John Andrews, Dos Passos resurrects the character that resembled him and from his first attempt at a novel. He is a well-educated and sensitive man with an artistic sensibility driven to share his experiences with others in some manner. Instead of writing, however, Andrews composes music. When Dos Passos has him perform the mindless washing that he had done at Camp Crane, the sight of the men drilling on the nearby fields inspires Andrews, and a musical rhythm comes to the would-be composer's mind. Almost unconsciously Andrews begins a composition.

He must make it into music; he must fix it in himself, so that he could make it into music, and write it down, so that orchestras could play it and make the ears of multitudes feel it, make their flesh tingle with it.

✣

Not far into his manuscript Dos Passos fashioned an oncoming catastrophe for Chrisfield that surprises the reader with deadly effectiveness. The conflicts between Chrisfield and Sergeant Anderson begun in the training camp stateside escalate and result in a court martial near the front in France when Chrisfield pulls a knife on his superior officer. His pay is docked, and he is confined to quarters. After the trial he meets up with Andrews by a trash-strewn brook where the men wash their clothes in the filthy water.

"Ah'm going to shoot that bastard," said Chrisfield, scrubbing at his shirt.

"Don't be an ass, Chris."

"I swear to God ah am."

"What's the use of getting all wrought up. The thing's over. You'll probably never see him again."

Shortly afterward Chrisfield is separated from his unit following a battle and finds shelter in a gray wet forest. Rising from his rest in a pile of leaves he spots an injured army officer hunched up on the ground. He walks over, and when the wounded man looks up, Chrisfield recognizes the face of his nemesis, Sergeant Anderson. The wounded officer petulantly demands to know the whereabouts of their colonel, and Chrisfield grows angry.

"First you was a corporal, then you was a sergeant, and now you're a lootenant," said Chrisfield slowly.

"You'd better tell me where Colonel Evans is. . . . You must know. He's up that road somewhere," said Anderson struggling to get to his feet.

Chrisfield walked away without answering. A cold hand was around a grenade in his pocket. He walked away slowly, looking at his feet.

Suddenly he found he had pressed the spring of the grenade. He struggled to pull it out of his pocket. His arm and his cold fingers that had clutched the grenade seemed paralyzed. Then a warm joy went through him. He had thrown it.

Anderson was standing up, swaying backwards and forwards. The explosion made the woods quake. A thick rain of yellow leaves came down. Anderson was flat on the ground. He was so flat he seemed to have sunk into the ground.

Chrisfield pressed the spring of the other grenade and threw it with his eyes closed. It burst among the new-fallen leaves.

After murdering Anderson, Chrisfield walks out of the woods and is reunited with his unit, where he gets his fill of a potato and gravy stew. The squad then begins to move out, following the same route back through the woods where Chrisfield had encountered Anderson.

"Here's an officer done for," said the captain, who walked ahead. He made a little clicking noise of distress . . .

Chrisfield looked straight ahead of him. He did not feel lonely any more now that he was marching in ranks again. His feet beat the ground in time with the other feet. He would not have to think whether to go to the right or to the left. He would do as the others did.

✦

Meanwhile an exploding shell wounds Andrews while he was resting by a pond some distance from the front lines. His long recovery from the shrapnel wounds causes him to reflect on Chrisfield, Fuselli, and his own experience in the army. To this point Andrews had avoided directly confronting his situation. His work, his musical composition, had been an escape. Dos Passos decides it would no longer suffice.

And he felt a crazy desire to join the forlorn ones, to throw himself into inevitable defeat, to live his life as he saw it in spite of everything, to proclaim once more the falseness of the gospels under the cover of which greed and fear filled with more and yet more pain the already unbearable agony of human life. As soon as he got out of the hospital he would desert; the determination formed suddenly in his mind, making the excited blood surge gloriously through his body. There was nothing else to do; he would desert. He pictured himself hobbling away in the dark on his lame legs, stripping his uniform off, losing himself in some out of the way corner of France, or slipping by the sentries to Spain and freedom. He was ready to endure anything, to face any sort of death, for the sake of a few months of liberty in which to forget the degradation of this last year. This was his last run with the pack.

Following Andrews's release from the hospital, Dos Passos sends him to Sorbonne, where he too had studied. In Paris he meets a beautiful French woman, Geneviève Rod, modeled after Dos Passos's friend the pianist Germaine Lucas-Championnière. Andrews's idyllic time with Rod is shattered when military police arrest him, wrongly presuming he is AWOL, and send him to a labor camp. Slipping into the Seine one night, he escapes with the aid of a sympathetic family living on a barge. Reunited with Geneviève Rod, he explains his motives to his skeptical lover in a forest scene.

"Things reached the breaking point; that was all. I could not submit any longer to the discipline. . . . I was quite willing to help in the killing of Germans, I had no quarrel with, out of curiosity or cowardice. . . . You see, it has taken me so long to find out how the world is. There was no one to show me the way."

He paused as if expecting her to speak. The bird in the willow tree was still singing.

Suddenly a dangling twig blew aside a little so that Andrews could see him— a small grey bird, his throat all puffed out with song.

"It seems to me," he said very softly, "that human society has been always that, and perhaps will be always that: organizations growing and stifling individuals, and individuals revolting hopelessly against them, and at last forming new societies to crush the old societies and becoming slaves again in their turn."

He returns to the room in an inn outside of Paris. The innkeeper, however, had alerted the military police that she believed she was lodging a deserter. When an MP arrives, he finds Andrews furiously composing a musical work about John Brown, the abolitionist who tried to spark an armed insurrection to end slavery in the United States. Andrews readily admits he had deserted. The MP blows his whistle and orders Andrews to get his stuff together.

"I have nothing."

"All right, walk downstairs slowly in front of me."

Outside the windmill was turning, turning, against the piled white clouds of the sky. Andrews turned his eyes towards the door.

The M. P. closed the door after them, and followed his heels down the steps. On John Andrews's writing table the brisk wind rustled among the broad sheets of paper. First one sheet, then another, blew off the table, until the floor was littered with them.

+

Done at last with his manuscript, Dos Passos emerged from Spain in April 1920 and spent several days in Marseille with Lawson. He thought the city's bawdiness—the place during the war where they had seen waitresses perform their unusual trick with coins—made it a fit place to celebrate. "Everyone eating, hating, loving, struggling, starving, fornicating—a bath in raw humanity," he wrote Rummy.

In Paris Dos Passos holed up in a small Left Bank apartment and typed up copies of *Three Soldiers* to submit to publishers. Dos Passos was aware that the manuscript was incendiary, especially the almost casual and nonjudgmental portrayal of the officer's assassination. But the work reflected the sense of urgency he felt. "Every written word should be thought of as the last that humanity will write," he told a friend a few months earlier, "every gesture of freedom the last before the shackles close definitely."

The more mature Dos Passos was a different author from the one who had penned *One Man's Initiation: 1917*. The war was no longer solely a cataclysmic horror that swept across Europe and maimed and killed 38 million people; rather, its unparalleled militarization was a harbinger of how society was robbing people of their individuality. The military life Dos Passos had seen and now tried to write about was not a unique response to war but instead reflected life in an industrial society. There was still a larger story he wanted to tell, and he vented his frustration through Andrews's deep drive to put to music what he had witnessed. "If he could only express these thwarted lives, the miserable dullness of industrialized slaughter, it might have been almost worth while—for him," wrote Dos Passos, "for the others, it would never be worth while."

In London Dos Passos offered his new novel to Allen & Unwin. The editors were impressed but declined the opportunity to publish it, especially as they were already about to release *One Man's Initiation: 1917*, another war book by the young, untested author. Dos Passos then sailed to Cuba on the familiar *Espagne* and caught a ride on the aging steamship *Monterey* to the United States.

Once back in New York City Dos Passos acquired an agent who took *Three Soldiers* around to publishers. He even placed the manuscript into the hands of well-connected people such as feminist and peace activist Crystal Eastman. She passed it on to her brother, writer and editor Max Eastman, with whom Dos Passos had spent time prior to shipping out to serve as an ambulance driver. The manuscript came "from a funny Portuguese boy," Crystal told her brother. "It would not have helped much if I had seen him," recalled Max Eastman, "for Dos is so shy that he seems cold as an empty cellar with the door locked when you meet him. Those flames of passion and sky-licking imageries that illumine his novels are damped down so they don't even smoke in social intercourse."

Eventually Dos Passos's agent found a home for the book at his fourteenth stop when Eugene F. Saxton, editor and publisher at George H. Doran Company, agreed to publish it. In October Dos Passos was reunited with E. E. Cummings, who came down to the city from New Hampshire. After having been arrested with his friend William Slater Brown, they spent three more months in captivity in a large room with other detainees before being released at the end of 1917 when the French decided not to press charges. Back in the United States, he had written an unconventional memoir of his incarceration, calling it *The Enormous Room*. "I thought *The Enormous Room* was one the best books ever written and begged everyone concerned that it be published intact," said Dos Passos. "The publisher had other ideas."

For editors, the war remained a risky subject. The patriotism fired up during the conflict now fueled a crusade against reds, anarchists, and most forms of dissent. The Bolshevik seizure of power in Russia convinced those in power in the United States to regard every labor strike as a potential spark of revolution and radical utterances in print or speech as accelerants. When radicals detonated actual bombs, with deadly results, the hammer came down. By the time Dos Passos was back in the United States the government had engaged in wholesale deportations of radicals, the film industry was cranking out anti-Soviet features, newspapers were leery of straying from a pro-America take on world affairs, and anything or anyone betraying a smidgen of un-Americanism was suspect. "It is said that people are quite terrified by unrespectable references to the flag and to the glories of war in the last part," Dos Passos told a friend.

At the George H. Doran Company a nervous Saxton decided that at the very least Dos Passos would need to tone down the language used by soldiers in his book, lest it seem disrespectful to their service. "All I'd done was put down the soldiers' talk the way they talked it," said Dos Passos, who vainly sought to preserve his slang. The *Jesuses* survived, but the *sons of bitches* and *buggers* were reduced to only two appearances, and *friggin* disappeared entirely. "In the end I told them to do what they goddamn pleased with it."

Even in London Dos Passos's language and tone ran into trouble as Allen & Unwin prepared *One Man's Initiation: 1917* for publication. Their printers had refused to work on the book unless some alterations were made to scenes, such as the ones that referred to prostitution and Christ in a potentially blasphemous fashion. In this case, as with the Saxton's objections, Dos Passos gave in.

In due time copies of *One Man's Initiation: 1917* arrived in New York. Along with Cummings and other friends, Dos Passos headed into Greenwich Village to celebrate his entry into the ranks of novelists with liquor that remained widely available although illegal. "You go into a restaurant and innocently order clam bouillon and before you know it you are guzzling vitriolic cocktails out of a soup tureen," he told Lawson. "You order tea and find it's gin."

Not many beyond the small group, however, took note of the slim book prompting the celebration. In fact, it sold only sixty-three copies, and Dos Passos knew who bought two dozen of those. Literary fame and success would have to wait for another day.

10

HEMINGWAY FOUND LOVE AGAIN IN CHICAGO. IT WAS OCTOBER 1920. HE had just moved into an apartment belonging to the brother of green-eyed Katy Smith of Michigan summers. Y. K. Smith and his wife, Genevieve, were glad to lend a room to Hemingway while he waited for his war friend William Horne to secure an apartment for the two of them. Horne had urged Hemingway to share a flat with him. It was an attractive idea, especially as Katy Smith now lived in Chicago. It seemed like everyone Hemingway knew was heading to the Windy City and working in advertising. "It's bushels of fun," Horne told Hemingway, "keeps you writing and thinking, teaches you quite a lot about a million things, pays you a little more than enough to live on and gives you plenty of spare time to really write."

Hemingway's move to Chicago held the hope of ending the nomadic life he had led following his celebrated return from the war in January 1919. Since then he had lived with his family, in their summer home, in a boarding house, and with another family in Toronto. This last spot had sprung up when he had been asked to give yet one more of his talks about the war, in this instance before the Ladies Aid Society in Petoskey, Michigan. There he met a friend of his mother's whose husband ran the F. W. Woolworth chain of stores in Canada. She invited Hemingway to come to Toronto and serve as a companion for their disabled young son. The stay opened a writing opportunity. Her well-connected husband introduced Hemingway to editors at the *Toronto Star*, who gave him free-lance writing assignments, sixteen in all, before he returned to Oak Park in May 1920 and to Michigan for the summer.

Now, as autumn descended and his mother, who had grown tired of her son's mooching off the family, barred him from moving back home, Hemingway jumped at Horne's proffered solution and took the Smiths up on their offer of a bed. He was drawn into their busy social life. On many evenings their place was chock-full of aspiring writers. For twenty-one-year-old Hemingway the evenings were dreamed-of social gatherings. For those who came he was the man who had seen Paris and the war, carrying the wounds to prove it. At a crowded party one night not long after Hemingway joined the gatherings, Katy Smith introduced Hadley Richardson, an old school chum, to the assembled group. The tall slim woman with long auburn hair tied in a loose coil caught Ernest Hemingway's eye across the room.

✛

Life had not been easy for Elizabeth Hadley Richardson. Born in 1891 to an affluent St. Louis family, she had experienced death early when a sister died in a fire, felt further loss when her father committed suicide, witnessed her sister hospitalized for emotional problems, and suffered her own nervous breakdown from living under her overbearing mother, all before the age of twenty-one.

Her mother's recent death, however, had released Richardson from her domestic purgatory and left an estate that provided the financial means to be independent. The invitation to come for a visit from Katy Smith, her classmate from an elite St. Louis girls' school, was perfectly timed.

When Richardson arrived, Smith accompanied her to Y. K. and Genevieve's place, where she could stay now that Hemingway had vacated the guest room and moved in with Horne. Smith eagerly told Richardson about her Michigan summer friends who were now all in Chicago. They loved words, poetry, and nicknames to such an extent they had created their own dialect. One spoke of seeds (money) to purchase eatage (food) and pills (cigarettes). None of them ever seemed to use their real names. Her hosts Y. K. and Genevieve were Yen and Doodles. Smith was known as Stut, and her friend Hemingway was Wemedge, with whom, she confessed to Richardson, she thought she might be in love.

As soon as they changed into evening clothes she would have a chance to meet them. Richardson pulled a new blue serge dress from her suitcase. She had spent eighty dollars on it in a time when gingham dresses sold for less than one dollar. It was so daringly short that it just barely covered her knee. "I had," she said, "a lot of confidence in that dress." That evening it took Wemedge no time to notice the woman who wore it.

Looking up as she played the piano, Richardson saw Hemingway's brown eyes fixed on her. He was hard to miss in an Italian officer's cape. She thought him the handsomest man in the room. But her insecurities rose. *He likes me because my hair's red and my skirt is a good length*, Richardson thought. She was also much older than he, a deficit in her mind. Hemingway didn't hesitate. The eight-year age difference, almost identical to that between himself and Agnes von Kurowsky, only made Richardson more appealing.

During the following weeks the two delighted in each other's company over steaks and bootleg wine, in back rows of movie theaters, and at the Smiths' continual stream of parties. Their romantic cavorting even included a nighttime visit to Lake Michigan's shore, where Richardson rolled down a dune into an embrace with Hemingway. "Your hands can make me do all sorts of nice things for you by the littlest touch—make me want to, I mean, but then, so can your eyes," Richardson wrote upon her return home. "I'd do anything your eyes said."

Richardson listened attentively as Hemingway talked unceasingly about his desire to be a writer. He even let her read some of his work. But unlike conversation between the two, this did not go well. Richardson thought his journalism was fine, but his fiction put her off. She told him she didn't get it. "It was not the kind of writing I adored," she said. "I adored Henry James." She was also unconvinced about his future as a writer. At the time, despite only having held some modest journalism jobs, Hemingway held a high estimation of his potential. "You know," Ernest wrote to his sister Ursula, "sometimes I really do think that I will be a *heller* of a good writer some day." Hadley did not share in that confidence but decided that loving him required doing so. "He was absolutely sure of what he wanted to do, and I learned to be sure of it too." But the seed of doubt remained in her mind.

When Richardson's three-week stay came to an end, Hemingway took her to the train station, where the breeze ruffled her skirt as he held her close and kissed her hair. Several days later the mail brought a photo of her in a bathing suit with a group of friends. The short accompanying note soon grew into a torrent of letters flowing between Chicago and St. Louis, usually overnight thanks to the new airmail service between the two cities. "Yes," Richardson wrote, "I think you are the nicest lover a person ever had."

+

In December Hemingway had good news for Richardson, who now went by the nickname "Hash." He had procured a job. The Co-operative Society of America, a new and startlingly successful venture—although financial observers doubted its viability—had launched a monthly magazine, *The Cooperative Commonwealth*. For forty dollars a week Hemingway joined its stable of writers. Richardson, however, did not think it a wise move. "Not having your name connected there may save a lot of trouble for your *litry* name later on," she said.

The verbal passion of their correspondence intensified as Richardson's love for Hemingway grew. "I'd like to hold you so and kiss you so that you wouldn't doubt whether I wanted to or not," wrote Hemingway, signing off with the Italian flourish of "sera." Hadley recollected the times they had walked the street of Chicago hand-in-arm and sat in lobbies or streetcars. "Not talking or anything," she wrote, "just loving you so hard, so longing to get hold of you to love you with my arms and lips when a certain look came into your eyes."

But the presence of Katy Smith in Chicago loomed threateningly. The girl who had been Hemingway's summertime teenage crush had grown into an educated and striking woman. Smith, noted one acquaintance, "could go anywhere, even a desert, not knowing a soul, and in ten minutes cause a riot." Hemingway did little to correct the impression of sexual sophistication he gave off that led friends to believe he had slept with Smith in Michigan and Kurowsky in Italy. Even Hadley presumed Smith had been a lover, especially as Smith seemed irked when they announced their engagement. "Of course," Hadley wrote Ernest, "I know it about you that Kate's affairs in relation to you are kept to yourself and you told me some of the points so's to keep close to me in every way."

The Smith threat receded briefly as Richardson accepted Hemingway's marriage proposal. But it resurfaced when, in January of 1921, he told her to keep their nuptial plans secret. Even when they became public, Richardson worried after Hemingway failed to come to St. Louis for the engagement party on the excuse of work pressures. He remained, after all, in Chicago where Smith lived while she was hundreds of miles away in St. Louis.

But on a warm and clear September 3, 1921, Ernest made good on his promise, and he and Hadley were married in the Hemingways' summer retreat in Horton Bay, Michigan, and set up home in a small rundown Chicago apartment. Ernest had an eye on using the savings from their frugality and Hadley's income from her trust fund to return to Italy until Sherwood Anderson came to dinner.

Hemingway had met Anderson through Y. K. Smith, who knew the writer from work. The now-successful author was an animated presence at the Smith soirees and was the envy of the men with literary aspirations. Hemingway listened carefully to what Anderson had to say. In return the older writer took a shine to him.

Born in an Ohio farming town, Anderson had begun life with a spotty education, worked in a wide variety of jobs, served in the Spanish-American war, and when at last he achieved a modicum of business success, he suffered a nervous breakdown. Renouncing business, he turned to writing. His third published work, *Winesburg, Ohio*, was already being regarded as an American classic. The book was neither a novel nor a collection of short stories. For lack of a better term, critics called it a story cycle united by characters in a common setting of a fictitious town in the 1890s. *Winesburg, Ohio* was a startling change from the formulaic short stories readers had come to expect in that Anderson jettisoned plot and replaced it with psychological insights.

Purists were hostile. "It seems to me," said one, "a distillation of the sort of leering gossip one would expect to find bandied about by male scandalmongers chewing tobacco on cracker barrels in a dirty cross-roads grocery store." But on the whole, critics recognized they had something new in their hands. The work's understated prose, unembellished scene setting, and sophisticated expectation of readers won them over.

In the summer of 1921 Anderson and his wife journeyed to Paris. There he found a thriving expatriate writing community and a bevy of new literary publications. During his time in the City of Light Anderson was given an audience with Gertrude Stein, the poet, author, and literary grande dame of the city. They became instant friends. When he perused the shelves of Sylvia Beach's bookstore, Anderson met Ezra Pound, the poet and critic, who had just moved to Paris. And at a Saint-Germain-des-Prés café, he drank beers with Dos Passos, who had published one war novel, which no one had read, and now had a new one in stores that everyone was talking about. Just before coming to dinner Anderson wrote a letter of praise to the author, who was said to be out of communication on a five-month odyssey across Asia Minor.

Over dinner with the Hemingways upon his return, Anderson urged the couple to abandon their plans for Italy—Paris was the place for them. They could get inexpensive rooms at a hotel where he had stayed until they found more permanent lodgings. He promised he would ease their way by writing letters of introduction to Stein and Pound as well as to journalist and playwright Lewis Galantière.

✤

The traveling Dos Passos was unaware of the success of *Three Soldiers* that the Doran Company had finally brought out in October. Discouraged by the disheartening failure of *One Man's Initiation: 1917*, Dos Passos had decided he wanted to be as far away from New York as possible when his second war novel was published. So after signing off on the proofs of *Three Soldiers*, he persuaded E. E. Cummings to catch a ride to Lisbon on a Portuguese steamer. From Portugal the men went to Spain, where Dos Passos took over as tour guide, taking Cummings to Seville for its annual festival and bullfights.

Meeting up with Jack Lawson in northern Spain, Cummings and Dos Passos hiked across the Pyrenees in dangerously foul weather, and from Saint-Jean-de-Luz in France they took a train to Paris. Dos Passos idled the summer days away in Lawson's flat working on chapters of a second book for Doran, hanging about with other writers, and drinking with visiting writers such as Sherwood Anderson.

In September, with a small amount of money from his shrinking inheritance and armed with his press credentials, Dos Passos boarded the *Orient Express* and spent the fall on a US destroyer getting a close-up look at the fighting between the Greeks and Turks; on an Italian steamer to Georgia, having been granted permission by the Soviets to travel overland to Tehran, he came down with malaria; and to Baghdad, where he met the intrepid English writer, spy, and archaeologist Gertrude Bell.

He escaped his world easily, but getting back from these far reaches proved to be a challenge. In Baghdad a caravan heading to Damascus was willing to take Dos Passos. Riding a camel called Rima, he set out with the group. For days on end they rode across sand-and pebble-strewn hills, in frigid cold and stifling heat, dodging bandits until the cold wind of Damascus, as it was known, signaled the near end of their journey. After thirty-nine days they reached their destination. Dos Passos removed the Arab keffiyeh, agal, and thobe he had worn and headed for a Western hotel, bidding his companions farewell. "I actually found myself crying after I said goodbye to them," he wrote Rummy.

Shaved and dressed in Western garb, Dos Passos took the short train ride to Beirut, where five months of mail had accumulated awaiting his arrival. Luxuriating in a bathtub at the hotel, Dos Passos discovered he was famous.

✢

On publication day in October nervous Doran executives had placed an unusual advertisement in the *New York Times*. The notice described how, when first reading Dos Passos's manuscript, the editors believed it deserved a wide readership because for the first time it put into words the thinking of the men who had gone to war. "It voices the protests of youth, its energy and progress," read the advertisement. "But it was also agreed that even after necessary editing the books would probably come as a distinct shock to many, especially those who had not previously been made aware of the intense anguish of many youths who suffered disillusionment in the decay of idealism that alone made possible their surrender of personal liberty." They needed only to look a few pages away from the advertisement to see their fears were well founded.

"This is the kind of book that any one would have been arrested for writing while the war was yet in progress," began the *New York Times* lengthy review. "It is so savagely explicit in its accusations that it deserves no quarter at the hands of the reading public." At length Coningsby Dawson, who had served in the Canadian military for most of the war, tore apart the book's facts, even though it was fiction. At its core, he charged, the novel was an attack on the men who had valiantly served and "a dastardly denial of the special chivalry which carried many a youth to a soldier's death with the sure knowledge in his soul that he was a liberator." *Three Soldiers* sparked a literary firestorm. So many letters poured into the *New York Times* offices that they published two collections of them, sometimes printing only extracts. A first lieutenant in the Air Service rose to Dos Passos's defense, claiming the book accurately portrayed military life, and an infantryman found it a legitimate cry of passionate indignation. But an infantry captain said anyone familiar with the training of its soldiers "does not need to be told the utter folly, balderdash, bathos and nonsense the chapters of his book contain," and another, who said he had served in the ambulance corps, described Dos Passos as representing a school of writing "from whose eyes the glory has gone and see in life nothing but a seething mass of putridity."

The paper took the unusual step of running a second lengthy review two weeks later. "Every one now seems to have taken part in the discussion of John Dos Passos's brilliantly written novel of the American Expeditionary Forces except those who know most intimately the material of which *Three Soldiers* professes to be made—the men who served in the ranks of the front line," began Harold Norman Denny, a former infantryman who had been wounded in the Argonne forest. Dos Passos's depiction of men crushed by the machine of war was "arrant tommyrot," and had the author served as a combatant, he would have written a big book in which the gospel of individualism "would have been sung instead of whined."

Other critics were of a different mind from those commissioned by the conservative-minded *New York Times* editors. The *Los Angeles Times* reviewer, for instance, joined in praising the book's passion and called it a "work of art." Columnist Heywood Broun, writing in the *Bookman*, praised its honesty and eloquence. And the *New Republic* hailed its brilliant expressiveness and beauty. "It shows what sins have been committed in this country's name," wrote one of the magazine's editors.

As often is the case, the negative review attracted sales-spurring curiosity in the book, perhaps even more than the favorable ones. Bookstores delighted in the sales. One Greenwich Village store placed the book in its window, posting with it a likeness of the Greek God Apollo being run over by a steamroller.

Along with the clippings that reached Dos Passos in Beirut were numerous letters from his friends in the United States. They wrote excitedly about *Three Soldiers*. The book had created a "grandiose rumpus" and was the subject of conversation from subways to churches, said Jack Lawson. "You are as famous as Wrigley's."

It was time to end his self-imposed desert exile and go home. From Beirut Dos Passos went to Paris and then to London to find passage back to New York.

✦

In Chicago the Hemingways decided to follow Anderson's advice and move to Paris. Hemingway convinced the *Toronto Daily Star* to take him on as a stringer covering European politics and sports. Next he booked passage on the French ship *Leopoldina*, leaving New York on December 8, 1921. On the eve of departure Hemingway showed up at Anderson's apartment building. He climbed the stairs, shouting Anderson's name as he went up, laden down with a rucksack full of canned goods. "Bringing thus to a fellow scribbler," said Anderson, "the food he had to abandon."

As John Dos Passos rushed back to United States to claim his literary fame, Ernest Hemingway set off to Paris to seek his.

11

REACHING PARIS A FEW DAYS BEFORE CHRISTMAS, THE HEMINGWAYS followed Sherwood Anderson's recommendation and took lodgings at the Hotel Jacob in the heart of Saint Germain-des-Prés arrondissement on the Left Bank of the Seine. The four-story white stucco hotel with a carriage door entrance was inexpensive and well known to writers. Eight years earlier American poet Alan Seeger stayed there prior to his death in battle at the Somme and posthumous fame for his poem "I Have a Rendezvous with Death."

By mid-January the couple found more permanent quarters, renting a Spartan fourth-floor apartment in the Latin Quarter of Paris. Their funds, limited in Chicago, now went far in the City of Light. They had money for meals in restaurants and a maid—what the French call a *femme de ménage*—who washed pots in the morning and cooked at night. On a short vacation in Switzerland Hemingway took time to report to Katy Smith about the new apartment and his *femme de ménage*, painting if not a luxurious vision of his Parisian life, certainly an alluring one. "What's the use," Hemingway asked, "of trying to live in such a goddam place as America when there is Paris and Switzerland and Italy?"

Within a month Hemingway sent to Gertrude Stein Anderson's generous letter of introduction. "Mr. Hemingway," Anderson had written, "is an American writer instinctively in touch with everything worthwhile going on here." An invitation for tea was issued, and the young couple came to the house that Stein shared with Alice B. Toklas. Under Cézanne, Renoir, Matisse, and Picasso paintings, Stein and Ernest sat by the fire deep in conversation about writing while Hadley was trapped in polite conversation with Toklas in another part of the room. Old enough to be Hemingway's mother, Stein displayed a maternal interest in his work. She read and critiqued the stories he brought her and shared with him her idea about parsing sentences to their simplest declarative form, as she had done in her *Three Lives*. A few weeks later she hiked up the narrow stairs to the Hemingways' apartment for dinner one night and read more of his work while perched on their mahogany bed. One of his stories, Stein said that night, was unpublishable because of its graphic depiction of an adolescent male sex fantasy set on a Michigan dock. In the tale the woman resists the man's advances.

Neither Jim nor Jim's big hand paid any attention to her.

"No we haven't Jim. We ain't got to. Oh, it isn't right. Oh, it's so big and it hurts so. You can't. Oh, Jim. Jim. Oh."

Anderson's letters also introduced Hemingway to Ezra Pound. Soon the aspiring writer was teaching the poet to box. In return Pound shared bits of literary wisdom and promised he might get some of Hemingway's short stories published in *The Little Review*, the small circulation Parisian journal known for having serialized James Joyce's *Ulysses*.

One day, when Hemingway was still getting his bearings, he strolled over to Shakespeare & Company, a pleasant twenty minutes' walk from his apartment. Owner Sylvia Beach, a thirty-four-year-old woman, kept the bookstore stocked with American and English books. Expatriate writers flocked to the store particularly to make use of Beach's lending library. On the day Hemingway came he was without money for a deposit. Beach, nonetheless, insisted he take some books home with him from the lending library. No one, he thought, had been so nice to him.

Before the cherry trees displayed their pink blossoms in the Trocadéro Gardens that spring, Ernest and Hadley were well established in their new life. In his letters home Hemingway not only provided his friends and family with an exaggeratedly romantic portrait of his and Hadley's Parisian life but also wrote as if he were an old Paris hand. He adopted this tone as well in the articles he sent the *Toronto Star*. Hemingway mocked his fellow expatriates. Calling Paris a Mecca for bluffers and fakers, he wrote that impostors thrive because of the provincial nature of the French people and the gullibility of its press. Even the impoverished artists and writers who nursed ten-*centime* cups of coffee for hours at La Rotonde, a café across the street from the Hotel Jacob, were subjected to his ridicule. "They are nearly all loafers expending the energy that an artist puts into his creative work in talking about what they are going to do and condemning the work of all artists who have gained any degree of recognition."

Sarcasm was Hemingway's weapon of choice when his achievements failed to match those around him. He had worn out his "typer ribbon" pounding out stories for the *Toronto Star*, but the fiction for which he had come to Paris to write filled only a few folders tucked away in a sideboard. Even the autobiographical war novel he had started remained skeletal at best.

✣

Dos Passos basked in his success back in the United States. The publication of *Three Soldiers* marked the beginning of the literary life he had sought. By April Dos Passos received $8,000 in royalties from the sale of more than forty thousand copies in the first few months of the book's publication. It was a tidy sum, more than a dozen times the earnings of the average American in 1922.

Even six months after the book's appearance *Three Soldiers* continued to cause a ruckus. In March 1922 the *Chicago Tribune* published a full-page review entitled "Propaganda of Novel Is 'Blow at Americanism'" by an anonymous writer described only as a "member of the first division, a legionnaire, a father and a citizen." In explaining his purpose the veteran said, "the reviewer writes as a citizen of a state to warn his countrymen of the anarchistic, Bolshevistic doctrine running through this story, and to call their attention to the book's affront to every just and decent principle upon which society is founded and organized business and government maintained."

In the thousands of words that followed, the reviewer offered up a screed that attacked every aspect of Dos Passos's portrayal of military life and challenged the actions of the book's characters as if they had been real people. "Dos Passos has become the Knight Errant of all that

America does not stand for," he wrote. Once again the attackers treated the novel as nonfiction, ironically proving the authenticity of the book's voice.

The *Los Angeles Times*, which liked *Three Soldiers*, offered Dos Passos space to rebut his critics. "A novel isn't a history," he told readers of the paper. Of course, he readily admitted, there were people for whom the war had been a different experience from the one his protagonists endured. But he insisted what he witnessed at the front was not patriotism but a madhouse atmosphere. More important, he had remained out of the country during almost the entire duration of the nation's participation in the war. "You see, I couldn't have written it to smash any illusions, because I didn't know this country has any illusions," he said. "I wrote it to get it off my chest."

Cummings's wartime book *The Enormous Room*, which after delays had also been published, faced similar hostility but did not sell well. The *New York Times* felt a need to editorialize on the two books. "It is a pity that men of peculiar sensitiveness and irritability so frankly confessed by Mr. Cummings ever entered any form of military service, and a greater pity that they will insist on writing books like this one and *Three Soldiers*— books of the 'now-it-can-be-told' sort—books that are utterly false because they are only a part, and a very small part of the truth."

The attention given to *Three Soldiers* won Dos Passos entry into the American literary fraternity. He was invited to come around to the offices of *Vanity Fair* and step out for lunch with two of its editors. A few months earlier, in February, the magazine had put Dos Passos's photograph on a page featuring nine members of "The New Generation in Literature," along with those of F. Scott Fitzgerald, Stephen Vincent Benet, Gilbert Seldes, John Peale Bishop, and Edmund Wilson. The latter two worked for *Vanity Fair*, which did not seem to preclude their appearance on the list. The New York literary world, all white and almost exclusively entirely male, was a cozy affair in the 1920s.

When the elevator door opened on the floor of the midtown New York City building housing the magazine's editorial offices, the shy Dos Passos exited unprepared for his newfound prominence. He waited in the hall while Bishop went to retrieve Wilson for their lunch date. Not yet thirty years old, Wilson was already among the nation's most influential critics. Three years earlier he had sent in an unsolicited parody that Dorothy Parker read and liked. It put Wilson on the path to becoming the magazine's managing editor and gave him a platform that he used eagerly to publish the work of his friends and those writers whom he admired. In fact, just prior to the lunch date he had published one of Dos Passos's poems in *Vanity Fair*.

Despite his intellectual reputation, Wilson, known to friends as "Bunny," was an imp. He drove a motorcycle to work each day from his childhood home in Red Bank, New Jersey, and did magic tricks and puppetry. When the three men stood by the elevator to head out for their meal, Wilson suddenly executed a somersault in his business suit before an astonished Dos Passos.

From his post at *Vanity Fair* Wilson knew everyone in the literary world. Among his friends was novelist F. Scott Fitzgerald, whose first two works, *The Beautiful and Damned* and *This Side of Paradise*, had launched his writing career and turned him and his glamorous wife into celebrities. Fitzgerald was taken by Dos Passos's new book and reviewed it for the *Daily News* in his hometown of St. Paul. Describing the author as an artist, Fitzgerald wrote that *Three Soldiers* was "the first war book by an American which is worthy of serious notice. Even *The Red Badge of Courage* is pale beside it." He told Wilson he wanted to meet Dos Passos.

✦

In Paris it was Italy that beckoned Hemingway. In May 1922 Ernest and Hadley traveled to a Swiss town on the northern border of Italy. From there they hiked across the Great St. Bernard Pass and took a train that delivered them to Milan. In a city in which he had once courted a nurse with blue-gray eyes, Ernest now escorted his wife about, pausing for a glass of Capri, a young Italian white wine, at the Galleria Vittorio Emanuel, whose glass-vaulted iron arcades connected two of Milan's main squares.

A bus delivered the couple to Schio, where Ernest had been posted with his fellow ambulance drivers.

Hemingway told the young woman perched on a stool behind the zinc-topped counter in Schio's principal bar that he had been there during the war.

"So were many others," she muttered, taking his money for his drink.

Everywhere he looked nothing matched his memory. He could not even locate the garden filled with wisteria where he and others drank beer on hot nights. Still, perhaps the space where he had been wounded was as it had been. He hired a car and a driver, and they drove to Fossalta. There he found new stucco houses painted in bright colors standing in place of the rubble he had known. Rather than being pleased by the restoration of normalcy and that the citizens of the town had new housing, Hemingway was disappointed that he could not bring his wife to the spot where the mortar had forever changed his life.

In an account of his trip he warned those *Toronto Star* readers who were war veterans to visit someone else's front. The green fields that have covered the expanses of shell holes and barbwire, he wrote, "will combine against you and make you believe that the places and happenings that had been the really great events to you were only fever dreams or lies you had told yourself."

They returned to Paris and passed an uneventful summer.

✢

Under a bright blue sky in late October 1922 Dos Passos walked fast up Fifth Avenue, late and anxious. F. Scott Fitzgerald had summoned him, through their common friend Bunny Wilson, for lunch. Breathless, Dos Passos knocked at the door of the Fitzgerald suite in the elegant Plaza Hotel. Scott answered and scolded his guest for being tardy. Once inside, Dos Passos found that Sherwood Anderson, in town from Chicago, was also joining them for lunch. As was their habit, Scott and Zelda Fitzgerald plied their guest with questions. "Their gambit," said Dos Passos, "was to put you in the wrong. You were backward in your ideas. You were inhibited about sex."

Dos Passos fought off the barrage of questions, and Anderson rescued him by talking about his writing. Dos Passos rose from the table, walked about the room, looked north out the window at the trees in Central Park, which had begun to turn. After a knock on the door, an elderly waiter entered and set a glittering lunch table with lobster croquettes and crisp French rolls with creamy sweet butter. They drank champagne and

Bronx cocktails, a martini with orange juice. "Scott," noted Dos Passos, "had good bootleggers."

After lunch the Fitzgeralds bid good-bye to Anderson and asked Dos Passos if he would pass the afternoon with them on Long Island, where they wanted to find a house. They were paying $200 a week for their suite, and the cash-strapped couple heard that houses on the fashionable North Shore of the island rented from $300 a month. Setting out in a chauffeur-driven red touring car, they came to Great Neck, where they paused briefly at a real estate office to pick up a salesman. He led them to see several mansions, but none of them satisfied Scott or Zelda, who were rude to the real estate man. "They parroted his way of saying 'gentleman's estate' until I was thoroughly disgusted with them," said Dos Passos. "I tried to stick up for him. The poor devil was only trying to do a little business."

Failing to find a suitable house, Scott directed the driver to take them to Ring Lardner's Great Neck home. Unlike Fitzgerald or Dos Passos, none of Lardner's dozen or so books had been much of a success. His fame rested on readers who delighted in his newspaper sports columns and magazine short stories. At the house, a large mansion like those the Fitzgeralds had toured that day, they came across the writer sitting alone in a drunken stupor in the darkened living room. His wife, Ellis, coaxed her husband to speak, but he stared back in silence. "He was literally out on his feet," Dos Passos said. They drank proffered whiskeys and got back into the car. As they drove away, Scott told Dos Passos that Lardner was his private drunkard and that everyone ought to have one.

After a stop for a ride on a Ferris wheel at a carnival they returned to the Plaza Hotel, ten hours after their lunch. Despite the amount of alcohol consumed, both Zelda and Scott emerged from the car with public faces of charm. "They were celebrities and they loved it," said Dos Passos. "It wasn't that I was not as ambitious as the next man; but the idea of being that kind of celebrity set my teeth on edge."

✦

In late November Hadley was stuck in Paris, ill with a cold, while Ernest went off to report on a peace conference in Lausanne, Switzerland, to settle a dispute between Turkey and Greece. Reporters from around the world were there. The attraction in the city by Lake Geneva, aside from a possible treaty, was the attendance of Benito Mussolini, who had just come to power in Italy. Hemingway had interviewed the Fascist leader earlier that year in Milan while he and Hadley were in northern Italy. "He was a great surprise," wrote Hemingway. "He is not the monster he has been pictured."

The Lausanne conference, like other gatherings of politicians that he covered, brought Hemingway into the company of American journalists. He saw Dos Passos's friend the socialist Max Eastman as well as the muck-raking journalist Lincoln Steffens. Hemingway had met Steffens before and had showed him a horseracing story. Steffens was so taken by the tale that he had mailed it to his friend Ray Long, editor of *Cosmopolitan*. Now, in Lausanne with Hemingway, Steffens asked whether he could see more of his stories.

Recovered from her cold, Hadley decided to respond to the entreaties from her lonely husband. He was pleased. "I do so hate for you to miss what is the most comfortable and jolly time for mums," wrote Hemingway, who tracked Hadley's menstrual cycle on a calendar.

Hadley wired Ernest that she would join him in Lausanne. Afterward they planned to vacation in a pension in the French skiing village of Chamby with a British war friend. Hadley raced about their flat packing for an extended absence from Paris. She filled a large suitcase with her clothes. Grabbing a valise, she went to the dining room, where she gathered up Hemingway's handwritten drafts, typed manuscripts, and carbon copies. Into the smaller bag she placed virtually the entire collection of her husband's work, what he hoped would launch his writing career.

As nightfall came the owner of the dance hall on the rez-de-chaussée of their apartment building drove Hadley to the Gare de Lyon. Aboard the Paris-Lausanne overnight train Hadley found a seat with legroom where she hoped she might catch some sleep. On the rack above she placed her suitcase, and at the foot of the seat she deposited the valise filled with the manuscripts she had presumed her work-obsessed husband wanted. She had gotten to the station with plenty of time before the scheduled departure, so Hadley left her seat and stepped off the train.

In the hubbub of the busy station vendors could be heard advertising their wares with shouts, and passengers called for porters. The engines let off clouds of steam, their boilers stoked in anticipation of hauling their loads into the night beyond the city.

"Tous à bord!" yelled the conductor of the Paris-Lausanne train, and Hadley climbed back on board. At first she thought she was in the wrong compartment—the valise was not where she had left it. But when she saw the suitcase on the rack, she realized to her horror she had found her seat. The bag was gone.

She looked furiously about for it. A newspaperman heading to the peace conference assumed that only her suitcase had been taken. "My wife will lend you some of her things," he kindly offered. Sobbing uncontrollably, Hadley explained what was missing, and a policeman was called to the car. He asked questions, left, and the train pulled from the station. Into the darkness it sped, with Hadley in tears.

In the morning the train pulled into the Lausanne station where Hemingway and Steffens were waiting. The tears still falling so profusely, Hadley could hardly get the words out. Hemingway listened stoically, but Hadley understood the enormity of the loss. "His heart was broken," she said. "I could see that."

Steffens and another journalist were heading to Paris. When they reached the Gare de Lyon they checked the lost and found but reported to Hemingway that nothing had been turned in. Hadley and Ernest continued on their way to Chamby, where they spent Christmas and returned to Paris after the New Year. The exuberance of a young marriage lived out in one of the world's most romantic locales was gone with the valise. Fault mattered less than the loss's association to Hadley. From now on, whenever Ernest picked up a pen to compose a new story, to try to recompose his missing work, or even to think about what was lost, the disaster would be tied to Hadley. For a marriage it was an emotional cancer.

As 1923 opened, Hemingway was further than ever from his goal of being a writer. "Sure seems there is a curse on me," Hemingway said. He told Pound of his loss at the hands of Hadley. "You, naturally, would say 'Good' etc.," he wrote. "But don't say it to me I ain't yet reached that mood. I worked 3 years on the damn stuff."

Since returning from the war he had told everyone he was a writer, but he had nothing to show for it except one unnoticed publication in a tiny New Orleans magazine edited by a friend of Sherwood Anderson. Certainly Hemingway's editors in Toronto were pleased with the news pieces he had filed, and he had made valuable connections with writers. But on the matter of actually becoming a writer of fiction Ernest had made little progress. His attempts at fiction had been stacked in the dining room cupboard, and were now gone except for one story. "My Old Man" had not been in the valise—it was the story Steffens had sent to a New York editor.

Hemingway gave this short example of his work to Ezra Pound's friend Edward O'Brien, who edited an annual anthology of best short stories. The piece deeply impressed O'Brien, and he asked whether he could publish it in the anthology even though it had not yet appeared in print. Hemingway was exultant, but once again literary progress was put on pause. Hadley announced she was pregnant.

12

ON BOARD THE SS *ROUSSILLON* HEADING OUT OF NEW YORK CITY'S HAR-
bor in late March 1923, Dos Passos looked forward to being back in
France for a new reason. For only the second time in his life a woman
had caught his attention, and Crystal Ross, he decided, was worth crossing an ocean for. He had met the prepossessing woman, who favored a
cloche hat pulled down over hair with a flapper cut, the previous summer
at a New York City funeral. Twenty-nine-year-old Wright McCormick
had been killed in a fall while mountain climbing in Mexico. Dos Passos had known the man at Harvard, and Ross had met him in New York
City. When they came to say their good-byes to a friend in common, they
found each other's company pleasing. But Ross was leaving the country
to pursue a doctoral degree in France. Rather than tête-à-têtes in New
York eateries, the venue to explore each other's feelings became the mail.
As Ernest and Hadley had done when separated by the distance between
Chicago and St. Louis, Dos Passos and Ross grew into avid and warm
correspondents across the Atlantic.

To his friends the shy and bookish Dos Passos, now twenty-seven, had
previously shown a notable lack of interest in the opposite sex. "Dos don't
you ever think about women?" Cummings once asked as the men traveled together through Spain a few years earlier.

"No," replied Dos Passos.

"Don't you ever dream about sex?" continued Cummings, whose visits with ladies of the night frequently inspired verses about prostitutes.

"No."

Dos Passos's thrashing about and groans when he slept led Cummings to suggest to his friend that sometimes dreams about sex are disguised. "You may be dreaming about sex without knowing it," Cummings told his friend.

The woman who had at last captured Dos Passos's heart was a Texan with an unconventional sense of adventure. Born in the small town of Lockhart, near Austin, the daughter of a country doctor with a big library, Crystal Ross graduated from the University of Texas in 1919. At Columbia University in New York City she obtained a master's degree in English and decided to study comparative literature at the university in Strasbourg, France. Few women in Dos Passos's experience were so intellectually motivated and daring to travel overseas on their own to pursue a degree.

✢

In Paris Hemingway continued in his struggle to balance the demands of the *Toronto Star* with his literary ambitions, now made more complicated by pending fatherhood. By April he had written more than twenty thousand words of journalism but hardly a word of fiction. A trickle of creativity ended the drought when Ernest and Hadley vacationed in Cortina d'Ampezzo, an Italian resort in the Southern Alps.

Away from Paris and work, Hemingway began typing a story. In almost a single take at his machine he pounded out a story of a young American couple staying in a hotel in a northern Italian village, much as he and Hadley were doing at the time. The couple in the story wanted to go fishing but was not permitted at the time. Nonetheless, they hire the hotel's gardener, the town's drunk, to guide them to a stream. Before they reach the stream the wife—who has been given Hadley's nickname "Tiny"—convinces her husband to abandon the risky plan of fishing illegally. As they return to the hotel, the husband still gives the guide more money, knowing it would be used to buy alcohol.

The emotional timbre of the story reflected Hemingway's inner turmoil. He felt trapped by the pregnancy after carefully tracking her menstrual cycle had failed him. He had lost trust in his partner after she lost all his work. The couple he created for the story spoke with the kind of fatalism he ascribed to his own marriage.

The flat mundane tone conveyed emotion without heavy-handedness, and a sparseness still provided details despite their absence. On paper Hemingway was trying to make those parts he left out an integral part of his story, much like the Paul Cézanne paintings Hemingway frequently went to see in Paris's Musée du Luxembourg. Staring at them, he saw a suggestion of a world beyond the surface of the canvas. "I was learning something from the painting of Cézanne that made writing simple true sentences far from enough to make the stories have the dimensions I was trying to put in them."

At his typewriter in the small Italian village, turning his own life into a story with a veneer of simplicity and directness, Hemingway was hitting his stride.

When Hemingway left Cortina he found that for the first time his work was in demand among the coterie of small Paris presses publishing in English. Ezra Pound planned on bringing out a half-dozen Hemingway miniature tales, some no longer than a paragraph in the literary journal *Little Review*, along with an amalgam of poetry and prose reflecting on the peace conference at Lausanne. Robert McAlmon, a wealthy American who befriended Hemingway on a trip to Spain that summer, had just launched Contact Publishing Company. On his list of forthcoming books, by such authors as William Carlos Williams and Mina Loy, he added "Short Stories" by Ernest Hemingway. The good turn of fortune continued when Bill Bird told Hemingway that his one-year-old Parisian hand press operation, Three Mountains Press, would also publish a collection of his stories.

This embarrassment of richness in opportunity was a moment of celebration tinged with apprehension. His cupboard of fiction was bare, both literally and figuratively. All he had in the way of short stories were "Up in Michigan," which Gertrude Stein said shouldn't be published because of the sex; "My Old Man," which Lincoln Steffens had fortunately saved from the valise by mailing it to an editor; and his new "Out of Season." To fill the remaining pages of the Contact Publishing book all Hemingway could offer was his unpublished poetry.

✦

As the summer months of 1923 passed, Hemingway worked on a series of short stories for a larger collection planned by Three Mountains Press. The vignettes were short, fewer than two hundred words, and much like the brief news items he had written as a cub reporter for the *Kansas City Star*. They appeared, on the whole, to be fragmentary memories. His romance with Agnes von Kurowsky, for instance, surfaced in "A Very Short Story."

Despite the passage of four years Kurowsky had been on Hemingway's mind recently. A few months earlier he had found a letter from his former lover in the stack of mail. It reopened the emotional scab left from her jilting of him. "I always knew," Kurowsky wrote, "it would turn out right in the end and that you would realize it was the best way, as I'm positive you must believe, now that you have Hadley."

For his response Hemingway turned to fiction. Crafting a story set in a wartime hospital in Italy, Hemingway portrayed a wounded young American soldier falling in love with a nurse named Ag with whom he secretly shared a bed. At the end of the war Ag and the soldier agree he should go to the United States and get a job so they could marry. The nurse professes her love in more than a dozen passionate letters but—just as Kurowsky had done to Hemingway—she suddenly announces she had fallen for an Italian major and would no longer join the soldier in the United States.

She loved him as always but she realized now it was only a boy and girl love. She hoped he would have a great career, and believed in him absolutely. She knew it was for the best.

For Hemingway love and war were inseparable. To his mind combat was a test of manliness, and who better to serve as a foil than a woman. That was how it had been for him when he recalled the front in the hills of northern Italy. The 457-word autobiographical story was the longest he produced for the planned collection.

✦

While Hemingway worked on his stories in his flat, Dos Passos entertained Crystal Ross in Paris. They spoke of going to Norway or Rome or crossing the Red Sea, visions inspired by an atlas he had given her. A life together was a possibility. But right now her studies couldn't be put off, and Dos Passos escorted her to a train for Strasbourg. In her absence he spent his evenings in the company of E. E. Cummings, editor and writer George Seldes, and critic Malcolm Cowley, who had a place in Giverny to the west of Paris.

Paris certainly had its artsy and literary set, and the life of the party among many expatriate gatherings was Donald Ogden Stewart. The twenty-nine-year-old Columbus, Ohio, native kept everybody in stitches with his humor. But he also harbored ambitions to use comedy in the cutting manner of Jonathan Swift and Voltaire. After graduating from Yale, Stewart had gone into the bond business. F. Scott Fitzgerald, a good friend of his, brought Stewart's work to the attention of John Peale Bishop and Edmund Wilson at *Vanity Fair*. For them Stewart wrote a parody of Theodore Dreiser and Fitzgerald. After its publication in the magazine he wrote a book-length spoof of H. G. Wells's *Outline of History* that became a hit.

Dos Passos knew Stewart in New York City, and in Paris the humorist was eager to introduce the novelist to Gerald and Sara Murphy. The wealthy American couple—Gerald's family owned the Mark Cross leather goods company—used their money to entertain writers and artists and generously invited many of them to spend time at their French Riviera villa. By 1923 the couple were the center of the growing artistic and literary expatriate circle. They had, said Stewart, "the gift of making life enchantingly pleasurable for those who were fortunate enough to be their friends."

One evening Stewart brought Dos Passos to the Murphys' Left Bank apartment overlooking the Île de la Cité. On this night they were giving a party for the entire cast of the Ballets Russes. Dos Passos was reluctant to attend. "I was shy," he said, "and hated small talk and I didn't like having to answer questions about my writing." As the evening progressed, Dos Passos found he liked Sara but judged Gerald to be cold and a bit of a dandy. "I refused to stay for the party and went off prickly as a porcupine," said Dos Passos.

A while later Gerald invited Dos Passos to lunch, after which they were joined by the painter Fernand Léger for a stroll along the quays above the Seine. The addition of Léger was a brilliant move on Murphy's part. Léger had spent two years on the front in the war and barely survived a gas attack, an experience to which Dos Passos could relate. Dos Passos also had never entirely renounced his own painterly ambition. When he went to Spain before the war it had been with his pencils and watercolors. Even during the war he had kept them near just as he did now.

Murphy, an accomplished painter himself, had been studying under Léger, and the two conversed animatedly as Dos Passos listened. Léger pointed out shapes and Murphy talked about their place in a vista. "Instead of the hackneyed and pasteltinted Tuileries and bridges and barges and *bateaux mouches* on the Seine," said Dos Passos, "we were walking through a freshly invented world."

Dos Passos was won over, and Murphy and he were soon fast friends. In time they even discovered their fathers had also known each other. Dos Passos took to dropping in to visit the Murphys when they were not in the midst of entertaining the world. Best of all for Dos Passos was to stop in when the children were present. "I had never had a proper family life and was developing an unexpressed yearning for it," he said.

✛

Now a successful American author, Dos Passos's presence did not go unnoticed among the writers who comprised the small clannish expatriate community in Paris. Hemingway and Dos Passos agreed to meet for lunch at the Brasserie Lipp on Boulevard Saint-Germain. Favored by poets, the forty-three-year-old café had been recently redecorated with murals of tiles, a painted ceiling, and moleskin seats.

The spot was significant for Hemingway. It had been while eating a meal in the brasserie that he had come to terms with the loss of his manuscripts and realized the story he had written in Cortina represented a new beginning. And perhaps he had stumbled onto a new literary idea in writing his Cortina tale. When writing "Out of Season" Hemingway cut out the ending he had planned in which the old man hanged himself. Omitting it didn't hurt the story. "The omitted part," he decided, "would strengthen the story and make people feel something more than they understood."

On the appointed day for lunch Hadley joined the two men. Customers were drinking *distingués*, as the regulars called a pint, and a permeating odor of the brasserie's cervelas sausage, made of beef, bacon, and pork rinds, and the pommes à l'huile filled the room. They were amused they had become wordfellows, a term they both mocked despite having been made up by their common friend Sherwood Anderson.

Dos Passos was impressed by how the eighteen-year-old ambulance driver had turned into a sophisticated twenty-three-year-old during the five years since they met on the Italian front. "He had one of the shrewdest heads for unmasking political pretentions I've ever run into," Dos Passos said. Hemingway showed Dos Passos one of the sketches he was working on for the Three Mountains Press book. "I right away," said Dos Passos, "put him down as a man with obvious talent for handling the English language." What caught his attention in particular was Hemingway's vocabulary that seemed to stem from his affection for prizefighting and his work as a political reporter. "Everything was in sharp focus," he said.

But further literary conversation would have to wait. The Hemingways were taking their leave from Paris and heading to Toronto so Hadley could give birth in Canada surrounded by doctors who, to her mind, were better by virtue that they weren't French.

Just before the departure from Paris a messenger brought Hemingway the proofs of *Three Stories and Ten Poems*, its rather unoriginal title given to it by Contact Publishing. It would comprise his first book. It seemed too slim, so lacking in heft, that Hemingway grew worried. "No body will buy a book it is too goddam thin," he wrote to McAlmon, who had launched the press. He went to his shelf and pulled down books to study how they were put together. "I've been checking up the blank page stuff on books here in the house," he reported to his publisher. "Find in Three Soldiers, *Daws* Passos, 8 blank pages without a goddam thing on them immediately after cover."

✦

Like Hemingway, Dos Passos returned to North America at the end of the summer of 1923. His next novel, *Streets of Night*, was scheduled for publication that fall. After *Three Soldiers*, the success of which seemed to promise further literary triumphs, Dos Passos's publisher had brought out *Rosinante to the Road Again*, an odd collection of essays and stories about Spain. Since his first trip to Spain in 1916 the country had captured

Dos Passos's imagination. Although this book met with critical success, it generated only modest sales. His insistence on publishing a collection of his poems accelerated his further descent from commercial success.

The situation grew even worse when *Streets of Night* arrived in bookstores. It was a novel Dos Passos had begun in college, and he would have been better off to have left it unfinished. It traced the fortunes of a woman studying music and two men, a Harvard art instructor and an anthropology graduate student. The professor hopes to marry the woman, but she is drawn to the student. Frustrated by her unwillingness to have sex with him, the student seeks the company of a prostitute, whom he flees when he sees her naked. Torn by love, lust, and racked with guilt from his upbringing under a stern clergyman father, he commits suicide.

Hardly anyone reviewed the book, and sales were nonexistent. F. Scott Fitzgerald, who had admired *Three Soldiers*, lost faith in Dos Passos upon reading an advance copy of this new book. Hemingway made no mention of the work. He was slavishly churning out political stories as well as travel tales for the paper in Toronto. But had he looked at the book he might have seen that Dos Passos was also toying with the concept of what to leave in and what to leave out. One anonymous reviewer noted it. "The things which Mr. Dos Passos has not said explicitly, but which he has left to the knowledge and insight of the readers, are by far the most significant," said the *Spectator*'s reviewer who gave the book a close reading. "He has set down the effects and inferred the causes."

Despite his disappointment in Dos Passos's newest work, Fitzgerald insisted the author come spend Christmas at his house in Great Neck. Edmund Wilson and Gilbert Seldes would be there as well as Esther Murphy, the younger sister of Gerald Murphy. Dos Passos agreed, but reluctantly. All fall he had been hiding in a boardinghouse in Far Rockaway at work on a new ambitious novel. He tolerated the holiday interruption but returned as quickly as he could to resume work on the book. He was taking to his typewriter with hopes like that of a horse breeder raising his next thoroughbred. There is always another day at the post.

✦

Both Dos Passos and Hemingway were back in Paris by April 1924. The Hemingways had returned from Canada with their new son, John Hadley

Nicanor Hemingway, who was being called "Bumby." The stay away from Paris had been awful, particularly for Ernest's writing. "Canada is the shit," he had written to Pound. "I cannot write anything but a dull letter." But the return to Paris was filled with anxiety about finances. He had quit his job with the *Toronto Star* and was now planning on supporting a family on his writing along with help, of course, from Hadley's trust fund.

The writing now went well. As the spring brought warm weather, Hemingway lingered increasingly at La Closerie des Lilas, meeting Dos Passos on many days. When the racers took to the vélodrome for the annual indoor six-day bicycle race, Hemingway and Dos Passos equipped themselves with pots of pâté, cold chicken, cheese, baguettes, and wine from the food stalls in the market streets. They found seats in the stands of the Vélo d'Hiver, and Hemingway filled in Dos Passos on the names, lives, and statistics of the riders. "His enthusiasm was catching," said Dos Passos, "but he tended to make a business of it while I just liked to eat and drink and enjoy the show."

On the days when the two met at the café they would down vermouth with cassis and take turns reading from the St. James Bible. Hemingway was invariably in a splendid mood. Unlike the previous year when they lunched together, he had stories in print now. The little collection *Three Stories and Ten Poems* and the modest chapbook with the lowercase title *in our time* could both be found in Sylvia Beach's Shakespeare and Company bookstore. The *Best Short Stories of 1924*, edited by Edward O'Brien, not only included, as he had promised, a Hemingway story but the volume was also dedicated to the author. The honor, however, was tainted slightly when Hemingway noticed his name on the table of contents was spelled "Hemenway."

Although not on equal ground by any means with Dos Passos—who had four full-length books and a collection of poetry from New York publishers willing to pay advances—Hemingway had standing and was acquiring a reputation. Dos Passos was eager to bring Hemingway's work to the attention of New York editors. "My story," said Dos Passos, "was that basing his wiry short sentences on cablese and the King James Bible, Hem would become the first great American stylist."

Their generation, which Gertrude Stein had told Hemingway was a "lost generation," needed its own voice. Both Hemingway and Dos

Passos believed something new, a different style of expression, was required. Hemingway was pursuing his notion that writing should be so minimalist that the words would convey imagery in the same manner painters were representing reality in geometric forms. Dos Passos, however, sought to fold modernity into text. In the manuscript back in his Paris rooms he was trying to put cinema on the page. If moviegoers could follow jump cuts and dissect visual imagery, couldn't readers? And following in Hemingway's footsteps, he was also withholding key details, leaving them to be intuited by readers.

Both men, vermouth in hand and Bible on the table, held ambitions to remake literature.

13

FOR DOS PASSOS, BEING IN PARIS WAS ALWAYS A JOYOUS OCCASION, MADE particularly pleasing this time as Crystal Ross came from Strasbourg to join him. Taking a break from her work on a thesis comparing the writers O. Henry and Guy de Maupassant, she took a room at the University Women's Club not far from the Hemingways' new flat. During this reunion with Dos Passos Ross at last relented and accepted his proposal of marriage. He was certain. She was not. She valued her intellectual pursuits and worried about her independence. "Dos for God's sake don't count on me," she told him. "I'm trying hard not to count on you."

One early summer evening Dos Passos brought his fiancée to meet Hemingway at La Closerie des Lilas. After drinks the group went to dinner at Lavigne's and then on to see a wrestling match. Ross found Hemingway to be hulking and handsome, but she was also struck by his manner of dress, from his canvas shoes to his Basque beret. "This fashion of dress is not an affectation," she decided. "It is a naturalism."

The group talked about Spain. Pamplona was the place to go, Hemingway said. On Gertrude Stein's advice he had taken Hadley to the northern Spanish city the year before. "By God they have bull fights in that town," he wrote a friend upon his return. Hemingway's idea to go to Pamplona excited Dos Passos. For him, time spent hiking in Basque lands, holing up in Iberian cities, or basking under the Andalusian sun were among the best moments in his life. There he had found an older world mostly untouched by the ravages of industrialization. "It's the most wonderful jumble," he told a friend, "the peaceful Roman world; the sadness of the Semitic nations, their mysticism; the grace—a little provincialized, a little barbarized—of a Greek colony; the sensuous dream of Moorish Spain; and little yellow French trains and American automobiles and German locomotives—all in a tangle together!"

But it irked Hemingway that Dos Passos had discovered Spain seven years earlier than he had—Dos Passos had even been to a bullfight four years before Hemingway. When Hemingway adopted a place, he made it his. Two years earlier he had only been in Paris for a few months when he wrote a scathing piece about American bohemians in which he called the café he first frequented a "showplace for tourists" and reveled about "the good old days" as if he were a Parisian. Now he already envied Dos Passos's literary success and chaffed that his friend turned out to be a more experienced Spanish hand than he.

With Dos Passos and Ross on board for a trip to Pamplona, Hemingway expanded his search for traveling companions by asking Bill Bird, along with his wife, Sally, and Robert McAlmon, his erstwhile Parisian publishers; Eric "Chink" Dorman-Smith, a friend from the Italian warfront who had accompanied Ernest and Hadley on vacation; George O'Neill, a young friend of Hadley's; and Donald Ogden Stewart to come along.

Hemingway had come to know Dos Passos's friend Stewart quite by accident several months earlier when Stewart came to Paris with instructions from *Vanity Fair* editor John Peale Bishop to look up "an interesting young writer named Hemingway." Dos Passos told Stewart that he must also eat at Madame Lecomte's restaurant on the Île Saint-Louis. In 1918 Dos Passos had rented a room above the place, and he so frequented the restaurant that the Lecomtes almost considered him a member of the family.

Following Dos Passos's culinary advice, Stewart went to Lecomte's for dinner soon after arriving in Paris. Looking around, he spotted the writer he was under orders to find. It was a lucky break that got even better when Hemingway took an immediate shine to Stewart. "He liked good food and lots to drink and he understood my kind of humor," said Stewart.

Hemingway's entourage was complete. Its members agreed to meet in Pamplona in time for the Feria del Toro, a bullfighting event held each July as part of the city's annual festival honoring its patron Saint Fermín. Ernest and Hadley left Bumby in the care of their *femme de ménage* and reached Pamplona ahead of everyone else. After checking in at the Hotel la Perla, situated on the main square, they strolled down to the Arga River that ran through the town. Hadley watched women washing clothes and drying them on the pebbly shore while boys forded the river jumping from one stepping stone to another. In her hobble skirt Hadley did her best to keep up with Ernest as he followed the boys.

Meanwhile Dos Passos and Ross took the train to Saint-Jean-Pied-de-Port in southern France. Five miles north of the Spanish border, the small town was the usual starting point for pilgrims walking the five-hundred-mile Camino de Santiago. Early the next morning the pair set off by foot up to the Roncevaux Pass that crosses the Pyrenees into Spain, famous for supposedly being the site of Roland's death recounted in the eleventh-century *Chanson de Roland*.

Dos Passos, a veteran of many hikes across Spain, delighted in the ascent but blithely gave no consideration to Ross, who couldn't maintain his pace, especially having made the rookie mistake of wearing new shoes that were not broken in. At last an amiable farmer came to her rescue and provided a donkey to carry her the remaining portion of the eighteen-mile hike to Burguete, across the border in Spain, where she recovered, resting by a stream.

Ernest and Hadley showed up the next day, and the four of them set off together for Pamplona. Over two days they crossed fields of corn and passed through groves of poplar trees until they looked up at the fortifications of the centuries-old city, once the capital of the Kingdom of Navarre.

There was confusion when they reached the Hotel de la Perla on the Plaza del Castillo at the center of Pamplona. When Hemingway had booked rooms earlier for the group he did not reserve any for Dos Passos and his fiancée. "He, speaking Spanish, can always get a place to stay," Hemingway told Stewart. Unwilling to admit his mistake in not securing a sufficient number of rooms, Hemingway claimed that one of the double rooms under his name was intended for Dos Passos and Ross. The pair was aghast that Hemingway presumed they were sleeping together. Rooms were quickly reallocated. Ross took the one Hemingway secured for Stewart, who then moved into a double room with Dos Passos.

+

The Feria del Toro began each night in Pamplona when a large number of bulls were hurriedly moved through the streets under the cover of darkness. Only the sound of their hooves on the cobblestones and the lingering bovine smell marked their passage. Early in the morning bands incessantly beating a drum roused the sleepy city, many of whose inhabitants were suffering from hangovers. Thousands rose from park benches or poured out of hotels and houses. Many went straight to the bullring. Others, however, found a spot along the nine hundred yards of streets that were lined with wooden barricades.

Soon the half-dozen bulls selected to fight that day were let loose from the corral where they had spent the night, and they charged down the barricaded streets. Those men and women who were daring ran ahead of the pack. Invariably some fell and were bruised or suffered broken bones from the hooves of the fast-moving herd. Others barely escaped injury by curling up in a gutter. In minutes the dash to the bullring was over.

The real danger to participants came when a bull got separated from the others and, in its disoriented fury, attacked. Hemingway, Dos Passos, and the rest of the group decided against running with the bulls. It was a fortunate decision because that summer the crowd mistakenly put itself into the path of an angry lone bull. The men were so tightly bunched that twenty-two-year-old Esteban Domeño Laborra was fatally gored when he could not jump over the fence. The death did not escape Hemingway's attention, and he recorded it, as he did with everything else he saw that week, in the notebook he carried with him.

It was, in fact, death that had brought Hemingway to Pamplona. In trying to write fiction in Paris he had struggled to capture feelings, events, or moments essential to bringing characters to life. He decided, instead, to begin with basics. "One of the simplest things of all and the most fundamental is violent death," he said. "The only place where you could see life and death, i.e. violent death now that the wars were over, was in the bull ring."

Every member of the group was conscious of Hemingway's obsession with bullfighting. Some, like Stewart, also grew enamored with the pastime. On the final day of the festival Stewart took up Hemingway's repeated challenge to join him in the ring during the *novillada*, the portion of the program when spectators, thinking themselves matadors, taunted heifers or aging bulls whose horns are padded with leather sheaths. "The only reason I got into the ring at all," said Stewart, "was because Hemingway shamed me into it."

Stewart was handed a cape. As he shook the hand of the toreador who gave him the cape, a bull charged. It tossed Stewart into the air. His glasses flew from his face, and the cape lay crumpled in the dust. The bull pawed the ground and made ready for another charge. "An amazing thing happened." Stewart said. "I lost my fear completely." He stood, put his glasses back on, grabbed the cape, and resumed his dance with the bull, this time more successfully. "I had shown that I could take it," Stewart said. His two cracked ribs were soon treated and became a badge of merit. Hemingway clapped him on the back, and the men went off to an evening of dancing and drinking.

An exaggerated account made it into the *Chicago Tribune* claiming that when the bull threw Stewart, it had been Hemingway who came to his rescue. Ever since the interview on the docks of New York City when he returned from his service in the Great War, Hemingway never minded guiding inflated accounts of his bravery into the press. The *Chicago Tribune* article, written no doubt by a colleague in the European press, also incorrectly claimed Hemingway had been a member of the American Expeditionary Forces and was the first American wounded on the Italian front.

Dos Passos had also followed Stewart into the ring, finding his excuse of nearsightedness insufficient against Hemingway's entreaties. "His American compatriots felt they had to show their mettle too," Dos Passos said. However, when he found himself face-to-face with one of the bulls, Dos Passos turned and ran. He made for the edge of the ring, where a wooden barrier created a kind of alleyway. The bull jumped the barrier and came up behind Dos Passos.

In the nick of time two Pamplonians hoisted Dos Passos up the footholds on the ring's wall and out of the bull's path. "My story," he said, "was that I was finding an elevated spot to make sketches from."

Indeed, sometime later Dos Passos took to his paintbrush rather than his pen to capture the American foray into the *novillada*. In the water-color he executed, Hemingway holds a heroic stance before a bull. Two men are on the ground, one is in the air, evidently having been tossed, and another figure—perhaps Dos Passos himself—is fleeing. The exaggerated features, poses, and rage of the bull make it seem like painterly sarcasm. It certainly fit Dos Passos's distaste for the adventure. "The sight of a crowd of young men trying to prove how *hombre* they were just got on my nerves," Dos Passos said. It was a manly week filled with heavy drinking and, for some, nightly visits to whorehouses, so busy during the festival that there were lines to get in. While Hemingway wished Hadley had not come, Dos Passos found that Crystal Ross's company preserved his sanity. "Between us," he said, "we built ourselves a sort of private box from which we looked out at all these goings on, in them but not of them."

+

The bullfighting at an end, at least for that year in Pamplona, the group broke up. Unfinished books, stories, articles, and academic studies awaited them in Paris, Strasbourg, and points beyond. Ross grabbed a Paris-bound train with Stewart. She and Dos Passos made plans to meet by summer's end. But first he wanted to hike. There were few things he loved better. It also leveled the playing field between him and Hemingway after a week-long pursuit of brawny bravura. Hemingway may have been a deft boxer, a practiced outdoorsman, and now a bullfighting aficionado, but when it came to hiking he was no match to Dos Passos. The man's long, indefatigable legs could stride across any countryside.

Leading the way out of Pamplona, Dos Passos set off in the company of Smith, McAlmon, and O'Neill on a planned 270-mile hike to Andorra, the miniature nation nestled in the midst of the Pyrenees. "We were going," Hemingway wrote his mother, "but Hadley did not feel absolutely fit when the time came to start and it was a trip where you need to be in absolutely perfect condition." What Hemingway didn't tell his mother was that he was in a foul mood. As usual he tracked Hadley's menstrual cycle on his calendar. The markings convinced him that she was pregnant again. He took out his frustrations on everyone. "Stop acting like a damn fool and a crybaby. You're responsible too," said Sally Bird, wife of the Paris publisher. "Either you do something about not having it, or you have it." A day later Hemingway wrote in his notebook, "Kitty commenced." The crisis had passed.

On the sixth day of the hike McAlmon's gout and blisters defeated him, and he returned to Pamplona. That left Dos Passos in the company of two. The weather remained good as they made their way over high passes of the Pyrenees. "Silence and solitude were a delight after the gabblegabble round the tables under the portales at Pamplona," said Dos Passos.

Averaging twenty to thirty miles a day, a little more on days when they tapped into their supply of brandy, they reached Andorra in just under two weeks. The final miles were hard. It poured rain, and in the darkness they lost their way. Soaked and so cold that their teeth were chattering, they entered the capital city Andorra la Vella in the middle of the night. Most everything was closed, but they found an inn with three beds. With sore legs and bruised feet and desperate for sleep, they made their way upstairs to a dingy and foul-smelling room. "The minute we stretched out in dry clothes," said Dos Passos, "the bedbugs came like shock troops, wave after wave."

Dos Passos soon traded his bug-infested bed for the luxury of a room in the Hotel du Cap in Antibes on the Côte d'Azur at the invitation of Gerald and Sara Murphy, who had rented the entire place for the summer. Almost like children who couldn't play on their own, the couple encouraged all their friends to come. The Fitzgeralds, in the midst of a marital crisis following Zelda's affair with a French naval officer, rented a villa down the coast. Stewart came from Paris for a quiet rest while his ribs recovered from the bull-induced damage. "The Riviera in summer is a strange and rather exciting place," Dos Passos wrote Jack Lawson after settling into a red-plush carpeted room.

In the mornings Dos Passos worked. After lunch with the Murphys he usually bathed in the sea or went with the whole group to a bookshop in Nice. The manuscript consuming Dos Passos's hours was different from anything he had written previously. When he began a year earlier in the rooming house of Far Rockaway his goal was clear in his mind, but the execution was not. He wanted, like Hemingway, to be free of the traditional strictures of writing. He enthusiastically promised a friend it would be "utterly fantastic and New Yorkish."

For a considerable time he had been scribbling down slogans he had read, bits of conversation he had heard, and odd facts he had learned on scraps of paper and in his notebooks. He drew from his collection for the openings of each chapter. In one, for instance, a man is impatiently shouting from a soapbox in front of a Houston Street café about how the wealthy, like vampires, are making wage slaves of the citizenry.

Then, sticking words together like heavy wet snowflakes, Dos Passos wrote on.

Through the plate glass the Cosmopolitan Café full of blue and green opal rifts of smoke looks like a muddy aquarium; faces blob whitely round the tables like illassorted fishes. Umbrellas begin to bob in clusters up the snowmottled street. The orator turns up his collar and walks briskly east along Houston, holding the muddy soapbox away from his trousers.

But the chapters Dos Passos was constructing that immediately followed these slice-of-life vignettes played like disjointed scenes in a movie with no transition from what came before. Gone was the traditional plot line he had used in *Three Soldiers*. In its place he worked at creating nearly two dozen stories dotted with snatches of song lyrics and newspaper headlines.

+

Back in Paris Hemingway seemed no closer to his goal of being a writer than when he had quit working for the *Toronto Star* eight months earlier. His only remunerative literary work came from helping Ford Madox Ford edit *the transatlantic review*, whose name was modishly set in lowercase. If it weren't for his wife's trust income, the Hemingways would have been out on the street. The review had published a Hemingway short story, "Indian Camp," a few months earlier but nothing more. Dos Passos, however, at the invitation of Ford, had a portion of his manuscript featured in the August issue.

If he were to be in the game, Hemingway needed to churn out a sufficient number of new stories to build a publishable collection of his work. He was discouraged. "I am going to have to quit writing because we haven't any money," he told Ezra Pound, lamenting Ford's drain on his time.

"The Transatlantic killed my chances of having a book published this fall and by next Spring some son of a bitch will have copied everything I've written and they will simply call me another of his imitators."

Still Hemingway labored on. Michigan and Italy became his most common backdrops as he began to conjure up a youthful version of himself— Nick Adams, the son of a doctor who fishes, hunts, and pursues love in Upper Michigan and faces battle in Italy.

Adams's name was an invention, but in the bundle of manuscript pages Hemingway carried with him each day to the café, other characters, such as Bill Smith, retained their true identity. This, he knew, might need to change when the book was prepared for publication. But as of now he reinhabited the halcyon days of Michigan, where his creation Nick Adams romped with Kate "Katy" Smith. For Hemingway one of the powers of writing was that he could have on paper what he did not have in real life.

Nick, going by Hemingway's nickname, takes Kate into the woods. Naked, under a blanket, Nick turns Kate over as she exclaims, "Oh, Wemedge. I've wanted it so. I've needed it so," and the action begins.

"Is it good this way?" he said.

"I love it. I love it. I love it. Oh, come, Wemedge. Please come. Come, come. Please, Wemedge. Please, please, Wemedge."

Hemingway drew a large X across the scene. He did not need Gertrude Stein to tell him the scene was unpublishable.

In other stories the war was never far from Hemingway's thoughts, but he had not yet made up his mind what about the war he needed to tell. In one of his longer stories Harold Krebs returns to his parents' home after participating in some of the worst battles of the war. Like many who have experienced battle, Krebs believes no one can understand what he went through. Hemingway, unlike Dos Passos, worried less about war itself than coming to terms with it. War was personal for him, not political.

The title *in our time* that he had chosen for his first collection of stories and wanted to use if a larger collection could be published came from the English Book of Common Prayer. In a responsorial portion of the prayers the minister requests, "Give us peace in our time, O Lord," to which the congregation replies, "For it is thou, Lord, only, that makest us dwell in safety." Hemingway, however, meant to apply the request for peace not as a request for a war-free world but for his generation who had been at war and carried the experience with them.

+

As the summer of 1924 came to a close, so did the Murphys' extended party. Dos Passos returned to Paris. He was running short on money and even tried pawning his typewriter. But he had credit at a hotel and in a few restaurants, and that's all one needed in Paris for a good time. He put on three elaborate dinner parties and caught up with Hemingway. The younger would-be author was feeling better about his prospects because he was closing in on his goal. "I have written fourteen stories and have a book ready to publish," he wrote O'Brien, who had published one of Hemingway's earliest stories in the annual collection he edited. "It is much better than anything I've done."

But the work had been hard. One night Lincoln Steffens, whom Hemingway knew from his days of reporting on peace conferences; his new wife, Ella Winter; and Dos Passos gathered in a Chinese restaurant. Winter was trying to decide what kind of work she might pursue. Both Dos Passos and Hemingway urged her to write. Tapping her chin with a soft left hook, Hemingway said, "It's hell. It takes it all out of you it nearly kills you; but you can do it. Anybody can. Even you can, Stef."

Dos Passos agreed. He knew his new book still needed more work, and now it was time to complete it. But before he could return to New York there remained unfinished business. He went to be with Ross. "Ate a great deal of choucroute in the rain under the dripping eaves of Strasbourg and drank riesling-muscat in rhomantick schlosses popeyed with weldschmerz and weiblich liebe until the cows came home," he wrote Rummy, using German to cryptically convey to his favorite correspondent his melancholy about Ross's unwillingness to agree on a date for their wedding—she was unwilling to commit to anything until she finished her thesis.

Further discussion of marriage would have to wait until both of them had completed their respective work. Dos Passos went to Le Havre and found a ship to take him home. Like many American readers who had been to France, he hid a copy of James Joyce's *Ulysses*, still banned in the

United States, in his suitcase that he hoped to sneak by customs. Also with him was a freshly typed copy of Hemingway's expanded *in our time*.

In New York City Stewart was awaiting him at the Yale Club. Together, they decided, they would use their publishing contacts to find a way for their friend Hemingway to break out from the small exile literary journals, with their ridiculously miniscule press runs, and onto the bookstore shelves.

14

AFTER HANDING OVER HEMINGWAY'S MANUSCRIPT TO STEWART IN NEW
York City, Dos Passos took up residence again in the small Brooklyn
apartment where a year earlier he had begun the novel he now needed to
finish. His editor, who had moved to Harper & Brothers and brought Dos
Passos along with him, wanted the manuscript on his desk by the end of
spring so as to include the book on the 1925 fall list. "I'll be a raving ma-
niac if I don't get this goddamn piece of work off my chest immediately,"
Dos Passos told Rummy.

The four-story brownstone on a sycamore-lined street away from the
distractions of Manhattan possessed a remarkable view. "Just imagine,"
wrote the poet Hart Crane, who also lived in the building, "looking out
your window directly on the East River with nothing intervening between
your view of the statue of Liberty, way down the harbor, and the marvel-
ous beauty of Brooklyn Bridge close above you on your right." In fact, the
view of the bridge was so perfect that fifty-five years earlier its engineer
oversaw the construction by telescope from the same brownstone after a
decompression accident crippled him with caisson disease.

The vista was uncannily appropriate. The city across the river was, in a
sense, the protagonist of Dos Passos's manuscript, now called *Manhattan
Transfer*. Even the iconic bridge in the view from his window earned a role
in the book. Bud Korpenning, one of a dozen characters created for his
book, comes to New York City from the country. Wandering the street,

he is unable to find work, and eventually feeling defeated, Korpenning walks on the Brooklyn Bridge.

The sun has risen behind Brooklyn. The windows of Manhattan have caught fire. He jerks forward, slips, dangles by a hand with the sun in his eyes. The yell strangles in his throat as he drops.

None of the other characters in the book fare much better. Individuals, far from heroic, come and go and sometimes connect with each other. But they have little or no say in their destiny. Joe Harland loses a fortune on Wall Street and becomes a beggar. Ellen Thatcher Oglethorpe parts with her integrity for a stage career. The man she loves leaves her for another actress and then perishes in a fire. Trouble follows all the rest, from bootlegger Congo Jake to politician George Baldwin. Dos Passos's characters illustrate Manhattan's decadence, a city of unbridled desires. Continuing his signature habit of combining two, sometimes three words into one, he wrote,

Bars yawned bright to them at the corners of rainseething streets. Yellow lights off mirrors and brass rails and gilt frames round pictures of pink naked women was looped and slopped into whiskyglasses guzzled fiery with tipped back head, oozed bright through blood, popped bubbly out of ears and eyes, dripped spluttering off fingertips.

Dos Passos sought to infuse the novel with the same kind of motion he felt traveling on the city's mass transit. Everyone in the book is constantly on the move. The title itself, *Manhattan Transfer*, he took from the railway station in Harrison, New Jersey, where New York–bound passengers moved from steam-powered trains to electric ones that dove into a tunnel under the Hudson River. The painterly style found in small doses in his earlier novels explodes here. Rather than asides in the story, his word paintings are imbued with action. When he wrote of the flags on Fifth Avenue, the stars "jiggle" in the blue background, the red and white stripes "writhe" and the flags themselves turn into "hungry tongues."

Dos Passos felt confident that the manuscript he delivered to his editor contained something expressively new. But his triumph exacted a cost. He had ignored his strep throat and succumbed again to rheumatic fever, as he had in Spain in 1919. The onset of the fever confined Dos Passos to the Midtown Hospital on East 57th Street. From his bed he wrote his Harvard friend and ambulance corps colleague Robert Hillyer. The attack,

Dos Passos said, "has ruined me in every way, reduced me to an immovable painful vegetable."

During the weeks that followed he was in and out of the hospital. Back in his Brooklyn apartment Dos Passos looked so weak that his neighbor Hart Crane believed he had come close to death. Matters of the heart complicated his recovery. Crystal Ross arrived in New York having completed her studies in France. Her Texan father and brother also came to the city to meet her. They were at the dock, along with a weakened Dos Passos feeling very much the fifth wheel, when Ross's ship made fast. She and Dos Passos managed to get together for some meals and even took in a play, escaping her father, who disapproved of her choice of suitor. But he needn't have worried. Ross made it clear to Dos Passos that she was breaking off their engagement. She was going back to Texas to teach at the university. She loved Dos Passos but could not imagine a life as the wife of a novelist—she had her own ambitions.

Ross, her brother, and father boarded a train for Texas, and Dos Passos headed back to the hospital. His rheumatic fever had returned.

✛

In the midst of his health and romantic traumas Dos Passos heard from Hemingway in Paris. The handwritten letter he received was uncharacteristic. Hemingway was writing to thank him for having helped, along with Sherwood Anderson, persuade Boni & Liveright to publish *In Our Time*. He would now have a real book to his name, and the company was sending him a $200 advance. Neither *Three Stories and Ten Poems* nor *in our time* published by small Parisian presses had earned Hemingway any money.

"Jesus I wish you were over here so we could get drunk like I am now and have been so often lately," wrote Hemingway, thanking Dos Passos for his help in getting a contract for the book. "You are a good guy and I wish to hell you were here." Not surprisingly, Hemingway reported, the editors were cutting the "Up in Michigan" story because "the girl got yenced," he said. "I suppose if it was called 'Way Out in Iowa' Mencken would have published it if the fucking would have been changed to a community corn roast."

Sherwood Anderson, who had just signed on with Boni & Liveright, contributed a blurb, and Dos Passos did so as well. Hemingway's entry into the world of publishing looked promising. In June journalist Robert Forrest Wilson told readers of *Bookman*, the leading American literary journal, that Hemingway was a writer to watch for. "His work promises to remove him from the three-hundred-copy class of authorship," Wilson wrote. "He pursues his own ways, and his friends expect him to go far."

The question facing Hemingway was what to write about next. It had been seven years since the mortar fell on him. A year earlier he had made a furtive attempt to tell his war story.

Oh, Jesus Christ, I prayed, get me out of here. Dear Jesus please get me out. Christ. Please, please please Christ. If you'll only keep me from getting killed I'll do anything you say.

At first his efforts didn't satisfy. He toyed with pronouns and decided, in the end, to make it an observed scene from the perspective of soldiers in a nearby trench. He called it "Religion" and set the 143-word piece into the stockpile he was building. Up until this moment, that had been the extent of his effort to make the war into a story.

Now he took out a blue notebook and wrote "ALONG WITH YOUTH A NOVEL" across its cover. As Dos Passos had done, he began his war story on board the *Chicago*, the ship that, at separate times, had taken them to the war. Nick Adams, the alter ego Hemingway created for his short stories, is deep in a drunken conversation with three other men as the ship neared Bordeaux. As he frequently did, Hemingway used the real names of the men on board. His effort endured for twenty-seven rambling pages before he put it aside. Perhaps, after all, he was not yet ready.

+

Hemingway began planning another trip to Pamplona. Of the 1924 contingent only Donald Ogden Stewart was available this summer. Dos Passos remained too ill to leave New York. So Hemingway filled out the group with his Michigan friend Bill Smith, who had come over to Paris, and compatriots of the Paris expatriate community: Duff Twysden, a British lady now on her second divorce; her fiancé, Pat Guthrie; and writer Harold Loeb. Hadley consented to join the group, leaving Bumby in the care of friends.

The intoxicating and adventurous spirit of the previous Pamplona trip was absent. "The Garden of Eden wasn't the same," said Stewart.

"Something had gone out of Pamplona." The companions became mired in sexual intrigue, roiled with jealousy, and almost resorted to fisticuffs, all fueled by drunkenness. The fetching Twysden took up with Loeb in Saint-Jean-de-Luz prior to the fiesta, and then she turned her sights on Hemingway. "When I got there," recalled Stewart, "I found that some-one had left the door open and Eve had walked into my male Garden of Eden." Eve's name was Lady Duff Twysden. As for the centerpiece of the fiesta, the bullfighting disgusted most of the group, except veteran Stewart and, of course, the leader of the pack.

Not only was the gathering different from that of the previous summer, Hemingway also appeared changed to Stewart. The affable guide of 1924 seemed ill-tempered in 1925. Absent of the calming influence of Dos Passos and Ross, the group frequently triggered angry outbursts from Hemingway. "You were not to disagree with the Master in any way from then on," Stewart said. Hemingway, in his eyes, had become "a dangerous friend to have."

Hemingway and Hadley went on by themselves to Madrid. There they were entertained by Cayetano Ordóñez, the matador who had wowed Ernest in Pamplona and had given Hadley an ear from a bull he killed. Seeing Ordóñez at work helped redeem the summer. Inspired, Hemingway began work on a story with a matador modeled on Ordóñez.

By the time Ernest and Hadley reached Valencia, their next stop in Spain, the short story he had envisioned about a bullfighter had grown past one hundred pages and was populated with the retinue of expatriates who had accompanied him to Pamplona. At first Ernest retained actual names. Later thinking it the wiser course, he rechristened the members of the group. Harold Loeb became Robert Cohn, Bill Smith and Donald Stewart merged into Bill Gorton, and Duff Twysden's fiancé became Mike Campbell. Twysden herself still had not yet undergone an authorial rechristening. Hem himself became Jake Barnes, with a few differences. He altered nothing of the settings. From the cafés in Paris to the journey in Spain, every detail is recounted with such accuracy that those who had been there would recognize what he was writing.

However, the story so closely resembled his Pamplona group that the name changes he adopted did little to mask his characters' identities. Everyone in the expatriate community of Paris would know who was who if the book were published. Hemingway gave no hint that he cared. Back in Paris he continued to fill the pages of his notebooks with his story. One night he strolled with Kitty Cannell, an arts correspondent for American newspapers, to dinner at the Négre de Toulouse. Ahead of them walked Hadley in the company of Loeb and Smith. "Well," Ernest said, "I've taken your advice at last. I'm writing a novel full of plot and drama. Everybody's in it." Then, with a gesture to the two men ahead, he added. "I'm tearing those bastards apart."

"But not you, Kitty," he continued. "I've always said you were a wonderful girl! I'm not going to put you in."

To see if she believed him, Hemingway turned and looked at Cannell. She stared back at his rosy cheeks and his smile full of white teeth that reminded her of an eight-year-old boy. "It made you feel like giving him an apple—or maybe your heart," she said.

Several days later Hemingway wrote "The End" in the seventh notebook.

✛

In New York Dos Passos was feeling sufficiently recovered to sail to Europe. He joined Gerald and Sara Murphy in Cap d'Antibes for a cruise on Gerald's new yacht. The *Picaflor*, Spanish for hummingbird, was a racing sloop with a Russian captain at the helm. Sara chose to leave the men to their sail, and they headed for Genoa, Italy. In the moonlight, with all sails up, the men reveled at the nighttime beauty of the Mediterranean. The sea, however, had less regard for them, and a strong wind came up. "Suddenly it seemed like one of those windstorms in Vergil's *Aeneid* when the winds blow from all directions at once," said Dos Passos. The men, clueless on proper handling of sails except for the Russian, barely managed to lower sufficient amounts of canvas before the wind knocked the yacht over. They limped into the port of Savona, almost foundering on the rocks of the channel into the harbor.

The *Picaflor* was swamped and listing and needed a tow in a hurry. As Murphy and the Russian bailed, Dos Passos tried to find the appropriate Italian word in a dictionary to call for help. The word he settled on was for *steamboat*. "It certainly didn't sound right, but for what seemed like hours

I hung in the shrouds drenched to the skin and howled *ayuto* and *pyroscafo* at dim figures round the lighthouse." They were eventually rescued.

Dos Passos said his good-byes and made his way to Paris for a reunion with a boisterously happy Hemingway. Autumn brought the publication of Hemingway's first book from a major publisher. Boni & Liveright printed thirteen hundred copies of *In Our Time*, publishing the title in upper and lower case to differentiate from the smaller Paris collection of stories that was sold under the name *in our time*. Reviews were complimentary, although the lack of a story in many of the stories puzzled a few critics. The *New York Times* greeted the book with enthusiasm. "Ernest Hemingway has a lean, pleasing, tough resilience," the paper said. "His language is fibrous and athletic, colloquial and fresh, hard and clean: his very prose seems to have an organic being of its own. Every syllable counts toward a stimulating, entrancing experience of magic." *The Bookman* was more reserved. The collection offered, it said, "sketches which show clear, vigorous beauty and a vigorous acceptance of life in its proper proportions." But the magazine did not list it as a recommended selection. That honor went to Sherwood Anderson's *Dark Laughter* along with some other titles.

Hemingway loaned his copy of *Dark Laughter* to Dos Passos, and the two talked about the book over lunch in Paris. Rather than be pleased for Anderson, Hemingway opted to bite the hand of the man whose advice had brought him to Paris, encouraged his writing, and contributed a strong endorsement on the cover of *In Our Time*. In a matter of only a few short weeks Hemingway penned a cruel parody of Anderson's *Dark Laughter*.

Literary parodies were much in vogue, and Donald Stewart had done well with his. But Hemingway's motivation was more than pecuniary: he planned on thrusting a literary rapier at Anderson to publicly break with his mentor as well as Gertrude Stein while he was at it. Any hint that he was an imitator was an affront. His parody, which he named *The Torrents of Spring*, made no pretention of being more than a hurriedly penned spoof. One chapter had been written in a mere two hours, Hemingway confessed to readers. "Then went out to lunch with John Dos Passos, whom I consider a very forceful writer, and an exceedingly pleasant fellow besides. This is what is known in the provinces as log-rolling." Over sole meunière and wild rabbit stew accompanied by bottles of Montrachet and Hospice de Beaune wine, 1919 vintages, as well as a bottle of Chambertin, Hemingway read the chapter to Dos Passos, after which he claimed his friend exclaimed, "Hemingway, you have wrought a masterpiece."

The still-unknown Hemingway was giving himself imaginary compliments from Dos Passos, his more famous and successful friend. It got Dos Passos to wonder whether Hemingway was getting back at him for strictures in the book contract he had helped obtain. It required that Hemingway provide an option on his next two works. The aspiring writer, with only a short story collection to his name, was not one to be contractually shackled, especially when he believed unperceptive editors were the only barriers to his eventual success.

Possibly this was Hemingway's motive, Dos Passos thought: "Was he deliberately writing stuff that Liveright, as Sherwood Anderson's publisher and friend, couldn't possibly print, or was it just a heartless boy's prank?" The work was certainly funny, and Dos Passos laughed at the table in La Closerie des Lilas where Hemingway read aloud from it. But publishing the book would be asking for trouble, and Dos Passos told him so. The book is not good enough to stand on its own, he said. More important, it was not a worthy successor to follow on the tails of *In Our Time*. When they parted, Dos Passos thought he had talked his friend out of publishing it.

+

Hadley also implored Ernest not to publish *The Torrents of Spring*. But another woman in Hemingway's world was of a different opinion. Pauline Pfeiffer was the newest member of the Hemingway court that drank at La Closerie del Lilas or ate cassoulet at Négre de Toulouse. She told Hemingway to disregard Dos Passos's advice and urged him to submit the parody to his publisher. He listened to what she had to say.

Hadley had only herself to blame, as it had been she who brought this woman into their circle. They met at a tea given by Kathleen Cannell in her apartment a few blocks from the Eiffel Tower. Cannell, who knew almost the entire expatriate community, frequently introduced newcomers. It was fur coat weather, and Pauline, accompanied by her sister Virginia, came dressed in a new chipmunk coat from a noted Paris couturier. The dark-eyed sisters were petite with black bobbed hair cut across the fore-head in such a way as to remind Cannell of Japanese dolls.

Pauline Pfeiffer and Hadley found they had much in common, having both grown up in St. Louis and sharing the friendship of Katy Smith, whom Pauline had met at the University of Missouri journalism school. As a matter of fact, it had been Smith who urged Pfeiffer to look up the Hemingways in Paris. In turn, after coming to Paris Pauline urged Katy to come as well. Her letter also included a suggestion that the city was fertile hunting grounds for a husband. Smith chose to remain stateside.

Disregarding the advice of his best friend and that of his wife as well, Hemingway wrapped up the manuscript of *The Torrents of Spring* and mailed it to his publisher, asking for a $500 advance, more than twice what he had been given for *In Our Time*. The money, however, was not what mattered: the move was strategic. If Boni & Liveright rejected the book, Hemingway would be contractually released from the publisher's option on future works. It had been a part of the deal he had agreed to, as most first-time authors do, feeling like a beggar at the table when being offered one's first contract. But now that Maxwell Perkins, Fitzgerald's editor at Scribner's, was interested in his work, Hemingway wanted his freedom.

Fitzgerald had told Max Perkins that, although he had not met Hemingway, this unknown writer in Paris had a significant literary future. Perkins, one of New York's leading book editors, was not one to miss out on the opportunity of signing a writer at the beginning of a career. In turn Hemingway told Perkins he would send him his manuscripts if he could get free of obligations to Boni & Liveright. Perkins was willing to suffer through publishing the frivolous *Torrents of Spring* in order to get his hands on the serious but incomplete manuscript set in Spain.

+

At the Dingo American Bar and Restaurant in Montparnasse, a new fa-vorite haunt of late-night drinkers, as it was open all night, Hemingway met Fitzgerald. His behind-the-scenes benefactor was drunk and, in his stupor, heaped high but slurred compliments on Hemingway. Friends brought an end to this first meeting between the writers when Fitzgerald looked like he might pass out. They took him back to his hotel room.

The second meeting a few days later at La Closerie des Lilas went better. Fitzgerald asked Hemingway to read *The Great Gatsby*, which had just come out. Hemingway found it to be terrific, and the two began a literary friendship.

Both from the Midwest and only three years apart, the two men took up in conversation and correspondence the themes common to their generation. For Fitzgerald, who had not witnessed the war, alcoholism, love, money, decadence, and despair were the stuff of his first three novels. The Great War earned a brief mention in his first novel *This Side of Paradise* when the protagonist takes a protracted leave from the pages when he serves in the army.

This was not the case for Hemingway. He believed the war had left an infection in its wake. It had fractured their generation's world. Its survivors—at least those in their circle—seemed to be on a hopeless search for meaning that took on a pursuit of sex, adventure, and conversation awash in booze. Hemingway was thinking of calling his book *The Lost Generation: A Novel*, after a comment Gertrude Stein had made to him. As Bill Gorton, a character in the novel-in-progress, explained, "You drink yourself to death. You become obsessed with sex. You spend all your time talking, not working. You are an expatriate, see?"

Writing about the war itself, not its later effect, remained a cathartic pursuit for Hemingway. He carried physical and mental scars from the moment when the mortar fell near him along the Piave River. He needed, as Dos Passos had done, to get it down on paper. The books Americans were reading that year included *Arrowsmith* by Sinclair Lewis, *An American Tragedy* by Theodore Dreiser, *The Great Gatsby* by Fitzgerald, and *Dark Laughter* by Anderson, which Hemingway described as "about 350 pages of perfect *diahorreah* or however it is spelled." They were the works of authors who had all missed being part of the Great War. Hemingway's frontline experience set him apart from them, with the exception of Dos Passos. Hemingway, after all, had the scars and shrapnel wounds to remind all that his near-death experience made him different.

Hemingway was like those soldiers who had returned from the war with varying degrees of psychological trauma. British doctors were only beginning to use the term *shell shock* and were among the first to come to terms with the neurotic cracks they found among the men they treated.

Typical of the soldiers seeking help in British hospitals was one who had suffered an injury similar to Hemingway's at about the same time in the war. "I was one of the first to be hit," he had told British doctors, "and, despite the pain of the wound and the terror that I should bleed to death before I was attended to, I kept on repeating to myself 'It's over now. It's over now.' And so it was, for me at any rate." But when the soldier was released from the hospital many months later, he found he was physically healed but not psychologically. "I was just twenty-one years of age, but I was an old man—cynical, irreligious, bitter, and disillusioned. I have been trying to grow young ever since."

W. H. Rivers, a British psychiatrist who worked at Craiglockhart War Hospital, was convinced the trauma his patients experienced was made worse by their belief that if they repressed the haunting memories, they would cease to be a problem; rather, Rivers sought to have his patients make the memories more bearable by confronting and examining them. One of the means to do so was by writing about the trauma.

✢

Feeling inadequate for having only made it as far as a stateside military training camp before the war ended, Fitzgerald admitted to Hemingway he regretted not having been part of the war. "The reason you are so sore you missed the war is because war is the best subject of all," Hemingway replied. Then in a remarkable admission for a man who had dined off exaggerated war tales, Hemingway continued. "Don't for Christ sake feel bad about missing the war," he told Fitzgerald, "because I didn't see or get anything worth a damn out of the whole show."

Hemingway confessed he had been too young when he went to Italy. But Dos Passos, said Hemingway—whose work both writers admired— there was a man who had seen and understood the war. "Dos, fortunately, went to the war twice and grew up in between." His first effort *One Man's Initiation* had been lousy, but not his second book, Hemingway continued. "What made *Three Soldiers* a swell book was the war. What made *Streets of Night* a lousy book was Boston. One as well written as the other." Fitzgerald shared Hemingway's dismal view of Dos Passos's Boston novel but now found the early faith he had in Dos Passos, based on *Three Soldiers*, had been restored.

Manhattan Transfer, which was in stores, was "astonishingly good," Fitzgerald told Max Perkins. The book was eclipsing Hemingway's modest success with *In Our Time*. The *New York Times* heralded *Manhattan Transfer* as "a powerful and sustained piece of work." Comparing his efforts to change the nature of novels with that of James Joyce, the lengthy review gave Dos Passos's book the prominent and expansive space reserved for works of importance. The reviewer, in breathless prose much like that of the author's, told readers that "the real 'meat' of his strange book comes in the host of human moths more or less singed or wilted, who flutter and swarm round the lights of Broadway and Fifth Avenue—tramps, drunkard, wastrels, homo-sexualists, prostitutes more or less accredited, 'Villagers,' waiters, bootleggers and ruffians, with the shadow of Jefferson Market Night Court somehow never far from their shoulders."

Sinclair Lewis told readers of the *Saturday Review of Literature* that Dos Passos's work was a novel of great importance. "I regard *Manhattan Transfer* as more important in every way than anything by Gertrude Stein or Marcel Proust or even the great whiteboard, Mr. Joyce's *Ulysses*."

It was a moment of triumph, but as was his habit, Dos Passos had elected to be in an inaccessible spot when the critics delivered their verdict. This time he was in the outer reaches of Morocco. When he reemerged and reached a city with international communications he learned critics had acclaimed *Manhattan Transfer* and that the book was already in its third printing. He picked up a postcard featuring a street scene of a cobblestone street in Algiers with a merchant wearing a white apron looking toward the cameraman with curiosity and veiled women making purchases. Addressing it to Hemingway, he scribbled, "Algiers is just like Belloc-Lowndes' description of Lacville—gambling everywhere and insufficient lights. It's swell. Met John the Baptist on the street, also Julius Caesar, Seneca, Tadius, Iscariost. . . . Up to neck in couscous. Love to Hadley."

It was time to emerge again from hiding. In March 1926 Dos Passos persuaded a pilot to let him sit with the cargo in a plane bound for Marseille. The flight was cold and rough, with stops in Spain. In the turbulence Dos Passos vomited into his hat. Once in France he went straight to Cap d'Antibes, where the Murphys welcomed him. Dos Passos learned from them that Boni & Liveright had rejected Hemingway's parody of

Anderson. Freed from his contractual obligations, Hemingway had made a rapid round trip to New York City and signed a contract with Perkins at Scribner's to publish both *The Torrents of Spring* and the novel he was finishing.

While Hemingway was in New York City the *Nation* magazine published an article comparing his work to that of Dos Passos. Both men are writers of unusual integrity, poet and essayist Alan Tate wrote. Dos Passos's *Manhattan Transfer* would alter American consciousness and Hemingway's style would be noticed, he predicted. "The passionate accuracy of particular observation, the intense monosyllabic diction, the fidelity of internal demands of the subject—these qualities fuse in the most completely realized naturalistic fiction of the age."

Back in Europe, Hemingway urged Dos Passos to join him and Hadley in Schruns, Austria, where the high, powdery snow that spring made for great skiing, and to bring the Murphys along. When they got there in the middle of March Dos Passos and Gerald Murphy looked over the scene with trepidation. Massive snow-covered mountains surrounded the village on all sides. As Dos Passos had not skied since his days in boarding school and Gerald had few of the necessary skills, the slopes looked daunting. They both knew it was useless to try to keep up with the more athletic Hemingway, an inequality their host greatly enjoyed. Murphy did his best, and Dos Passos resorted to using his backside to slow his downward speed whenever he spotted a tree or obstacle. By the end of several runs he had a hole in the back of his pants.

As they did whenever together, Dos Passos and Hemingway talked shop. Hemingway had been reading *Manhattan Transfer* and had mixed feelings about it. "Twice I didn't think I would be able to finish it—or care about finishing it and each time when I started reading again it was much more interesting," he confided to his new editor, Max Perkins. What disturbed Hemingway the most was Dos Passos's conjoining of words such as in the sentence: "It was a narrowwindowed sixstory tenement. The hookandladder has just drawn up." The two argued about it. Hemingway believed the additional shade of meaning gained by combining the words is lost by the jolt given the reader by its oddity. "Dos himself," Hemingway reported to Perkins, "says now he thinks it was a mistake coupling the words."

In the evenings, spent and exhausted, the Hemingways, Murphys, and Dos Passos gathered around radiating porcelain stoves, where they ate trout and drank hot kirsch. Feeling the warm comfort of friends, one night Hemingway brought out his much-revised manuscript, due in New York in two months. For the first time an audience listened as he began to read aloud from his first novel.

15

IT WOULD HAVE TAKEN ONLY A FEW MINUTES BEFORE DOS PASSOS, THE Murphys, and Hadley recognized where Ernest had found the material for the novel they were now hearing. As they sat around the porcelain stove in Schruns in March 1926, descriptions of their Paris and its cafés, Pamplona and its bullfights, and the sexually tense and boozy world of their expatriate life filled the room. Even Dos Passos's former fiancée, Crystal Ross, provided an early line of conversation in the novel. "I know a girl in Strasbourg who can show us the town," the main character tells a friend. "She been there two years and knows everything there is to know about the town. She's a swell girl."

The staccato stream of the words Hemingway read aloud gave the prose a startlingly muscular sparseness like that of the vignettes contained in *In Our Time*. Devoid of metaphors and similes, and an almost-complete absence of adjectives and adverbs, the unadorned sentences still managed to convey a story.

In it Parisian-based American journalist Jake Barnes, who was wounded in World War I, downs coffees and *fines* as he moves from cafés to bars populated by expatriates such as Princeton graduate Robert Cohn and Bill Gorton, both of whom Barnes had met during the war. The beautiful British divorcée, Lady Brett Ashley, arrives and becomes everyone's object of desire. Barnes, however, has long been in love with her and she with him. They first met when she served as a volunteer nurse in a hospital where he was recuperating from wounds during the war. But the extent of his battle wounds thwarted their romance—the war had made him impotent.

The group, along with Ashley's fiancé, Michael Campbell, eventually reunites in Pamplona. Wine, lust, and Ashley's spurning of her past and current lovers to pursue the handsome torero Pedro Romero—too young to have been affected by the war—brews a toxicity inspiring fights, boozy confrontations, and confessions. Everyone departs depressed and anxious.

When Hemingway ceased reading, his audience praised him in unison. He brought out photographs of the bullfights that he kept with him. It stirred the Murphys to announce they too wanted to accompany Hemingway on his next return to Pamplona in July. Dos Passos demurred—one Hemingway-led trip to Pamplona was sufficient. But for now the perfect weather; ideal skiing conditions; nights of trout, beer, and kirsch; and this moment of literary intimacy had created an "unalloyed good time," said Dos Passos. "We were brothers and sisters when we parted company."

Ernest and Hadley remained in Schruns. On his Corona typewriter Ernest set about revising the last five chapters of the novel. He typed out a coda in which Barnes, tending his wounds in San Sebastian, receives an urgent telegraph from Ashley asking that he come to Madrid. There he learns she has broken up with the bullfighter. They get into a taxi.

Working with short sentences, almost all composed solely of words of two or fewer syllables, Hemingway struggled to give his novel a breathless ending of lost opportunity.

"Oh, Jake," Brett said, "we could have such a damned good time together."

Ahead was a mounted policeman in khaki directing traffic. He raised his baton. The car slowed suddenly pressing Brett against me.

Then Hemingway debated the final words that Barnes would utter.

"Yes," I said. "It's nice as hell to think so."

No.

"Yes," I said. "Isn't it nice to think so."

No, again. Finally.

"Yes," I said. "Isn't it pretty to think so?"

Like the final words of Fitzgerald's *The Great Gatsby* that Hemingway so admired—"So we beat on, boats against the current, borne back ceaselessly into the past."—Hemingway had found the closing words for his book on his generation whose fate seemed largely beyond its control.

✛

As Ernest and Hadley stayed on in Schruns, Dos Passos made his way to Cherbourg, France, where he boarded the *Berengaria*, a ship that had once belonged to Germany but had been given over to the British as reparation for the *Lusitania*. Landing in New York City, Dos Passos arrived in time to catch one of the last performances of a play of his, which critics panned and left audiences baffled. Off and on he had tried his hand at writing plays. The year before the Harvard University Dramatic Club had put on his "The Moon Is a Gong," the modest success of which led to a very short run in a New York City theater. But things other than playwriting were on his mind.

Unlike Hemingway, who sought to describe the desolate postwar world with honest clarity, Dos Passos wanted his writing to change it. Itzok Isaac Granich, who had adopted the pen name Mike Gold during the notorious Palmer Raids when the government rounded up radicals, asked whether Dos Passos would help bring out a new incarnation of *The Masses*, a radical left-wing magazine that authorities had closed during the war. For six years it had published radical critiques of society, capitalism, and the war by John Reed, Dorothy Day, and others as well as literary contributions from Jack London, Carl Sandburg, Upton Sinclair, and Sherwood Anderson. Most striking, however, were the pages of illustrations by John Sloan, Stuart Davis, and Art Young. They served up macabre representations of war, uncomfortably frank depictions of poverty, and daringly direct political cartoons. The writing and illustration had been too much for the government, which successfully shut the magazine down in 1917 using its powers under the Espionage Act.

Dos Passos stood ready to help resurrect *The Masses*. "I'm absolutely with you," he wrote to one of the organizers. "*The Masses* was the only magazine I ever had any use for." Since the success of the government's repression efforts, Dos Passos was glad for an opportunity to bring to the fore what he called, "the pacifist 'radical' tendency of the old *Masses*." His friend, John Howard Lawson, whom he had met on the ship heading to the war in 1917, also joined the effort.

Leftists were up in arms about the impending execution of Nicola Sacco and Bartolomeo Vanzetti, two anarchists in Massachusetts who had been convicted—wrongly in the eyes of many—of murder and robbery. On April 15, 1920, a paymaster for a shoe company in South Braintree, Massachusetts, and his guard had been killed and the money they carried stolen. The murderers, who were described as two Italian men, escaped with more than $15,000. After going to a garage to claim a car that police connected to the crime, Sacco and Vanzetti were arrested. Considering the two were known anarchists, carried guns, and lied to the police, the authorities were convinced they had their men. Soon after, Sacco and Vanzetti were convicted and sentenced to execution, despite seemingly exculpatory evidence. They might have died unnoticed as two perpetrators of a botched robbery, but in the six years since, protests on their behalf had made the names of Sacco and Vanzetti world famous and symbols of injustice.

The American public on the whole, however, was unmoved. After the war Americans nurtured a rising abhorrence of foreigners and radicals. Not without reason, a wave of deadly bombings perpetrated by anarchists terrified the public. But Dos Passos placed greater blame for the intolerance on the war. A massive propaganda campaign—including a poster that depicted Germany as a giant, drooling monster carrying the limp body of a bare-breasted woman in his arms—fueled a xenophobic revulsion that Dos Passos believed continued in the 1920s. Even before the end of the war Dos Passos had sensed the growing hostility while attending Harvard. "I personally felt," he said, "the frustrations that came from being considered a wop or a guinea or a greaser." With both personal and political motives, Dos Passos offered to go to Boston and report on the case for readers of the *New Masses*.

On a June 1926 day when the blue sky reminded him of robin's eggs, Dos Passos walked up to the jail in Dedham, Massachusetts, that held one of the two men. He was surprised to find lawns leading to a building flanked by trees. Inside he traversed a spacious reception area and was admitted to the warden's office, whose light brown–varnished floor was so clean, it gleamed. After greeting Dos Passos, the warden, who had seen his share of writers and reporters, told his newest visitor to take a seat while Sacco was summoned from his cell.

After a bit, Sacco arrived. He had a waxy countenance as if he had been ill for a time. The two men sat side by side. They chatted about Dos Passos's effort to publicize the case, and Sacco answered his questions. Dos Passos decided the accused was the decent man described in the character witness depositions he had read before coming. It was now time to meet the other alleged murderer.

At the Charlestown State Prison Dos Passos found crowds milling about the front of the prison. The atmosphere was like that of a circus. As at the Dedham jail, he was permitted to interview Vanzetti. His meeting with the second man left no doubt in Dos Passos's mind that the two were incapable of the crime with which they were charged.

Returning to New York City, Dos Passos wrote up his account of the case for the *New Masses*. Drawing on his skills as a novelist and the kind of urban-realism style he had honed for *Manhattan Transfer*, he provided sympathetic biographies of the two men, a summary of the events leading to their arrests, and attacked the thinness of the evidence. Dos Passos focused his defense of Sacco and Vanzetti on the court's prejudicial handling of eyewitness testimony in a separate trial of Vanzetti, where he was convicted of a lesser charge in connection with a preceding robbery on December 24, 1919. The prosecutors hoped the conviction would strengthen their hand when they tried the two men together for the Braintree robbery.

More than a dozen people claimed they saw Vanzetti selling eels at a North Plymouth fish market on the morning of the crime. The courtroom discounted the testimony, believing it unlikely that so many people would have bought eel on the same day. They did not know, as Dos Passos pointed out, that a traditional Christmas Eve dish for Italians is *capitone*, otherwise known as eel. For Dos Passos the ignorance was symbolic of the misunderstanding stemming from Americans' hatred of new immigrants.

In writing his report Dos Passos blamed Dedham, the site of the second and more significant trial, for the unfairness done to Sacco and Vanzetti. The town's genesis story, as described by Dos Passos, was one of racial purity dating back to the Puritans. It was a place of elms, beeches, barberry bushes, and cultivated citizens standing united in a belief of Anglo-Saxon supremacy. "When the Congregational God made Dedham," wrote Dos Passos, "he looked upon it and saw it was good."

When he came to the end of his work Dos Passos had only produced a short book, padded with testimony and documents. It was not much of a persuasive text to buttress his support for an impartial commission to review the case. "If they die what little faith many millions of men have in the chance of Justice in this country will die with them," he wrote. "Save Sacco and Vanzetti."

Discouraged by the Sisyphean nature of the campaign on behalf of Sacco and Vanzetti, Dos Passos left New York City to hike along the Outer Banks of North Carolina in the company of Rummy, who was now twenty-six years old, and two other friends. They spent days walking the beaches, stripping off their clothes and dipping in the ocean to cool off, drinking moonshine at night, and dancing with women. "There are more beautiful girls at Buxton than any place in America," Dos Passos said, noticing women for the first time since his breakup with Crystal Ross.

✦

In Paris, when the Hemingways returned from Schruns, Hadley joined Pauline Pfeiffer and her sister Virginia Pfeiffer on a motor trip to the Loire Valley. As they drove away from the city, Pauline, carrying a copy of *Moll Flanders* from Sylvia Beach's lending library, lapsed into uncharacteristically long silences. One afternoon on the grounds of a château Hadley turned to Virginia. "Don't you think Ernest and Pauline get along awfully well together?"

"I think," she replied, "they're very fond of each other."

The manner—not the words—of the reply was devastating. Hadley knew. Her husband had fallen in love with the woman who had been their constant companion for months. The steps Ernest and Pauline had taken to conceal the affair right under her nose suddenly became clear. While she and Ernest had been in Schruns Pauline wrote to inquire about Dos Passos's supposed amorous interest in her, to throw Hadley off the scent. "Hadley," she said, "this is of course private, but was there any where about him in addition to the regular luggage, anything resembling a jewel casket?" Possibly betraying the ruse by suggesting this imagined lover had Spanish rather than Portuguese blood, Pauline continued her confidences. "Everything between me and the hot Spanish suitor has now been placed on the high love plane, and this I suppose must be maintained," she closed, making a stab at humor about jewels being the material reward of passion.

But clues of her husband's infidelity specifically hinted that Pauline was working her way into Ernest's life. "She is a swell girl," Ernest had written Bill Smith, Katy's brother, a few months earlier telling how Pauline was with them all the time. While Hadley tended to their child, it had been Pauline who had become Ernest's drinking companion. "Pauline and I killed on a Sunday two bottles of Beaune, a bottle of Chambertin and a bottle of Pommard and with the aid of Dos Passos a quart of Haig in the square bottle, and a quart of hot Kirsch." Like Hadley, Dos Passos remained unaware that there was more to the friendship than shared booze. But then again, despite his novelist's observation skills on most matters, relationships with women remained a mystery to him.

Upon her return to Paris from her motor trip Hadley confronted Ernest. He was livid that she brought it up, almost as if he believed he could carry on with both women. He and Hadley fought for several days and nights, but she knew the battle had been lost. For Pauline's part, now that it was out in the open, she wanted Ernest to herself.

On the streets of Paris one day Kitty Cannell spotted Hadley and asked why she had not gotten in touch with her since returning from Schruns. Then she asked about Pauline.

"Well, *you* know what's happening," Hadley replied. "She's taking my husband."

+

As the rain poured down steadily from April to May, Hemingway grew sullen, torn between two women. He missed his friends, all of whom, including Dos Passos, were out of town. "I feel low as hell," he wrote Fitzgerald. "I've not had one man to talk to or bull shit with for months." He had mailed the finished *The Sun Also Rises* to editor Max Perkins, who was bringing out *The Torrents of Spring* that month as a payment of sorts for this much-awaited manuscript. Hemingway's parody of Sherwood Anderson attracted some notice, mostly complimentary, and accomplished its goal of publicly ridiculing Anderson, but it did little more. Hemingway's hope for literary success, the kind Fitzgerald and Dos Passos enjoyed, would rest on the manuscript on Perkins's desk. All he could do was wait. He planned to escape Paris and go to Spain as he had each previous summer for three years. But for now, Hemingway told Fitzgerald, "I am thinking of going out, in a few minutes, and getting very cock eyed drunk."

Hemingway did go to Spain, but on his own. Hadley and their son went to stay with the Murphys in their fourteen-room mansion on the Riviera, where she hoped Bumby would recover from whooping cough in the warm sun. She wrote Ernest that she had accepted Pauline's request to join them, using one of his nicknames for her. "It would be a swell joke on *tout le monde* if you and Fife and I spent the summer at Juan-les-Pine or hereabouts instead of Spain." Taking a page from Machiavelli, she brought her husband's lover close to keep her under constant watch.

When Ernest came up from Spain, Pauline was there. An odd stillness, like that in the eye of a storm, descended upon the three. Together they rented bicycles and took long rides, swam for hours by the beach, and drank into the night. Hadley bided her time thinking her husband would eventually come to his senses. Pauline and Ernest tried to act civil, as if this ménage à trois were possible. From Ernest's point of view, it certainly was. But Pauline did not agree—she wanted him to herself. She grew bolder while Hadley became increasingly passive. Perhaps thinking she had the upper hand, one day Pauline invited Hadley out to sunbathe. After they reached a spot, Pauline stripped off her swimsuit and lay naked in the sun, showing off her slimmer figure to the matronly mother of Ernest's child.

✦

Dos Passos's summer was rapidly consumed with work on his literary defense of Sacco and Vanzetti. He remained mostly in New England, revising the book about the case that would be published by the Sacco-Vanzetti Defense Committee. While conducting his research Dos Passos went occasionally to Provincetown, at the tip of Cape Cod. A literary and artistic spot where Hemingway's friend Katy Smith lived with her brother, the town was familiar to Dos Passos. While at Harvard he had been there on a number of occasions.

On one visit Dos Passos went to a party at the home of playwright and novelist Susan Glaspell. He admired Glaspell for her role in creating the

Provincetown Players. He hadn't given up on trying to be a playwright himself. The group had begun in 1915 with two plays, and its popularity led to more summertime performances and eventually several seasons in New York City. The company no longer performed, having closed three years earlier, but it was widely credited with having helped gain interest in the works of American playwrights such as Eugene O'Neill.

Wearing a rumpled suit punctuated with a bright orange knit tie, Dos Passos met artist Eben Given. The two Chicago natives had a shared past, both having served with the Red Cross in Verdun. Dos Passos talked with Given about the Sacco and Vanzetti case and his work on his book about the case, but Given noticed that his new friend grew increasingly animated as he discussed another book. Dos Passos said he had agreed to write a review for the *New Masses* of a first novel by a writer unknown to Given. It was called *The Sun Also Rises*.

16

ON FRIDAY, OCTOBER 22, 1926, ERNEST HEMINGWAY'S *THE SUN ALSO RISES* went on sale. Wrapped in a yellow and gold dust jacket with an illustration of a woman whose loose vestments exposed her thigh and shoulder, Hemingway's first novel was added to bookstore shelves already crowded with best-sellers such as *Gentlemen Prefer Blondes* by Anita Loos and *Beau Geste* by P. C. Wren. But Charles Scribner's Sons knew it had something special. Its staff worked on advertisements to place in newspapers, promising the novel would "command the sharpest attention even in a season so crowded with good fiction."

The *New York Times* was the first to agree with the publisher's assessment. "This novel is unquestionably one of the events of an unusually rich year in literature," the reviewer wrote a week after the book's appearance. "No amount of analysis can convey the quality of *The Sun Also Rises*. It is a truly gripping story, told in a lean, hard, athletic narrative prose that puts more literary English to shame."

Other reviews soon echoed the *Times*'s assessment. "The dialogue is brilliant," said the *New York Herald Tribune*. "If there is better dialogue being written today I do not know where to find it." The *New York Sun* also came up empty in seeking a comparison. "There is no one writing whose prose has more of the force and vibrancy of good, direct, natural, colloquial speech."

Those reviews that did find fault with the work objected to the descriptions of the free-spirited irresponsible life led by expatriates while most Americans remained at home and at their jobs as well as to the perceived promiscuity on the part of the character Ashley. As one critic asked, "Why does Mr. Hemingway, who *can* draw flesh-and-blood, waste his time on the bibulous shadows?"

Hemingway's hometown newspaper reflected its pride in the Oak Park youth who had become a noted writer but carped that he was wasting his immense skill on an unworthy subject. "Ernest Hemingway can be a distinguished writer if he wishes to be," said the *Chicago Tribune*. "He is, even in this book, but it is a distinction hidden under a bushel of sensationalism and triviality." His mother was less kind. Grace told Ernest she had avoided attending her book group when it discussed *The Sun Also Rises*. "It is a doubtful honor to produce one of the filthiest books of the year," she wrote. "Surely you have other words in your vocabulary besides 'damn' and 'bitch'—every page fills me with a sick loathing." Had her son not written it, she concluded, she would have pitched the book into the fire.

But in the end even some of his most vociferous critics capitulated when it came to Hemingway's ability to write. "A writer named Hemingway has arisen," announced *The Atlantic*, "who writes as if he had never read anybody's writing, as if he has fashioned the article of writing himself."

Like many others, Dos Passos was in awe of the writing as he read the passages of the book in preparation for review in the *New Masses*. Its bedazzling nature, however, befuddled Dos Passos. "It's an extraordinarily well written book," he said, "so well written that while I was reading it I kept telling myself I must be growing dough-headed for not getting it."

He turned to his typewriter and began his review by chastising his friend, with whom he had once read biblical passages in a Paris café, for beginning the book with a quotation from the Bible. It leads readers to believe the book will be substantial, Dos Passos wrote. "Instead of these things of deep importance you find yourself reading about the tangled love affairs and bellyaches of a gloomy young literatizing Jew, of an English Lady of title who's a good sport, and a young man working the Paris office of an American newspaper, the 'I' who tells the story."

Frustrated by Hemingway's plot—or lack of one—Dos Passos said the lost generation needed an epic, but *The Sun Also Rises* was not it. "This

Hemingway, around five years old, tries his luck fishing a stream near his family's summer place in northern Michigan. Hemingway developed a love for the outside, for fishing, and for hunting as a young boy.

(Courtesy of the Ernest Hemingway Collection, John F. Kennedy Presidential Library and Museum, Boston)

Clad in a sailor's suit, Dos Passos poses stiffly for the camera. Much of Dos Passos's childhood was lived out of hotels in Brussels, Biarritz, and Boulogne-sur-Mer—places where his parents could meet openly before they married. "He never grew to like formal dress and was never happier than dressed plainly working in his garden or walking around the farm," according to his daughter Lucy Coggin.

(Courtesy of the University of Virginia)

Dos Passos entered Harvard University when he was only sixteen years old. By the time he graduated in 1916 he decided he wanted to be a writer and had completed his first novel. He also made lifelong friends at Harvard, including E. E. Cummings.

(Courtesy of the University of Virginia)

At age sixteen, Hemingway was in high school in Oak Park, Illinois. Like Dos Passos, Hemingway was also thinking of a writing career; he published short stories in the school's literary magazine and contributed articles to the school newspaper.

(Courtesy of the Ernest Hemingway Collection, John F. Kennedy Presidential Library and Museum, Boston)

When Dos Passos joined the ambulance corps in 1917, volunteers had to purchase their own uniforms from a Parisian couturier on the fashionable rue de la Paix. The tailor fitted Dos Passos for an olive drab tunic made of worsted wool, held closed by gray metal buttons and cinched with a wide brown leather belt. Jodhpurs, a soft trench cap, and knee-high laced boots completed the outfit.

(Courtesy of Lucy Coggin)

Hemingway was fitted with US Army officer's uniforms in 1918 because the volunteer ambulance corps had been disbanded after the United States' entry into the war and taken over by the US military. "Our uniforms are regular United States Army Officers' and look like a million dollars," Hemingway wrote his family.

(Courtesy of the Ernest Hemingway Collection, John F. Kennedy Presidential Library and Museum, Boston)

Dos Passos was among the American volunteer ambulance drivers who navigated treacherous roads on the French battlefront. The skills required to drive an ambulance were not easy to acquire. A driver had to control various levers and use his feet, like an organist, to operate three pedals that controlled the transmission's various speeds.

(Courtesy of the Dos Passos family)

Although Hemingway is posed in the driver's seat of an ambulance, he mostly rode a bicycle to reach the Italian soldiers confined in trenches. It was while making a delivery of chocolates and cigarettes that he was wounded in a mortar attack.

(Courtesy of the Ernest Hemingway Collection, John F. Kennedy Presidential Library and Museum, Boston)

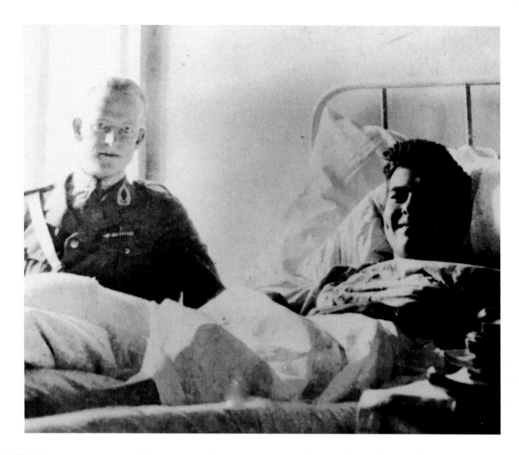

Captain Meade Detweiler, a fellow ambulance driver, was among the first to visit the wounded Hemingway at the Ospedale Croce Rossa Americana in Milan where he had been taken to recover from his wounds in July 1918.

(Courtesy of the Ernest Hemingway Collection, John F. Kennedy Presidential Library and Museum, Boston)

Twenty-six-year-old Agnes von Kurowsky met Hemingway while he was recuperating from his war wounds in Milan. The two fell in love. For Hemingway, still only a teenager, the romance seemed to come right from the pages of a war novel he had read the summer before.

(Courtesy of the Ernest Hemingway Collection, John F. Kennedy Presidential Library and Museum, Boston)

After returning to the United States from the war in 1918, Hemingway frequently wore a uniform. One day he brought an Austrian helmet, a revolver, and his blood-stained and torn uniform to his high school where he addressed the students.

(Marcelline Hemingway Sanford Collection, courtesy of the Ernest Hemingway Foundation of Oak Park and the Oak Park Public Library)

Dos Passos met Walter Rumsey Martin (right) on a train ride to California shortly after his mother's death. In "Rummy," as he called Martin, Dos Passos found a confidant and a lifelong friend.

(Courtesy of the University of Virginia)

In September 1921, Hemingway married Elizabeth Hadley Richardson in the Hemingways' summer retreat in Horton Bay, Michigan. Like Hemingway's Italian lover Agnes von Kurowsky, Richardson was an older woman; in this case, eight years older. Hemingway's friend Katy Smith introduced him to Richardson.

(Marcelline Hemingway Sanford Collection, courtesy of the Ernest Hemingway Foundation of Oak Park and the Oak Park Public Library)

In 1923, Hemingway went to Spain on the advice of Gertrude Stein and fell in love with bullfighting. But it irked Hemingway that Dos Passos had discovered Spain seven years earlier than he had—Dos Passos had even been to a bullfight four years before Hemingway. When Hemingway adopted a place, he made it his own.

(Courtesy of the Ernest Hemingway Collection, John F. Kennedy Presidential Library and Museum, Boston)

In 1924, Ernest and Hadley Hemingway, Donald Ogden Stewart, Dos Passos, and other friends went to Pamplona for the Feria del Toro. Hemingway persuaded Dos Passos and Stewart to follow him into the bullring for the portion of the program, the *novillada*, where spectators taunt heifers or aging bulls with horns padded with leather sheaths. Afterward, Dos Passos executed a watercolor with Hemingway in a heroic stance in front of the bull.

In March 1926 the camera captured Dos Passos, Hadley and Ernest Hemingway, and Sara and Gerald Murphy in Schruns, Austria. It was what Dos Passos called "the last unalloyed good time I had with Hem and Hadley." Not long after, Hemingway divorced Hadley and married Pauline Pfeiffer.

Skiing was a constant pastime in Schruns. Hadley and Ernest Hemingway were very comfortable on skis but Dos Passos, standing here near an instructor, could hardly keep up. "When the slopes got too steep," he said, "I used to sit down on my skis and turn them into a sort of toboggan."

After divorcing Hadley, Ernest married Pauline Pfeiffer in 1927. Pauline was a friend of Katy Smith, who had also introduced Hadley to Ernest. In fact, it was Smith who had urged Pfeiffer to look up the Hemingways in Paris.

(Courtesy of the Ernest Hemingway Collection, John F. Kennedy Presidential Library and Museum, Boston)

In 1927, as the execution of anarchists Sacco and Vanzetti neared, Dos Passos was arrested in Boston with other protesters. The trial and execution pushed Dos Passos further to the political left and strengthened his resolve to use his writing as a tool of social change. It also painfully placed a wedge between him and Hemingway as his friend remained unmoved when Dos Passos urged him to also join the campaign to save the two anarchists.

(Courtesy of the University of Virginia)

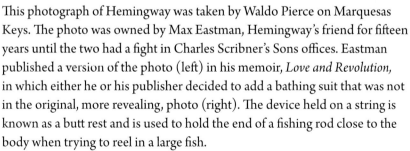

This photograph of Hemingway was taken by Waldo Pierce on Marquesas Keys. The photo was owned by Max Eastman, Hemingway's friend for fifteen years until the two had a fight in Charles Scribner's Sons offices. Eastman published a version of the photo (left) in his memoir, *Love and Revolution*, in which either he or his publisher decided to add a bathing suit that was not in the original, more revealing, photo (right). The device held on a string is known as a butt rest and is used to hold the end of a fishing rod close to the body when trying to reel in a large fish.

(Courtesy of Colby College, Special Collections, Waterville, Maine)

In 1928, Ernest and Pauline Hemingway moved to Key West, Florida, on the recommendation of Dos Passos. When Dos Passos visited, the two men fished, drank, and read. Sometimes they did all three at once.

(Courtesy of the Ernest Hemingway Collection, John F. Kennedy Presidential Library and Museum, Boston)

Dos Passos, Hemingway, an unidentified man, and Edward "Bra" Saunders, a Bahaman pilot who frequently went out to sea with Hemingway, reach dry ground at Dry Tortugas on the Florida Keys in 1928. Dos Passos went to sea to fish at Hemingway's insistence but he rarely enjoyed it.

It was in Key West in 1928 that Dos Passos met Katy Smith, whom
Hemingway had known since his days summering as a teenager in
Michigan. Playful, she soon gave Dos Passos the nickname "Monsieur
Muttonfish." It was his favorite seafood at dinner, even though it was less
prized than other dishes. It also differed from the rest of the fish in the
region's waters—muttonfish preferred to swim solitarily among the reefs
of Key West, avoiding its own kind. A writer herself, Smith provided the
kind of companionship he had long sought.

*(Courtesy of the Ernest Hemingway Collection, John F. Kennedy Presidential Library and
Museum, Boston)*

"From the first moment I couldn't think of anything but her green eyes," Dos Passos said of Katy Smith. The two married in 1929.

(Courtesy of the University of Virginia)

After getting married, John and Katy Dos Passos lived in Provincetown, Massachusetts, and frequently saw her brother Bill (center), who had also known Hemingway since childhood.

(Courtesy of the University of Virginia)

In 1937, Dos Passos and Hemingway went to Spain to make a documentary in support of the embattled Republican government. During their time in the war zone, their friendship unraveled acrimoniously.

(Courtesy of Bettmann)

novel strikes me," Dos Passos wrote, "as being a cock and bull story about a lot of summer tourists getting drunk and making fools of themselves at a picturesque Iberian folk-festival."

Dos Passos read what he had written. The review, which would be read by all their friends, praised Hemingway's writing but came down hard on the book's subject. He took a carbon copy of the review, scribbled "God this is a rotten review" at the top, and stuffed it, along with a note, into an envelope addressed to Hemingway. "I've written a damn priggish mealy mouthed review that makes me sick," he told his friend. "The book makes me sick anyway, besides making me very anxious to see you, and homesick for good drinks and wisecracks and Pamplona and bullfights and all that sort of thing, god damn it and them."

"I've never felt so rotten about anything," he continued. "Hem, please forgive all this rubbish." Dos Passos was in a dark mood brought on by the impending execution of Sacco and Vanzetti and the evident futility of what he had written about the case. "Everything I write seems to be crap and everything everybody I like writes seems to be crap." As writers, they often found it easier to share intimacies on paper rather than in person.

He was not done yet. He rambled on, almost incoherently, comparing Hemingway's masterpiece to his own *Streets of Night*, which both Hemingway and Fitzgerald had denigrated, and saying that neither of them could write and should take up charcoal burning. But in the next instant he confessed his enviousness. "You write so damn well and the book is damn readable," he said. "I'd like to get cockeyed in *fine a l'eau* in your company."

Instead Dos Passos packed his bags and grabbed a train.

✦

Getting out of town was a favored way out of problems for Dos Passos. "Locomotion even under the most adverse conditions always cheers me up," he told his war buddy Robert Hillyer two years earlier while on a ship. After a brief stop in northern Virginia to visit his half-brother, Dos Passos went for a three-day walk in the Blue Ridge Mountains. "Nobody in the Virginia mountains had ever heard of Sacco and Vanzetti or Marx or expressionism in the theater," Dos Passos said. "If they had they didn't give a damn. What a relief!"

He rode the train on to Louisville, St. Louis, and eventually to Dallas. The ride and stops so far had been to gather material for an expansive novel beginning to take seed in his mind about the United States. The stop in Dallas had a more personal purpose. It was where Crystal Ross lived. Since the last time they had been together Ross had taken a job as a professor at Southern Methodist University. When Dos Passos caught up with her in Dallas, she was also preparing an article for the *Dallas Morning News* that both recounted their time with Hemingway in 1924 and reviewed *The Sun Also Rises*. "To say it quickly," Ross wrote, "Ernest Hemingway's style is remarkable and exciting, and his book valuable; it is not so valuable as his style." The story of lost Americans and Brits, drifting and drinking in Paris and Pamplona—in which she appears as the "girl in Strasbourg"—was not the point of the work, she perceptively told readers of the Dallas paper. "The things he writes about seem scarcely worth the care of his artistic energy. But what of it? The thing is perfectly done."

The suitor who had replaced Dos Passos's place was a Harvard-educated lawyer. Deciding there was little point in trying to win her back, a defeated Dos Passos returned to the train station. Romance continued to disappoint him. "My private life is such a disorganized menagerie of ill fed desires that I'm no authority on Hymen," he had written earlier in the year to Rummy when he first heard of Ross's engagement. "I've never understood exactly why people get engaged—The only time I did the most disastrous things happened." But there was no bitterness between Ross and Dos Passos, and they parted as friends.

✛

In Paris Hadley was sorting out her relationship with Hemingway now that Pauline had muscled in. At first Hadley had—acting, in her words, like Emperor Tiberius—ordered that her husband and his lover remain apart for one hundred days. To fulfill the terms of the edict Pauline had left for the United States. If at the end of such time they were still in love, Hadley said, she would consent to a divorce. But before many of the hundred days had passed, Ernest began pelting his wife with pleas. "She's going crazy without me," he would tell a dumbfounded but resigned Hadley when he visited her in the hotel where she had moved.

She capitulated. In the end Hadley knew the marriage was over, and vindictiveness was not among her character traits. But in his desire for the new, Ernest failed to see what he was losing in the old. For a man obsessed with writing the one true sentence, he was giving up his one true love. Pauline got word and rushed back to Paris from her exile in the United States. A French court soon granted the Hemingways a divorce on the grounds of desertion and gave Hadley custody of their three-year-old son.

Dos Passos heard of the breakup when he saw Pauline in New York City during her exile. "I'd like to knock your and Hadley's head together," he wrote Hemingway. "Hem," he quickly added, "please forgive all this rubbish. The trouble with me is that I am expatriated—from Paris. Silly hell, ain't it, we'll all be expatriates from the Garden of Eden." But Dos Passos readily admitted liking Pauline. "Why don't you get to be a Mormon?" he suggested.

Instead Hemingway became a Catholic. To avail himself of a commonly used loophole in the Church proscription regarding remarriage after divorce, Hemingway claimed a priest had baptized him in Italy when he had been wounded in case final unction was needed. If so, it meant he had been Catholic when he had married Hadley in a civil ceremony. This was sufficient for the Roman Catholic Church to consider his first marriage defective in form and thus not a barrier to a wedding. On May 10, 1927, Ernest Hemingway and Pauline Pfeiffer were married in the Église Saint-Honoré-d'Eylau in the Place Victor-Hugo.

In addition to winning the church's approval for his new marriage, Hemingway had placated Hadley with a promise of financial support, especially as she had custody of their child. He agreed to give over all income from *The Sun Also Rises* to Hadley, to whom he had dedicated the book along with their son, Bumby. As a result, except the advance, he was earning nothing from his first moneymaking book, which was now well into its third printing. "The Sun has risen," his editor Max Perkins said, "and is rising steadily."

✦

When Hemingway read Dos Passos's review he sloughed off the main criticism but took exception to his comment that the Pamplona described in the book was not as exciting as the place itself. "It would be easy to write about for Dos and make it exciting—because he has been there," Hemingway wrote Perkins. "But written for him it wouldn't mean anything to the quite abstract reader that one tries to write for."

Besides, Dos Passos was becoming a convert to the book's legion of fans. "The funny thing about *The Sun Also Rises*," he wrote to Hemingway from Mexico, where he had gone after seeing Ross in Dallas, "is that in sections it isn't shitty. It's only in *conjunto* that it begins to smell. Of course, it's perfectly conceivable that it's really a swell book and that we're all of us balmy." Being out of the country in the early part of 1927, Dos Passos was unaware of the book's popularity. Now into its sixth printing, in April students at Yale had selected the book as their favorite, and even some young women took on the mod dress style of the character Lady Brett Ashley and young men the aloof airs of the protagonist Jake Barnes.

But while Dos Passos begrudgingly admitted to Hemingway that his book had hit the mark, he held his ground in his opposition to his friend's use of real people for his stories. Beginning in *The Torrents of Spring* and continuing in *The Sun Also Rises*, Hemingway's stories were thinly veiled accounts of the real lives of his friends. It was a dishonorable technique in Dos Passos's eyes. "I think that all the tendency to write about friends is rotten," Dos Passos told Hemingway "Writers are per se damn lousy bourgeois parasitic upperclass shits and not to be written about unless they are your enemies."

Although Dos Passos certainly recognized his former fiancée's appearance in the novel as the "girl in Strasbourg," he was unaware that he too had been originally slated for a cameo appearance in *The Sun Also Rises*. Hemingway struck the passage from the second chapter of the book when he cleaned the manuscript of real names. His blue-penciling, however, was insufficient. Everyone in the Paris expatriate community knew who was who in the book. Some, like Donald Stewart, were amused— but he made a living writing satire. Others, like Kitty Cannell, whom Hemingway had told earlier when he was writing the book that it would tear "those bastards apart," were furious.

The book revolted Cannell. Hemingway had been untrue when he told her she would not be in it. Frances Clyne may not have looked like her, but there was no question she spoke in Cannell's manner, right down to her jokes. When the poet Hart Crane arrived in Paris and went for a drink at the Coupole brasserie in Montparnasse, he overheard a woman speaking near him at the bar. "Why you're Kitty Cannell!" he exclaimed. "I'd recognize you anywhere from descriptions."

"So apparently did everyone in Montparnasse," Cannell ruefully wrote.

But what irritated Cannell the most was Hemingway's portrayal of Harold Loeb, her former lover. She took to bed where she remained for three days. For his part, Loeb put on a public face and claimed not to have read the book. Later he admitted how offensive he had found Hemingway's use of him and decided it came from Hemingway's jealousy over his weekend tryst with Duff Twysden on the way to Pamplona. When Hemingway later ran into Twysden at the Dingo bar she told him she had not been bothered by the book but made sure to point out that unlike the character Ashley in the book, she had not slept with the "bloody bullfighter."

In the United States, readers took pleasure from the voyeuristic view of the lives of their country's expatriates. "He drank with them, played with them and in their company watched many an hour slip by," wrote Joseph Hilton Smyth in the *Boston Globe*. "Then he went home and wrote a book about them." The transgression darkened the City of Light, and Hemingway began, for the first time, to consider living elsewhere.

In the end Hemingway accepted Dos Passos's criticism. "You are right about sticking people's names in," Hemingway told him. "You *shdn't* do it." But he couldn't resist, now that he too had a novel to his name, adding some smug advice regarding Dos Passos's current writing travails. He did so with a sexual reference, keenly aware of his friend's discomfort with the topic. "Lay off," said the younger writer to his older mentor. "What is the use of trying to screw if you are dry. Lay off and it always comes back."

+

Ernest and Pauline honeymooned in a small fishing village in Southern France. As he did each summer, Ernest wanted to go to Pamplona. But worrying that his Spanish friends would not approve of his divorce, he left Pauline in San Sebastian and went on in the company of a new friend, a fan actually. Maine native Waldo Peirce, a gregarious talkative painter, had sought out Hemingway in Paris after reading *The Sun Also Rises*, and the two had hit it off. After a while Ernest went back to San Sebastian to fetch Pauline for the final days of the fiesta. For a brief moment Pamplona was like the July days of 1924 and 1926 and unlike the disastrous one of 1925. Hemingway possessed literary success and the woman he thought he wanted, but monetary riches still escaped him, especially after having given over to Hadley all the royalties from *The Sun Also Rises* that continued to sell. So he went to work assembling a collection of stories that Perkins could bring out in the fall in hopes of cashing in on his newfound fame.

His parents wrote, not having heard from him in months. Hemingway paused from his work on the story collection to send a six-page reply, apologizing for the shame and suffering his divorce had caused them, telling them that he had not committed adultery and that he would have stayed with Hadley if she had wanted him to. At age twenty-eight he was still lying to his parents and remained angry at his mother for her disapproval of his writing.

"My work," he wrote, "is much more important to me than anything in the world except for the happiness of three people and you cannot know how it makes me feel for Mother to be ashamed of what I know as you know that there is a God in heaven is *not to be ashamed* of."

His new collection of stories was set to appear in October. The title he chose was *Men Without Women*.

✛

Dos Passos returned to New York from Mexico but was still disconsolate about work. "I can't seem to get any writing done and I am in a great state of mental and moral decay," he told his friend John Lawson. He pined for the productive days of Paris, hours at cafés, and mostly for times with Hemingway, "For Christus' swoote sake Hem you old ostrich," Dos Passos wrote Hemingway. "Why didn't you wire me that you wanted to go to Mexico. Geezus I hate mighthabeens."

The Sacco and Vanzetti case still weighed heavily on Dos Passos's mind. He had assembled his book on the case, and the Sacco-Vanzetti Defense Committee had published it under the title *Facing the Chair: Story of the Americanization of Two Foreignborn Workmen*. Loaded with documents and long excerpts of testimony, the work was more than a defense of the accused; it was a prosecution of American attitudes toward immigrants. "The attitude of press and pulpit, howling about atrocities, civilization (which usually means bank accounts) endangered, women nationalized, put the average right-thinking citizen into such a state of mind that whenever he smelt garlic on a man's breath he walks past quickly for fear of being knifed," Dos Passos wrote. "A roomful of people talking a foreign language was most certainly a conspiracy to overturn the Government."

Emotionally spent from completing the book and his rheumatic fever resurfacing, Dos Passos took a boat to St. Thomas in the Virgin Islands to hide and rest. St. Thomas's sun and glasses of "Barbadian enfuriators" and "green swizzles" and planters' punch worked. "My God Sir," he wrote to Hemingway, "the drinking down here is amazing."

After a short stay Dos Passos left St. Thomas refreshed, his fever checked. But back in New York City he learned that a committee appointed by the Massachusetts governor, which included the president of Harvard, A. Lawrence Lowell, decided the trial had been fair. Incensed, Dos Passos circulated a letter he sent to Lowell. He accused the president of being party "to a judicial murder that will call down on its perpetrators the execration of the civilized world."

Dos Passos was convinced that Lowell had contributed Harvard's name to a whitewashing of the state's failures in the case. Venting his outrage in the Communist paper *The Daily Worker*, whose press credentials he carried in his pockets, Dos Passos said the actions of Lowell and the committee "draped a pall of respectability over the frame-up and had effectually silenced the 'best minds.'"

Demonstrations on behalf of the two convicted men grew in number and size in both the United States and abroad. Dos Passos went to Boston to join a small band of protesters on the day before the scheduled execution. At the gold-domed capitol at the top of Beacon Hill five or so policemen looked on, seemingly uninterested in the small band of protesters. But as the protesters marched back and forth, a crowd gathered. A police captain decided matters had gone far enough. "Loitering and sauntering is against the law," he announced as he stepped into the path of the protesters. "You have seven minutes in which to disperse. Move on."

The protesters continued marching. Two patrol wagons pulled up, and dozens of police officers spilled out and rushed at the protesters. They grabbed the men by the coat collars and the women by their arms. Dos Passos made a run for it. But he ran smack into a state police officer who obligingly turned him over to a member of Boston's finest. Along with Dos Passos, writer Dorothy Parker was among those taken into custody. Charged with "loitering and sauntering," Dos Passos and thirty-nine other protesters were freed after a few hours of custody.

The following day at 11:27 p.m., thirty-three minutes before the first of the men was to be escorted to the electric chair, the Massachusetts governor postponed the execution for eleven days to give the courts a final chance to review last-minute appeals. Dos Passos grew frantic and telegraphed his friends to come to Boston. He wired Edmund Wilson, who was close by in Provincetown. Wilson sent a curt reply of no. Only John Lawson came.

On August 22, as the hour drew near for the execution, Dos Passos went to the Boston Commons, where this time a large numbers of protesters had turned out. As the crowd of two thousand began to march toward the state capitol, the police lining both sides of Beacon Street tightened their ranks and warned the oncoming marchers that they were violating the law. After the first group was arrested, Dos Passos and Edna St. Vincent Millay, the poet and playwright, came up the hill next, leading a contingent of writers and poets. The police repeated their warning, waited the prescribed seven minutes, and took the group into custody.

Dos Passos, having been previously arrested, now faced a second set of charges. He pleaded not guilty in a courtroom packed with sympathizers. The judge ordered a trial date. Millay's husband, the wealthy Eugen Boissevain, provided the bail money for everyone, and the group was freed.

✦

At eleven past midnight that night Nicola Sacco was strapped to the electric chair. He cried out "Long live anarchy" as the guards attached the electrodes to his body. Eight minutes later he was dead. Bartolomeo Vanzetti was brought into the execution chamber, and a few minutes later he was dead as well.

Overseas, condemnation of the American execution of the two Italian immigrants came swiftly, and protests frequently turned into riots. Paris saw the worst street violence since before the war. Rioters surged in cafés, turning the saucers, glasses, and tables into weapons against the police attempting to restore order.

Dos Passos was glad to take his leave of Boston, a city in which his most recent novel—as well as Hemingway's—was banned from sale under the state statutes that prohibited the sale of indecent literature. He fled to Provincetown. He rudely turned down an invitation to his friend Wilson's party, still angry at his failure to come and join the Boston protests. Dos Passos soon apologized. "You can't imagine how queerly your wire jangled my nerves—Jesus X Columbus—man didn't you realize that we were virtually all mad up in Boston—You try battering your head against a stone wall sometime."

The execution of the two anarchists was for Dos Passos like the European battlefield horrors he had witnessed a decade earlier. But what he had considered an unprincipled and unnecessary war led him to indict the military, not the nation. Now his disillusionment was complete. The United States had let him down. He rushed a thirty-one-line poem into print in the *New Masses* filled with a sense of despair.

> They are dead now
> The black automatons have won.
> They are burned up utterly
> Their flesh has passed into the air of Massachusetts
> their dreams have passed into the wind.

The horror of it all was such that Dos Passos renounced even the form of his response, closing the last stanza with,

> Make a poem of that if you dare!

The execution of Sacco and Vanzetti pushed Dos Passos further to the political left and strengthened his resolve to use his writing as a tool of social change. It also painfully placed a wedge between him and his most cherished literary collaborator. It had been only a few years since he and Hemingway had plotted a radical new course for postwar fiction at a Paris café. But now his friend remained unmoved when Dos Passos urged him to also join the campaign to save the two anarchists. "So Papa Primo won't let his little innocents hear about the atrocities in the U.S.A.," Dos Passos caustically wrote. "I'm not sure he's not right—Well it's all over now and gone down in History—as far down as the public press can push it."

A decade earlier, near the French front, Dos Passos and his friend Robert Hillyer had ambitiously begun work on the "G.N.," referring in code to the "Great Novel" by its initials, like the Jewish prohibition of spelling the name of God. The time had come, Dos Passos decided, to resurrect that ambition and embark on an all-consuming attempt to write the Great American Novel in which he would put the United States on trial. Let Hemingway write about the meaningless life of expatriates, a symptom of a great societal sickness. He would take on the malady itself.

17

ON A SUNNY AFTERNOON IN EARLY APRIL 1928 THE PENINSULAR AND Oriental Steam Navigation Company ferry drew up to its dock in Key West, Florida, after completing its hundred-mile crossing from Havana, Cuba. An exhausted Ernest and Pauline Hemingway took their first steps together as a married couple on American soil. They were a different Mr. and Mrs. Hemingway from the couple who had left the United States under that name on the Cherbourg-bound *Antonia* out of New York City in 1924. In the four years since, Ernest had divorced and remarried, converted to Catholicism, lost custody of his son, and become a renowned writer.

Ernest chose Key West as his and the now-pregnant Pauline's destination based on a recommendation from Dos Passos. Four years earlier his friend had been in Florida on one of his walking trips. Exhausted and dehydrated from the Florida heat, Dos Passos sought refuge in a small out-of-the-way railroad station. A train pulled in, and he asked the conductor where it was headed? To Key West, he replied.

The ride was unlike any he had taken. The train barreled off the shore of Florida on viaducts that spanned azure watery expanses across the archipelago that lead to the United States' southernmost city of Key West. At first the tracks laid by millionaire Henry Flagler were regarded as "Flagler's Folly," but since its completion in 1912 they were considered a marvel of the age. "Passengers in the railway trains," said one traveler, "may sit at the windows of Pullman cars in serenity and have an opportunity of seeing how the Atlantic Ocean looks in a gale."

When Dos Passos reached the four-mile-long island that held the town of Key West, he was bewitched. He looked at the fishing boats cramming the harbor and drank in the sultry Gulf Stream air. Meandering down a dirt road that passed for a main street, he strolled by unpainted sun-bleached houses that stood anchored to the coral rock to survive hurricanes and whose roofs collected rain providing the island's only drinking water. "It was like no other place in Florida," he said. He told all his friends including Hemingway, whom he saw a few months later in Paris.

The Hemingways' journey from Paris to this bit of tropical paradise had been unpleasant. The ship *Orita*, a large, lumbering liner that ferried them from La Rochelle, France, to Havana, Cuba, was badly appointed, poorly equipped, and understaffed. The two did their best to amuse themselves. Pauline passed Ernest a note suggesting they "fondle far into the night—despite the smallness of the beds."

"Dear Miss Pfeiffer or ~~should~~ may I call you 'Mrs. Hemingway,'" he replied on ship stationery. "We are five or ten days out on a trip or tripe to Cuba which promises to extend indefinitely into the future. I have often wondered what I should do with the rest of my life and now I know—I shall try to reach Cuba."

When they completed the final portion of their journey from Havana to Key West there was no one to meet them. The town looked deserted, especially to a couple coming from a cosmopolitan setting like Paris. The Ford Model A Coupe that Pauline's Uncle Gus had purchased for them was nowhere to be found. The apologetic managers of the Trevor & Morris Ford dealership informed them it was still awaiting assembly in Miami, 129 miles to the north. Undoubtedly not wanting to further upset a pregnant Pauline, the car dealers installed the couple in an apartment above their offices.

Despite the unpromising start of a new life in the United States, Hemingway resumed work on the new novel he had begun while still an expatriate in Paris. Only a week after arriving in Key West he telegraphed Perkins in New York that he was working hard on it. In the mornings he wrote; in the afternoons he fished with Pauline. They caught red snapper, barracuda, and even shark, which they sold to a company that made shoes and luggage from its skin. "This is a grand place," Ernest told Waldo Peirce, the painter who had accompanied him to Pamplona the previous summer.

✦

It was only natural that Dos Passos would be the first to accept Hemingway's invitations to come to Key West. He was worn out from his most recent playwriting efforts. An internecine war among the politically charged writers who ran the New Playwrights Theatre in New York City had left him exhausted. And the latest campaign he had joined to save two more Italian immigrants from the gallows had failed. Tropical rest was appealing.

Returning to Key West, this time by boat rather than rail, Dos Passos found Hemingway and an entourage waiting for him on the dock. The group escorted their guest to the three-story clapboard Overseas Hotel to drop off his bag and change from his city clothes. The hotel's postcards claimed it was the "Largest and Only Modern Hotel in the City." Considering the Spartan nature of accommodations in Key West, it was not a hard boast to make. Then it was off to fish for tarpon, four-to six-foot-long aggressive fish that are considered great sport because they jump out of the water when hooked.

Hemingway was exuberant. He had been told his next royalty check from Scribner's for his short-story collection *Men Without Women* would be nearly $4,000, and five dollars a day bought a good life in Key West. Unlike Paris, there were no expatriates angry over being used in a book or a literary community with petty rivalries to spoil the moment. Ernest and Pauline could not have escaped to a world more different from this island. The population, which had fallen from twenty-six thousand to ten thousand since the last cigar factory closed a few years earlier, comprised an unpretentious sort of people who spoke Caribbean Creole, Cuban Spanish, and English and cared little about books. "Nobody believes me when I say I'm a writer," Hemingway told Perkins, pleading that he send copies of his books to prove them wrong.

Hemingway and Dos Passos settled into a pattern of work, fishing, eating, and drinking—no one seemed to pay attention to Prohibition on the island—punctuated by discussions of their writing. Dos Passos was as angry as he had been when Sacco and Vanzetti were executed a year earlier. For the first time in his life he had become an activist—joining in protests, speaking at rallies, and even getting arrested. But his heart had not been in it; rather, he wanted to use his skills as a writer to point the way. "Knowledge is the first thing necessary to reform a thing," Dos Passos believed, "one must first know the conditions."

In solitude following the defeat of the campaign to save Sacco and Vanzetti, Dos Passos had begun sketching out his most ambitious novel yet. Unlike *Manhattan Transfer*, which was set in New York City, the backdrop of this book would be the American landscape along the forty-second parallel that ran across New York State, through Chicago, and marked California's northern border. The story would be built around the lives of five Americans buffeted by industrial capitalism, the oppression of modernity, and the betrayal of democracy; the chronology would mirror that of his life. Still enamored with his attempts in *Manhattan Transfer* to capture bits of modernity on paper, he toyed with interspersing the narrative in this new book with miniature biographies and sections of text that imitated newsreels and cameras. He wanted his writing to mirror the way the visual media was altering people's perception of the world. All of which would put heavy demands on the casual reader.

✢

Ernest was ten to fifteen thousand words into his novel as Pauline's due date neared. He hoped to have a finished manuscript prior to leaving Key West for Piggott, Arkansas, Pauline's hometown where she wanted to spend the last part of her pregnancy. The writing pace slowed to a halt with the arrival of Waldo Peirce. The large, bearded painter had also been an ambulance driver in 1915 after graduating from Harvard. His presence added a bond of commonality to the group.

Further adding to the distractions was the arrival of Hemingway's old Michigan compatriots Bill and his sister Katy Smith. Hemingway had not seen Katy since the day he married her friend Hadley; however, she also knew his new wife, having gone to the University of Missouri journalism school with Pauline. The congenial group took to the waters. They swam in the shuttered Navy Yard, poled skiffs to fish in nearby waters, and took to further reaches in a motorboat. On some trips Hemingway would add bottles of champagne to the ice bins used to keep the bait fresh. The rule was that no bottles were to be opened until someone caught a fish. On some days the wait could be long.

Before going to bed the group often stopped in one of the town's few restaurants. Over plates of deep-fried yellowtail and bonito with a tomato sauce, they talked about whatever was on their minds. "No taboos," said Dos Passos. "After the ideological bickering of the New York theater, Key West seemed like the Garden of Eden."

Generously paying the $15 fee for a day's boat rental and covering other expenses, their host had things the way he wanted them. "Hem was the greatest fellow in the world to go around with when everything was right," recalled Dos Passos. "The place suited Ernest to a T." In his enthusiasm he confided to Hemingway that it was the best time he ever had in his life.

Amid the swimming, fishing, and merriment Dos Passos found himself distracted in a way he had not been since he broke up with Crystal Ross two years earlier. Katy Smith had his attention. "From the first moment I couldn't think of anything but her green eyes," he said.

Smith knew about Dos Passos through her friendships with Hadley and Pauline. As a consummate reader, she was also aware of his work. She herself had literary aspirations. Since giving up a job as a copywriter for an advertising agency and moving to Provincetown, Massachusetts, with her brother, Smith had been writing stylish romance stories and submitting them to popular magazines, often under a pseudonym.

But now, thirty-four and unmarried, Smith's curiosity was piqued meeting the balding, nervous author in person. Soon she gave him a nickname, a sure sign of acceptance among the old Michigan gang who knew her as Stut and Ernest as Wemedge. "Monsieur Muttonfish" is what she decided to call Dos Passos. It was his favorite seafood at dinner, even though it was less prized than other dishes. It also differed from the rest of the fish in the region's waters—muttonfish preferred to swim solitarily among the reefs of Key West, avoiding its own kind.

Oddly, Smith and Dos Passos had not crossed paths in Provincetown. But now that they had met and taken a liking to each other, a romantic relationship would have to wait. Dos Passos was departing for New York to embark on a lengthy trip to Russia to see whether his friend Lincoln

Steffens had been right when, several years earlier, he said, "I have seen the future; and it works." The long-planned journey could not be postponed. He scribbled down E. E. Cummings's Greenwich Village address and gave it to Smith.

A month later, back in Provincetown, Smith took out a postcard featuring the railroad crossing in Provincetown and addressed it to Dos Passos, putting his name and Cummings's address on the left-hand side of the card under "correspondence here," and under "Name and Address Here" she scribbled "Pleased to have met you." She signed it "Home Girl." It was an inside joke. But by the time the card reached Cummings's New York City apartment, Dos Passos had sailed for Russia. The relationship between them had gone past the friendship stage—while Dos Passos explored the Soviet Union, Katy was telling her friend Pauline she hoped one day to be Mrs. Dos Passos.

✛

The guests gone, Hemingway returned to the 108 pages of his new novel sitting in the walk-up flat above the car dealership. The pressure was enormous. *The Sun Also Rises* had brought Hemingway a lot of attention, and the collection of stories *Men Without Women* was selling briskly. "But," he told his editor, "this next book *has* to be good."

It was not the book he intended to be writing. A few months earlier, while still in Paris, he had gotten forty-five thousand words deep into a manuscript that he described to Perkins as a "modern Tom Jones" novel. Late one night, after dining with Archibald and Ada MacLeish, he went into his bathroom and tugged what he thought was the chain to the water tank mounted on the wall high above the toilet. It was the chain connected to the skylight. Instead of triggering a flow of water to the toilet, Hemingway brought the skylight crashing down, raining glass everywhere and slicing open his forehead. Stacks of toilet paper sheets applied by Pauline failed to stem the flow. A tourniquet made of a dishtowel tightened by twisting a stick of kindling wood finally had some effect. Pauline summoned Archibald MacLeish, who took her husband to the American Hospital in Neuilly, where doctors stitched him up.

For Ernest the time on a surgeon's table had been like the moments when he had lain on one in the Milan hospital ten years earlier. When he got home that night his head was bandaged as if he had suffered a war wound. When he returned to his writing he set aside the novel in the style of Tom Jones and began to write about the war. The writing flowed. When he had written *The Sun Also Rises* he had mostly recorded the behavior of others whom he had observed. Now his personal experience with combat shaped the narrative.

Set in wartime Italy, the story had three main characters: Frederic Henry, an American ambulance driver wounded by a mortar; Catherine Barkley, a beautiful British nurse who tends to his wounds; and Rinaldi, a womanizing Italian surgeon. There was no outline. Hemingway built the story as he went, but then again he knew it well, especially the section he had completed after the accident in Paris.

Through the other noise I heard a cough, then came the chu-chu-chu-chu—then there was a flash, as when a blast-furnace door is swung open, and a road that started white and went red and on and on in a rushing wind. I tried to breathe but my breath would not come and I felt myself rush bodily out of myself and out and out and out and all the time bodily in the wind.

Had he a choice, Hemingway would have stayed on his island of solitude to finish his new book. But the impending birth of their child as well as Pauline's anxious family demanded she go home. Ernest put her on a train. In the awkward company of his father-in-law, he piloted the Ford Coupe the thirteen hundred miles to Piggott, Arkansas. When he got there he reported to Perkins that it was a "christ offal place" but that he was working again on the manuscript, now more than two hundred pages long.

Hemingway was not entirely honest in conveying optimism to his editor. He still did not know where the story would take him as scene after scene from Milan came to life on the page. Recollections of Agnes von Kurowsky surfaced when he wrote how Henry loved to take the pins from Catherine Barkley's hair as she lay on the bed kissing him.

I would watch her while she kept very still and then take out the last two pins and it would all come down and she would drop her head and we would both be inside of it, and it was the feeling of inside a tent or behind a falls.

Barkley, who embodied elements from his first two wives, took over the story. But to what end? Hemingway could not conclude the story of wartime passion with a quiet breakup by mail, as it had been for him with

Kurowsky. Pauline's pregnancy showed the way, and Henry got Barkley pregnant. He now had a story in which love and pregnancy bound his protagonists, adding urgency to the scene before Henry returns to the front that Hemingway composed as Pauline's due date neared.

So that Pauline could deliver their child in a modern hospital, Ernest put down his pen and drove her the four hundred miles from Piggott, Arkansas, to Kansas City, Missouri. On June 27, 1928, Pauline went into labor. After eighteen hours doctors freed a nine-and-a-half-pound Patrick by Caesarean section. "It was a very near business for Pauline," Hemingway told Peirce. "Nothing for a guy to watch when his affections are involved. Nor in any sense the ideal way to kill time while *woiking* on a novel."

A month later Hemingway returned to his novel, leaving Patrick and mother in Piggott and taking the car to Wyoming. Staying in a succession of dude ranches, Hemingway churned out the remaining pages. By this point Henry had returned to the front. It was not the one Hemingway had seen in 1918; rather, he set the book earlier than his own time in Italy. Using newspaper accounts he read, books he bought, and stories he heard from soldiers, Hemingway recreated the humiliating Italian retreat at Caporetta in 1917.

Hemingway had Henry lead the ambulances away from the front, picking up to two Italian sergeants who are also fleeing. When the ambulance bogs down in mud, Henry orders the two sergeants to help, but they walk away. When they refuse to halt, Henry takes out his pistol and shoots at them. One escapes, but the other falls wounded in the bushes by the side of the road. An Italian ambulance driver borrows Henry's pistol, walks over to the bushes, and put the barrel up against the skull of the sergeant. But when he pulls the trigger, it fails to fire.

"You have to cock it," explains Henry. This time the gun fires and the soldier drags the dead man to a spot by the side of the road. As in the moment in Dos Passos's *Three Soldiers* when Chrisfield murders his sergeant, Hemingway sought to capture the anger felt by those under the command of others. "All my life I've wanted to kill a sergeant," said Hemingway's man who pulled the trigger. But the scene also echoed the moment when, as a child, Hemingway had gone hunting with his father, found the dead quail his father had shot, and claimed it for himself.

In the confusion of the retreat Henry deserts and returns to his lover, as Dos Passos's main character had also done. Reunited, Henry and Barkley flee to Switzerland, rowing across Lake Maggiore as Hemingway had done with Kurowsky years earlier. For a while they have the life they had hoped for, away from the war.

As Ernest closed in on the end of his novel in Wyoming, Pauline arrived for a visit, having left their son, Patrick, with her family. For several days they toured Yellowstone Park and fished. Then Ernest went back to his manuscript and in three days wrote the concluding thirty-six pages in which Barkley goes into labor. At the hospital she begins hours of hard labor. In the room alone with her, Henry controls the valve on a cylinder of nitrous oxide from which Barkley inhales copious amounts to try to ease the pain. "Give it to me quick. Give it to me," she says.

"You'll stay with me?"

"Not to watch it."

"No, just to be there."

"Sure. I'll be there all the time."

'You're so good to me. There, give it to me. Give me some more. It's not working!"

I turned the dial to three and then four. I wished the doctor would come back. I was afraid of the numbers above two.

Barkley is taken into the operating room for a Caesarean section. Unlike with Pauline, Hemingway's Catherine delivers a dead baby boy. Soon after, the mother begins to hemorrhage, and Henry stays with her until she dies.

The manuscript complete, twenty-nine-year-old Ernest Hemingway had his armistice with the Great War.

18

BACK ONCE AGAIN IN PIGGOTT BY OCTOBER 1928, HEMINGWAY SECURELY locked his 652-page manuscript in a safe deposit box at the bank. In Paris he had learned his lesson about protecting manuscripts and was not going to take any chances. The following day he drove alone to Oak Park, Illinois, returning home for the first time in almost a decade. There he found a father whose faculties were failing and whose bouts of depression were worsening. Hemingway's mother was unchanged, especially in her ability to irritate him.

Pauline caught up with her husband a few weeks later, and they eventually made their way back to Key West. Instead of returning to the cramped apartment above the car dealership, the couple and their newborn son, Patrick, moved into a two-story house, with plenty of room for guests.

At times it must have seemed as if family was an elaborate conspiracy to keep Ernest from his work. Hadley wanted their son, Bumby, to get a dose of the curative Florida sun to shake off a winter grippe, not to mention spend time with his father. So Ernest packed the manuscript into his bag and took the forty-hour-long train ride to New York City, where Hadley delivered their son over to his custody. When the train carrying Ernest and Bumby south stopped in Trenton, a porter delivered a telegram from Oak Park that his father had died.

Hemingway confined his son to the care of the porter—unwilling to expose Bumby to his grandmother. The man astonishingly agreed to accompany the five-year-old boy the remainder of the trip to Key West. Armed with money F. Scott Fitzgerald wired to the station's telegraph office after receiving a telegram from his friend, Hemingway boarded a Chicago-bound train. When he reached the city he learned that his father had killed himself while sitting alone on the edge of his bed with the .32-caliber pistol Hemingway's grandfather had carried in the Civil War.

To outsiders it seemed as if money troubles had led to the doctor's death. The financial problems were real enough, as Hemingway learned when going through his father's personal papers. But what drew him to pull the trigger were his depression, mounting health problems, and a growing paranoia.

Hemingway went to work putting family matters in order. "Have everything fixed up except they will have damned little money," he wrote Perkins. "Realize of course that thing for me to do is not worry but get to work—finish my book properly so I can help out with the proceeds. What makes me feel the worst is that my father is the one I cared about."

Hemingway didn't wait to return to Key West or even for the long train ride to resume work. In his father's office immediately following the funeral he began revising the manuscript he had brought with him.

✦

Dos Passos returned to the United States in December 1928 after almost six months in Russia. "Drop me a line as to the life and habits of Key West, or thereabouts," he wrote Hemingway on a postcard. "I don't know where I'm going to live, if at all." In New York City he received a reply from Hemingway. "Well kid how does it feel to be back?" he wrote, urging him to come south. "I want like hell to see you."

"Every other day we shoot snipe for the day after," Hemingway continued. "My old man shot himself on the other hand (not in the other hand. In the head) as you may have read in the paper."

Dos Passos was glad for the invitation but had to put off a visit. He had come home brimming with ideas for the New Playwrights Theater, and the company planned to put on his play about a labor organizer who is framed for murder and put to death. When it did open, critics hated it, and it lasted for a few weeks—only because Dos Passos fronted almost

$1,000 of his own money. His friend Edmund Wilson was the sole writer with a kind word for the work.

Dos Passos was "less expert as a dramatist than as a novelist," Wilson wrote in the *New Republic*. But the play possessed an eloquence lacking in the novel and was perhaps the best thing Dos Passos had written. More to the point, Wilson continued, Dos Passos should be admired for his efforts to write about the social forces at work in America. "Most of the first-rate men of his age—Wilder, Hemingway, Scott Fitzgerald—cultivate their own little corners and do not confront the situation as a whole," he said. "Only Dos Passos has attempted to confront it."

Smarting from this latest costly theatrical failure and tired of the infighting among the company's directors, Dos Passos resigned from the New Playwrights Theater and fled to Key West in late March 1929. "As soon as the drama has you on your ass or as you get the drama visa versa come down here," Hemingway had said in his letter inviting him south. Dos Passos's effort to add playwright to his biography had been an ordeal, and he was glad it had come to an end. "Am down here licking my wounds," he wrote Wilson after reaching Key West, "fishing, eating wild herons and turtle steak, drinking Spanish wine and Cuban rum and generally remaking the inner man, somewhat shattered by the encounter."

✛

Over drinks and meals Dos Passos filled Hemingway in on his Russian adventures. It had been an opportune time to go. The power struggle between Joseph Stalin and Leon Trotsky, following Vladimir Lenin's death, had abated for a brief moment. The country was savoring a respite from turmoil, and Americans were welcomed.

Dos Passos had begun his Soviet explorations in Leningrad, where he met playwrights, poets, and writers, even one who had translated one of his novels. But the men who interested Dos Passos the most were movie directors. Among them was Sergei Eisenstein, famous for his use of film montage in which he layered short shots, condensed time, and produced a third visual perception. Its use three years earlier in his film *Battleship Potemkin* had attracted wide attention.

Dos Passos set off to explore the country armed with a teach-yourself-Russian book published by the Hugo Institute of London and a pocket dictionary. Traveling by boat down rivers, by bus on rudimentary highways, and by foot across mountains, he saw a Russia few other outsiders got to see. The magnificence of the landscape enthralled him, but living conditions were harsh. "The towns are little stone villages and the country between is wild as hell," he wrote Hemingway during a stop in Dagestan.

Sometimes Dos Passos went on his way alone, sometimes in the company of others. W. Horsley Gantt, a young American doctor whom Dos Passos met in Leningrad where Gantt was working with Ivan Petrovich Pavlov, joined the walking trip in the Caucasus Mountains. The travel was hard, and food was often difficult to obtain. "The Caucasus has been entirely neglected by Swiss hotelkeepers," Dos Passos quipped to Hemingway. Spending the night in the home of a widow who was a relative of a guide they employed, the travelers asked for hot water to make tea. Their host said she couldn't boil water because she could only afford to make a fire once a day.

In the months he traveled about, Dos Passos encountered a great deal more poverty. But he was struck by the generosity of the Russians who would share what little they had with a stranger. "People are so hospitable here and so nice that it is heartbreaking," Dos Passos wrote to E. E. Cummings.

In Moscow, where he settled in for the fall, he fell again into the company of writers and intellectuals. But being in the capital, he also began to get the jitters like those that infected other Westerners who had been in the Soviet Union long enough to see the strong hand of the state. His passport, for instance, remained ominously in the custody of the government. When the bureaucrats finally returned it to him, he immediately obtained the necessary visa and train ticket west.

At the train station a friend Dos Passos had made during his stay came to say good-bye, bringing along with her the teenage cast of the Sanitary Propaganda Theater company, which acted out skits in factories about the danger of syphilis or the necessity to brush one's teeth.

"They want to know," said the woman pointing to the children. "They want to know where you stand politically. Are you with us?"

"Let me see," Dos Passos replied, hedging for time to formulate an answer. The steam from the engines swirled around them in the twilight dimness of the day. His head throbbed. There had been too many men, too many women, and too many youngsters whom he had seen and talked with during his stay, too many foreign languages misunderstood for him to speak with confidence.

"But maybe I can explain," he blurted. "But in so short a time . . . there's no time."

The train began to move, and Dos Passos jumped aboard. "How could I answer that question," Dos Passos wrote years later. "I liked and admired the Russian people. I had enjoyed their enormous and varied country, but when next morning I crossed the Polish border . . . it was like being let out of jail."

✦

Early in his Key West reunion with Hemingway Dos Passos was handed a carbon copy of his compatriot's new novel. It was now called *A Farewell to Arms*, a title Hemingway had taken from a sixteenth-century poem by George Peele. Months of revisions had resulted in a polished manuscript. The last time Hemingway had shared an unpublished work with Dos Passos was the evening in Schruns, Austria, when he had read aloud from *The Sun Also Rises*. He had regretted the experience but remained so eager for Dos Passos's blessings that he was willing to chance it again.

Unlike *The Sun Also Rises*, which was written in a matter of weeks, *A Farewell to Arms* was the product of a long gestation. Each day Hemingway claimed he had reread the entire manuscript from the beginning until he reached the spot where he had left off and would then write new pages. As he repeated the process, the story developed, but the earlier pages grew tighter from the constant cutting and revisions. From its first page the tone of the writing was different from his previous work. Sentences were longer, and thoughts were connected loosely with a lavish use of the conjunction "and."

The trunks of the trees too were dusty and the leaves fell early that year and we saw the troops marching along the road and the dust rising and leaves, stirred by the breeze, falling and the soldiers marching and afterward the road bare and white except for the leaves.

In reaching for dust to illustrate the bareness of the wartime landscape, Hemingway's words were look-alikes for those in Dos Passos's first novel

One Man's Initiation. In it Dos Passos had described fictionally the scene he had seen as an ambulance driver when near Verdun: dust raised by trucks and soldiers covered the flowers and the soldiers were so shrouded in white dust they looked dead.

Even as Hemingway held a typed and completed manuscript, he still tinkered with the ending, as he had with *The Sun Also Rises.* He knew the final words of his literary composition would hang in the air like the last chords of a symphony in a concert hall. It took Hemingway nearly fifty tries to produce a suitable coda for the moment when Henry is alone with his dead lover after telling the nurses to leave the room. In his efforts he chose to scrap such closings as:

That is all there is to the story. Catherine died and you will die and I will die and that is all I can promise you.

or

When people die you have to bury them but you do not have to write about it. You meet undertakers but you do not have to write about them.

Until he finally settled on the one that pleased him most.

But after I got them out and shut the door and turned off the light it wasn't any good. It was like saying good-by to a statue. After a while I went out and left the hospital and walked back to the hotel in the rain.

Perkins let Hemingway know that *Scribner's Magazine* was prepared to pay an unheard-of $16,000 for the serial rights, the largest amount it had ever paid. The news brought immense financial relief to Hemingway, as he now supported his widowed mother. When Perkins came in person to retrieve the final manuscript he told Hemingway the novel was magnificent. It pleased Hemingway, but he continued to anxiously await the judgment of his closest literary friend. It had been only a little more than two years since Dos Passos had severely criticized Hemingway's first novel, deeming it a cock-and-bull story about a worthless group of drunken expatriates. "He's always been my most bitterly severe critic," Hemingway admitted to Perkins. To Hemingway's relief, Dos Passos was quick in rendering a verdict. It was spectacular, he said. "Dos liking it is the best news I've had since you did because he's always been hard as can be," Hemingway told Perkins.

The novel was not the only thing to Dos Passos's liking. As planned, Katy Smith timed her visit to Key West so they could be together. However, it was hard be alone. Also visiting was painter Waldo Peirce. The tall, barrel-chested handsome man with an enormous beard—"looked like a Neptune out of a baroque Roman fountain," thought Dos Passos—was also attracted to Smith. Some in Provincetown, where they both lived, presumed the two had been occasional lovers. If not, they certainly projected an intimacy when together that was off-putting to the shy Dos Passos.

But when together with Dos Passos, Smith reciprocated his growing affection. They took long walks, swam, and picnicked, leaving the Hemingway crowd to fend for itself. As a writer herself, Smith understood—as Crystal Ross had—the things central to Dos Passos's life. But unlike Ross, she was not hesitant about a romantic commitment. After less than a month together under the Caribbean sun, they pledged to meet up in Provincetown in the summer.

Before Dos Passos took his leave of Key West a wooden crate arrived from Chicago. It was from Hemingway's mother. The crate sat unopened for days among the trunks and suitcases they were packing for a trip to France. "For heaven's sake, Ernest," Smith said one day, "haven't you opened your mother's box yet?" Pauline got a hammer and pried it open. Inside they found canvas rolls that, when unrolled, revealed landscape paintings of the Garden of Gods in Colorado; they had been painted by Hemingway's mother. They were stained in places, as chocolate cake his mother packed in the crate had gone to mold and leaked. The box also held the .32-caliber pistol with which Hemingway's father had ended his life. Ernest had asked for it. Smith, who had met Grace Hemingway on many occasions, explained to Dos Passos "that Mrs. Hemingway was a very odd lady, indeed." Dos Passos, who had never met her, certainly knew Hemingway's feelings toward her. "Hem was the only man I ever knew who really hated his mother," he said.

Soon everyone was off. Dos Passos had a manuscript to finish, and Hemingway had galleys to proof. It had been a little more than a decade since the end of the war, six years since the two began plotting their literary plans in a Paris café. Dos Passos had eight books in print and Hemingway five. Along with their friend F. Scott Fitzgerald, they had become the voice of the war generation—the Lost Generation.

✦

Dos Passos took up an old friend's offer to stay in their Bucks County Pennsylvania farmhouse where he could work undisturbed. With a draft of the *The 42nd Parallel* almost complete, he went next to North Carolina to cover a textile workers strike for the *New Republic*. Finally, in June Dos Passos arrived in Provincetown where Smith lived.

Katy and her brother Bill had moved to Provincetown in 1924, sharing a succession of rentals in the resort town with two women. Using bits of the group's last names, town residents dubbed whatever house they rented "Smooley Hall." The housemates all held writing aspirations but also played together. "The group at Smooley Hall were at that time the essence of joyous freedom in life and booze," recalled novelist Hutchins Hapgood, "but never did they forget their first job was to think and do."

Smith had carved out a life of considerable freedom, and nothing up to this moment had enticed her to give it up. "Katy never encouraged anyone to speak of marriage back then," said one of her neighbors. "Katy loved the single, carefree life of Smooley Hall, but when Dos Passos visited we wondered what was in the making."

Smith gave a party to introduce to her friends John Dos Passos, the man who had broken down her barriers. The two decided to get married but not before Dos Passos had finished a draft of *The 42nd Parallel*. Smith also wanted to return to northern Michigan, where she had summered with Hemingway years earlier, to check up on the farmhouse that her recently deceased aunt, who had raised her and her brother, had owned.

Dos Passos hid in a friend's lake house near Syracuse, New York. There he worked steadily on the manuscript, interrupting his writing and revisions only for dips in cold spring water, long walks, or meals. The mail soon carried passionate missives between Smith and Dos Passos.

Needing to conduct research for his newsreel and camera eye sections of his book, Dos Passos next moved to Chicago, bringing him closer to Michigan where Smith was. She implored him to come to her. "Mutton-fish my deary," she wrote. "It's damn beautiful and I'd love to show you where we all grew to vigorous manhood and womanhood depending on sex and age. . . . This place reminds me a lot of Wemedge."

Dos Passos came quickly and toured the summertime paradise of his friend Ernest Hemingway with Katy Smith as his guide. Then, in the company of her brother, the couple headed back east via Canada, which was beyond the reach of Prohibition, and crossed back into the United States at the border with Maine. On Monday, August 19, 1929, John Roderigo Dos Passos and Katharine Smith stood before E. E. Gorielus, a Unitarian minister, in Ellsworth, Maine. Dos Passos wore a raincoat Bill Smith had urgently draped around him when it was discovered the groom had split open his pants. With marriage vows said and bourbon taken out from its hiding spot in a lobster pot, the small gathering celebrated the moment.

"I feel so swell I don't like to mention it," Dos Passos wrote Hemingway a few days later.

"Damned glad to hear you men are married," replied Hemingway from Madrid. "I'm happy as hell about it!"

As if torn from the pages of the romance stories Smith penned, the girl of Hemingway's teenage summer dreams was now the wife of his best friend.

19

ADOPTING DOS PASSOS'S HABIT OF BEING FAR AWAY WHEN REVIEWS OF his books appeared, Hemingway was in Paris when *A Farewell to Arms* neared its publication date. It had been a long editorial battle to preserve the salty vocabulary sprinkled about the book. "If a word can be printed and is needed in the text than it is a *weakening* to omit it," Hemingway told Perkins. "If it *cannot* be printed without the book being suppressed all right." In the end his editor conceded to *son of a bitch* and *whore* but *fuck* and *cocksucker* had been struck from the book, replaced with dashes.

The battle over these words in the manuscript had ended in a draw, but not so with *Scribner's Magazine*, which was publishing excerpts. Its editor insisted on such a rigorous cleaning of the excerpts that even the rather chaste scene in which Barkley and Henry have sex was reduced to a mention of beating hearts. The expurgation was insufficient for the Boston crowd. The Watch and Ward Society, whose original name the New England Society for the Suppression of Vice revealed its purpose more clearly, succeeded in barring newsstands from selling issues of *Scribner's* with the book excerpts. "Hey you old pornographer," Dos Passos teased Hemingway. "They've nailed Scribner's family journal in Boston."

On September 27, 1929, *A Farewell to Arms* appeared in bookstores. "First reviews splendid," Perkins telegraphed Hemingway in Paris the next morning. Indeed, the critics were saying the kinds of things writers dream of hearing. They certainly gratified the author with an insatiable appetite for praise. Critic Percy Hutchison, reviewing the book for the *New York Times*, was so thoroughly smitten by Hemingway's prose that he referred to "what may be termed the Hemingway school." Best of all for this critic as well as others, the daring nature of the writing in the earlier novel, *The Sun Also Rises,* was now accompanied by a dramatic story of war and love in this new work. "It is a moving and beautiful book," Hutchison concluded.

Paper after paper joined the chorus of approval. The *Chicago Tribune*, which had complained about *The Sun Also Rises*, said readers would find in this book "a blossoming of a most unusual genius of our day." Its critic, Fanny Butcher, confessed that she sobbed uncontrollably reading the final pages. Even Hemingway's mother, who had wanted to burn *The Sun Also Rises*, wrote an ecstatic letter of praise.

Dos Passos put into print the compliments he had conveyed privately to Hemingway earlier that year when he read the carbon copy of the manuscript. "Hemingway's *Farewell to Arms* is the best-written book that has seen the light in America for many a long day," Dos Passos wrote in his review for the *New Masses*. "The stuff will match up as narrative prose with anything that's been written since there was an English language."

The book took off. Within a month it had sold nearly thirty thousand copies and had displaced Erich Maria Remarque's *All Quiet on the Western Front* on the best-seller's list. "Hem," wrote Dos Passos, "do you realize you're the King of the fiction racket?"

✛

In October Dos Passos faced an editorial fight of his own, similar to what Hemingway had endured with *A Farewell to Arms*, over what four-letter words the public could handle in print. His editor at Harper's, Eugene Saxton, was more willing to accept impolite words in *The 42nd Parallel* than when he had published *Three Soldiers* eight years earlier while working at the more conservative Doran. "Clap," "hard on," "crissake," and "they loved each other on the sofa and she let him do everything he wanted" survived the editorial blue pencil but not "feeling her tongue in his mouth."

The ambitiousness of Dos Passos's project was visible on every page of the manuscript he turned over to Saxton. The book held three streams of action braided together. Making their way through a tangle of modern challenges until their lives slowly converge were a member of the International Workers of the World, a stenographer, a public relations man, an artist, and a mechanic from Fargo, North Dakota. Between their tales Dos Passos interspersed his newsreels filled with scraps of news and songs. Their appearance marked off time. Additionally, the camera eye contained fragmentary autobiographical scenes. If those elements alone didn't complicate the manuscript sufficiently, he added finely written poetic renderings of famous figures such as Eugene V. Debs, William Jennings Bryan, Andrew Carnegie, and Robert M. La Follette, among others.

Fortunately for the reader he greatly cut down the use of made-up compound words, but he retained the sense of urgency and the sense of constant motion of his earlier novel *Manhattan Transfer*. Unlike anything he had written before, Dos Passos was now working on an immense canvas, one that could not be contained in a single book. He realized it would require three books to execute his plan. He shared his plans with Hemingway. "You can always think that if volume one is shit, volume two will be swell," Dos Passos told him. "Jesus, I hope it's not the beginning of the end." Hemingway tried to soothe his friend's nerves. "Trilogies are undoubtedly the thing," he replied. "Look at the Father, Son and Holy Ghost—Nothing's gone much bigger than that."

Dos Passos was already deep into the second volume as he proofed the galleys of the first one in October 1929. He was calling it *1919*. It also featured five characters, several of them from the first book, but their lives would be easier to follow as Dos Passos reduced the nonfictional elements. Instead, the book revolved more around the often-autobiographical tale of a pacifist ambulance driver who gets in trouble with his superiors for disloyalty while in Italy, carries buckets of severed limbs out from a Paris war hospital, and falls in love with a woman who like Crystal Ross was from Texas, but unlike her becomes pregnant and meets a tragic end when she agrees to take a ride in a French officer's plane that crashes.

The 42nd Parallel had left readers at the moment in 1918 when Charley, the Fargo mechanic, signs up as an ambulance driver and boards the

Chicago, the same ship that took Dos Passos and Hemingway to the war. In *1919* Dos Passos returned to his memories of the European battlefields. Hemingway may have worked the war out of his system with *A Farewell to Arms*, but Dos Passos was not yet done.

✦

With *The 42nd Parallel* proofed and consigned to his editor, John and Katy Dos Passos took what little money they had and headed to Paris. The decline in the cost of passage by ship helped make the trip more affordable. Since the collapse of the stock market in October ocean liners were departing from New York with empty cabins. As neither Dos Passos, who never had much money, nor Hemingway, despite his recent financial success, held investments or factory jobs, they were less buffeted than many others by the Great Depression. Sales of *A Farewell to Arms* also seemed unaffected. "My books," said Dos Passos, "could hardly have sold less anyway."

When they reached Paris in late November 1929 Dos Passos was the happiest he had been in years. He eagerly took Katy on a Bateaux Mouches ride on the Seine, looking up at the ancient buildings of Paris bathed in the winter sun. Another day they rode the train to Sceaux-Robinson, a small town eight miles southwest of Paris renowned for its scenery. There they ate lunch in one of the restaurants built on the branches of massive chestnut trees, the presence of which had inspired residents to add Robinson of the book *Robinson Crusoe* to their town's name. Back in Paris they made the rounds of the cafés in the company of the poet Blaise Cendrars and took a meal in the home of artist Fernand Léger, whose wife cooked the best blanquette de veau Dos Passos had tasted but didn't remain in the house at night because she had a lover. "They lived up to the rest of the obligations of matrimony in a curious formal French way," said Dos Passos.

John also introduced Katy to Scott and Zelda Fitzgerald. Scott and Ernest Hemingway had been quarreling by mail over remarks Gertrude Stein made comparing the two authors that Fitzgerald had taken as a criticism. Hemingway, usually willing to hold his position to the bitter end, tried assuaging Fitzgerald's feelings. "I'll be damned if I going to lose you as a friend through some bloody squabble." It was clear, as the Dos Passoses soon learned when they visited, that not all was well in the

Fitzgerald household. Scott was drinking heavily, and Zelda was exhibiting the beginnings of a mental breakdown, telling Dos Passos she wanted to dance in the Ballets Russes. "For anyone who was fond of the Fitzgeralds," said Dos Passos, "it was heartbreaking to be with them."

The Dos Passoses and the Hemingways caught up with each other a few days later. Ernest's mood surprised them. He should have been celebrating his success with his new book and the financial security it provided, especially as royalties from his first successful book, *The Sun Also Rises*, still went to Hadley, but he was downhearted about the mysterious death of Harry Crosby. A former ambulance driver, Crosby had been an important part of expatriate literary life in postwar Paris. He had been found dead from a bullet wound in a hotel in what the newspapers deemed a suicide pact with his lover, who was also found dead at the scene.

Crosby's death added to Hemingway's growing sense of loss about Paris. His use of friends in *The Sun Also Rises* book had closed the door on any return. "The Hemingway who sat nightly in the Latin Quarter is no more," wrote a reporter for the *New York Evening Post*. "*The Sun Also Rises*," he continued, "marked his permanent exodus from the Dome, the Rotonde, and the rest of the Bohemian resorts of Montparnasse."

Equally responsible for Hemingway's foul disposition was gossip. He had discovered the cost of fame. Among the most stinging bits of malicious talk came from Robert McAlmon, his first publisher, who claimed that Ernest was a homosexual whose lover was Fitzgerald and that Pauline was a lesbian. Zelda Fitzgerald, apparently dissatisfied with her husband's bed skills, added to the tempest by saying publicly that Scott had "an unusual attachment" to Ernest. There was probably no other single thing that could rile Hemingway as much as an attack on his much-cultivated masculinity.

Hemingway sought, as he often did, to put geographical distance between himself and his woes. He and Pauline left town and followed John and Katy Dos Passos to Montana-Vermala, a tiny village in the Swiss Alps where the Murphys had gone for the winter. Their nine-year-old son Patrick had tuberculosis, and doctors had urged he get mountain air. Dorothy Parker, who had gotten arrested with Dos Passos during the Sacco and Vanzetti protests, joined the group. Parker had just published an adulation of Hemingway in the *New Yorker* rife with errors, and he had little patience for her. But she did her best to enliven the gathering with her celebrated humor. John and Katy Dos Passos joined the effort. "We skied and laughed our heads off over cheese fondue and the magnificent local white wine evenings in front of the fire," he said. "We were all set on keeping the Murphys cheered up. For a while it worked."

Hemingway contributed little to the jollification. He came down with a cold, and he and Pauline soon returned to Paris. As soon as Ernest left the Alps, Donald Stewart showed up. He had also been invited but delayed his arrival until Hemingway was gone. They had not spoken since the publication of *The Sun Also Rises*. What remained made for a morose gathering. "Trapped on this desolate snow-covered silent mountain," Stewart said, "with Death seeming to be waiting mockingly in the cold clear air outside, were two people who had been our models for the Happy Life."

The Dos Passoses took their leave. John had known the Murphys' son Patrick since he was little child and had no idea whether he would see him again. The couple went next to Schruns, Austria. John wanted to show Katy the spot where in 1926 he had spent what he deemed "the last unalloyed good time" with Ernest, who was then still married to Hadley. Katy knew of the moment because Hadley had written from Schruns, urging her to come as well. The couple went back to Paris and then down to Spain, again revisiting many of John Dos Passos's favorite places. When they finished their tour of Europe in February, which had amply substituted for a honeymoon, they headed across the ocean bound not for their home in Cape Cod but for Key West via Havana.

+

The first reviews of *The 42nd Parallel* reached Dos Passos soon after settling in for a long stay in Key West. "The Great American novel has never been written, perhaps never will be," proclaimed *Time* magazine. "But author Dos Passos has made a bold bid for it. Certainly no U.S. novel has ever been more comprehensive than *The 42nd Parallel*, none has ever given a broader, more sweeping view of the whole country."

Edmund Wilson, who by now had become one of the nation's premier critics, predicted that Dos Passos's trilogy "may well turn out to be the most important novel which any American of Dos Passos's generation has written." Again, as he had earlier, Wilson told readers Dos Passos was the only novelist concerned with the important political and social issues of the time. "*The 42nd Parallel* is not superior to Hemingway, for example, from the point of view of its literary originality and its intellectual interest, it seems to me by far the most remarkable, the most encouraging novel which I have read since the War."

Other complimentary reviews made their way down to the tip of Florida. On the whole they shared Wilson's estimation of the book's importance, but some complained about Dos Passos's continued efforts at experimentation. *The Nation*, for instance, was so put off that the magazine decided the only unifying aspect of the novel was its binding.

Ernest persuaded John to accompany him on a ten-day fishing trip to the Dry Tortugas. The men went and left Katy and Pauline in Key West. As usual, being on the water with a fishing pole was Hemingway's ideal way of spending time. If not a nightmare for Dos Passos, it certainly was not his idea of fun. But whenever he was in Hemingway's company Dos Passos worked to overcome his insecurities. He tried to keep up with Hemingway on all fronts, even imitating aspects of his friend's braggadocio behavior and coarse language in his letters.

Dos Passos wished he had Hemingway's financial success, as he was always having to rapidly dash off articles just to make ends meet. But Dos Passos had something Hemingway coveted: with or without cause, Hemingway was jealous of the critical praise Dos Passos got. "It is true," Hemingway confessed to Fitzgerald a little more than a year earlier, "Mr. Hemingway sometimes envies Mr. Dos Passos."

The revolution they had set off to make in literature had, in large measure, succeeded. Everyone who read books knew of Hemingway. Literary circles admired Dos Passos's work, even if they had not read it. The two men had come to a juncture in their lives. They were both in their thirties, and instead of being in the position of having to write an attention-getting work, they were under pressure to write a better book than the last one.

Dos Passos returned to his ambitious multivolume fictional portrait of America. Done for the time being with writing about war, Hemingway set off to write a book about bullfighting.

+

In October 1930 Dos Passos sorely needed a break. His manuscript *1919* was being obstreperous, and he felt mired in the morass of politics. Between his rabble-rousing in the *New Republic* and the *New Masses* and trying to finish the book, he had not rested since his springtime fishing trip with Hemingway. Meanwhile his friend had continued his pursuit of killing things with a hunting trip south of Billings, Montana.

Hemingway's letters were filled with news of his most recent slaughter of elks, rams, and bears. Pauline's wealthy and generous uncle funded the trip to polish Hemingway's marksmanship before a planned African safari. "Grizzlies are best training for Africa—the only dangerous animal in North America," Hemingway wrote to an old friend. The rich uncle now offered to pay for Dos Passos to join Hemingway for ten days of hunting. Pauline had returned home to care for their child, and as everyone knew, Hemingway liked an appreciative audience.

Nearsighted and fainthearted, Dos Passos was no hunter, but time with Hemingway far removed from the pressures of writing promised to be restorative. Besides, Katy was all for it. In late October Dos Passos descended from a train in Billings, Montana, and found Hemingway waiting to take him to the ranch.

Early the next morning Hemingway, Dos Passos, and the ranch owner set off on horses followed by a string of mules loaded down with supplies, including an ample supply of liquor. They soon came across big animal tracks in the snow but not the creatures that had made them. For Dos Passos this was a measure of comfort. Hemingway had given him a Mannlicher rifle that was very popular with deer and big-game hunters. But in Dos Passos's hands it was an unwieldy contrivance. He couldn't release the safety fast enough when game was present, and when he did the gun jammed. Soon he knocked the telescopic sight out of line. Elks, bears, and antelope had little to fear from Dos Passos, who spent his time reveling in the open western landscape and watching Hemingway hunt. "He'd smell a bull elk almost as soon as the elk would smell him," said Dos Passos.

After ten cold days of tracking and shooting, the men returned to the ranch. Dos Passos was due to take a train but instead accepted Hemingway's offer to return east by car with him. They packed their belongings in a Ford roadster Hemingway had once used to motor to Pamplona that had been shipped home by boat from Bordeaux. A ranch hand seeking to hitch a ride took the rumble seat in the back.

They spent the first night camping in Yellowstone Park. At the end of the next day they approached Park City, a few miles to the west of Billings. Conversation was animated as they made their way down Route 10, which ran along the north side of the Yellowstone River. The two-lane road had been recently resurfaced, leaving it without a centerline, and the sun was setting behind them. As in Spain, time together included booze. "Of course," said Dos Passos, "we had been drinking right much bourbon."

The headlights of a car emerged from the shadow-lined dips and rises of the road. Hemingway was momentarily blinded and steered to the right to give the oncoming automobile room. He discovered—in his words—"there wasn't enough road." Their car plunged into a ditch and flipped over. Dos Passos and the ranch hand crawled out uninjured. But Hemingway was pinned behind the wheel. They helped him out of the car. When he stood up the men saw Hemingway's right arm hanging limp and askew.

A passing car stopped and gave them a ride to the St. Vincent's Hospital in Billings forty minutes away while Hemingway kept his arm immobile between his legs. Once in Billings Dos Passos wired Pauline, who was with her family in Piggott, Arkansas. She immediately boarded a train, and Dos Passos met her at the station two days later. By then her husband had the good fortune of being seen by Dr. Louis Allard, a noted orthopedic surgeon. Allard opened Hemingway's arm above the elbow and discovered the fracture traversed the bone in a twisting angle. He drilled holes through the bone that he then threaded with kangaroo tendons to bind the injured portion, a technique developed, not surprisingly, by Australian surgeons.

With Pauline by her husband's bedside, Dos Passos returned to the car, which had been pulled back onto the road. Its doors were mangled, but it was drivable. He took it to a mechanic in Columbus, some twenty-five miles to the west, and then found a train to take him home to Provincetown.

Archibald MacLeish flew out to see Hemingway. After enduring terrifying flights on Northwest Airlines, he reported finding Hemingway "in bed with a magnificent black beard, full of suspicion of my motives and convinced—or so he said—that I had come out to see him die."

Instead, Hemingway began months of convalescence, frustrated at having lost the use of his writing arm. In the race to get their next book to readers, Dos Passos had the lead.

20

WHEN JOHN AND KATY DOS PASSOS ARRIVED IN KEY WEST IN FEBRUARY 1932 they found Ernest and Pauline Hemingway happily ensconced in a two-story, old limestone house with iron-railed balconies. They had bought the rundown place the year before for a modest payment of back taxes owed to the city. After years of rented flats in Paris, extended stays in hotels and resorts, long visits with in-laws, and more rentals in Key West, Ernest finally lived in a place he owned. It pleased him enormously.

It was the first time the two writers had seen each other since Hemingway ran the car off the road in Montana fourteen months prior. His hospital confinement had lasted seven weeks. Even out of the hospital, his damaged arm remained in a sling for a long time. When Hemingway did manage to type with his left hand the result was distressing. "This damned typer skips like a stammering flannel mouthed nigger," he wrote Peirce almost a year after the accident from Kansas City where he was with Pauline awaiting the birth of their second child.

Nine-pound Gregory Hancock Hemingway made his way into the world on November 12, 1931, by Caesarean section, as had his brother Patrick three years earlier. Also coming after a prolonged labor was Hemingway's new manuscript, a massive paean to bullfighting. Hemingway put to words his love for what some saw as a sport, others an art form, and yet others a horror. As he wrote, he returned to his pursuit of the one true sentence.

I suppose from a modern moral point of view, that is, a Christian point of view, the whole bullfight is indefensible; there is certainly much cruelty, there is always danger, either sought or unlooked for, and there is always death, and I should not try to defend it now, only to tell honestly the things I have found true about it.

Bullfighting, bulls, and matadors were the subject, but underneath the accounts, explanations, and anecdotes was a meditation on death. He even recounted the first deaths he saw in war-torn Italy when he collected the mutilated corpses following the explosion at a munitions factory.

In Hemingway's view death was the one inescapable reality he found among residents of the Old Castile region where bullfighting was most cherished. It was the one thing of which they could be sure, he believed, the only security that surpassed material comforts, and the concept that supported a religion in which life is shorter than death. By the end of the manuscript thirty-two-year-old Hemingway sounded old. Piling on one reminiscence after another, he spoke wistfully of the Spain he had known, lamenting that he would never again ride back from Toledo in the dark washing away the dust with Spanish brandy.

He titled the book *Death in the Afternoon* and sent it to his typists.

+

After the car accident Dos Passos had retreated from everyone's company to finish *1919*. By summer's end in 1931 he had a completed manuscript. Unlike in *The 42nd Parallel*, he decided to close this book with a poem. It was the single-best poetic work of his life, and it unleashed the rage he had felt since Verdun. Entitled "The Body of an American," it began with a paragraph, mimicking the Preamble to the Constitution and dotted with Dos Passos's inimitable compound words, describing the 1921 establishment of a tomb of the Unknown Soldier at Arlington Cemetery.

His pencil churned out the gruesome and frank stanzas that followed.

> how can you tell a guy's a hundredpercent when all
> you've got's a gunnysack full of bones, bronze buttons
> stamped with the screaming eagle and a pair of rull puttees?
> . . . and the gagging chloride and puky dirstench of
> the yearold dead . . .

And so on for several pages, describing the idiocy of militarism and the end of the soldier's life where

> The blood ran into the ground, the brains oozed out of
> the cracked skull and were licked up by the trenchrats, the
> belly swelled and raised a generation of bluebottle flies,
> and the incorruptible skeleton,
> and the scraps of dried viscera and skin bundled in khaki
>
> they took to Chalons-sur-Marne
> and laid it out neat in a pine coffin
> and took it home to God's Country on a battleship
> and buried it in a sarcophagus in the Memorial Amphi-
> theatre in the Arlington National Cemetery
> and draped Old Glory over it
> and the bugler played taps.
> All of Washington brought
> flowers.
> Woodrow Wilson brought a bouquet of poppies.

Done, Dos Passos sent the manuscript to Eugene Saxton, his editor at Harper. The book went into production rapidly, which pleased Dos Passos because he felt its contents were timely. All was well until Saxton received a cable from the company's former president and now a trusted adviser. Gene Wells wired instructions that the biographical poem called "The House of Morgan" be stricken from Dos Passos's book. The Morgan banking operation had provided crucial financing when the publishing company reorganized a few years earlier, and the executives were in no mood to castigate their savior by publishing a poem that referred to war, starvation, lice, cholera and typhus as providing "good growing weather for the House of Morgan."

"Sorry," said Wells, "I could not have taken another position. It is difficult to be a businessman and a gentleman at the same as you have often heard me argue." Dos Passos refused to cut the section. His book, after all, was an attack on industrialization, capitalism, and the materialism of which J. P. Morgan was a patron saint. His agent quickly placed the edited manuscript with Harcourt, Brace. "This is certainly a lousy break all round—but it's no use worrying any more about it," Dos Passos wrote Saxton, adding, "Hell it's only a book after all."

✛

Hemingway's *Death in the Afternoon* manuscript was typed by the time Dos Passos arrived in Key West in February. Hemingway was eager to get his friend's evaluation, especially as Dos Passos had lauded *A Farewell to Arms* after panning *The Sun Also Rises*. Praise from an author and friend whom Hemingway regarded as his "most bitterly severe critic" would be sweet. Dos Passos was bringing with him the galleys of *1919*, the second volume of his projected trilogy. The two men fished, drank, and read. Sometimes doing all three at once.

On board a ship heading home and perhaps feeling he was at a safe distance, Dos Passos delivered his verdict on *Death in the Afternoon*. "The Bullfight book—is absolutely the best thing can be done on the subject— I mean all the description and the dope—it seems an absolute model for how that sort of thing ought to be done," he wrote.

Compliments given—Dos Passos knew his audience—he set forth his criticisms. The discursive sections, the portions that sounded like a lecture where "Old Hem straps on the long white whiskers," and the pontifications about writing need to go. The book is so good, Dos Passos implored, "that it would be a shame to leave in any unnecessary tripe— damn it I think there's always enough tripe in anything even after you've cut out—and a book like that can stand losing some of the best passages." As always, after delivering a blow, Dos Passos backpedaled. "But I may be packed with prunes with all this so for God's sake don't pay too much attention to it—the Book's damn swell in any case."

But Hemingway did pay attention. Once Dos Passos had been the one with the money and fame. But no longer, especially in comparison to the Key West scribe. Yet Hemingway still valued his advice and promised to "try to cut the shit as you say." Within a few months he discarded large sections from the book in galleys. "I cut out all you object to," Hemingway reported to Dos Passos when he finished, adding, "seemed like the best to me God damn you if it really was." In turn, Hemingway offered up his take on Dos Passos's *1919*.

"The book is bloody splendid—it's four times the book the *42nd* was—and that was damned good," Hemingway told Dos Passos. He wasn't flattering his friend. At other times that year Hemingway told others that he believed Dos Passos could be an excellent writer and was getting better with each book. But Hemingway worried that the characters were too perfect in *1919*. "Remember it was Bloom and Mrs. Bloom that saved Joyce," he said, referring to the main figures in *Ulysses*. "If you get a noble communist remember the bastard probably masturbates and is jealous as a cat. Keep them people, people, people, and don't let them get to be symbols."

In this moment the path the two writers had followed since the ambulance-driving days led them in separate ways. Hemingway still believed that the perfect representation of an imperfect world alone was sufficient. Dos Passos wanted his writing to change the world. "For Christ sake don't try to do good," Hemingway said. "Keep on showing it as it is. If you can show it as it really is you will do good. If you try to do good you'll not do any good nor will you show it."

✢

The politics that animated Dos Passos's prose were not confined to the page. During the past year he had worked with novelist Theodore Dreiser to draw attention to the plight of striking mine workers in impoverished Harlan County, Kentucky. Miners were battling coal mine operators who cut wages after the start of the Great Depression. Violence, the involvement of the United Mine Workers union, and the popularity of the folk song "Whose Side Are You On?" written by the wife of a strike organizer, brought national attention to the struggle.

Dos Passos admired the sixty-year-old Dreiser and had read his novels growing up. Meeting him at last, Dos Passos found that the author's long nose and the way his skin wrinkled around his eyes reminded him of an elephant. In November 1931 Dos Passos traveled with Dreiser and other members of the National Committee to Aid Striking Miners Fighting Starvation to Harlan County. Local officials did their best to thwart the outsiders. When Dreiser entertained a woman in his hotel room vigilantes propped toothpicks against the door to see if it would open again before morning. They were still upright at dawn, resulting in an indictment against Dreiser for adultery. The case never went to court.

Dos Passos was dismayed when he saw the miners' living conditions. Their houses were up on stilts. The thin walls had cracks stuffed with newspaper, and the tarpaper roofs were barely able to ward off rain. He had seen similar shelters in the shantytowns of Florida, but here in the cold of the Kentucky mountains, he wondered how the families stayed warm in the drafty houses burning coal, mostly bought from the mine companies. "It wrings your heart," Dos Passos wrote, "the way the scantily furnished rooms have been tidied up for the visitors."

Dos Passos watched as the witnesses, whose speech reminded him of Elizabethan lyrics, came one by one to the county's main hotel where Dreiser masterfully conducted the committee's hearings. "These were fine people," Dos Passos said. "I desperately wanted to help them." As he had done during the fight to save Sacco and Vanzetti, Dos Passos helped the committee write a report. For his efforts Dos Passos was among those indicted on a charge of criminal syndicalism—criminal acts conducted for a political purpose—a few weeks later after leaving Kentucky. Like the adultery charge against Dreiser, nothing came of it.

As it had been with the Sacco and Vanzetti case, none of what Dos Passos told Hemingway moved him to lend his support. Hemingway remained uncommitted to political causes of any sort. He told his friend he could not be a Communist because he hated tyranny and perhaps government. "But if you're ever one its swell with me. I can't stand *any* bloody government I suppose." Paul Romaine, whom Hemingway had known in Paris and was now a Milwaukee book dealer, wrote Hemingway and urged him to join American leftists in their efforts to end the Great Depression through economic reforms. Hemingway replied. "There is no left and no right in writing. There is only good and bad writing."

Worse, Hemingway said, is that writers who are on the left will eventually swing to the right. "Dreiser is different. He is an old man and old men all try to save their souls in one way or another," he wrote. "Dos Passos doesn't swing. He's always been the same."

✛

Dos Passos's *1919* received a warm welcome when his new publisher brought it out in March 1932. Of course, Dos Passos was nowhere to be found. He and Katy had gone to Mexico after leaving Key West and did not return until long after the book had been published. But the reviews he saw when they got back home were gratifying.

The *New York Times* compared him at length to Hemingway, linking Dos Passos's method of interspersing mood changes through newsreel, camera eye, and biographical sections with those found in Hemingway's *In Our Time*. But critic John Chamberlain believed that when it came to subject material Dos Passos stood on his own. "One may safely call him the most adventurous, the most widely experienced, the man with the broadest sympathies (we do not say deepest), among our novelists since Sinclair Lewis bade goodbye to Martin Arrowsmith."

Chamberlain complained, as Hemingway had, about characters serving as symbols. But he judged this war novel far superior to *Three Soldiers*, praising Dos Passos for its broad reach. "Hemingway who is Dos Passos' closest competitor in exploring the jungle," Chamberlain said, "has been almost solely oriented in personal problems raised by the war."

Hemingway had his turn with book critics six months later when his *Death in the Afternoon* appeared. It wasn't fun. "One's guess is that it will be less successful than the novels in making new Hemingway addicts," decided the *New York Times*. "Action and conversation, as the author himself suggests, are his best weapons. To the degree that he dilutes them with philosophy and exposition he weakens himself." It was an echo of Dos Passos's observation. As it was Hemingway's first book since *A Farewell to Arms*, his new work garnered considerable interest but not the praise given to Dos Passos's most recent work.

Publicly Hemingway shrugged off the critic's view of *Death in the Afternoon*, telling Dos Passos, "a man *should* be pooped on by the Times." The hometown *Chicago Tribune*, whose Fanny Butcher had become a Hemingway fan following the publication of *A Farewell to Arms*, provided praise amid the lukewarm batches of reviews sent to Key West. *Death in the Afternoon*, she wrote, "is death incarnate, and Mr. Hemingway looks upon it and records its functioning with an art which is supreme."

Nonetheless for an author who had been the darling of the literary scene for his first three books, he was unprepared for the less-than-charitable treatment given to a famous writer when his work falls short in the minds of critics. Max Perkins mailed a stack of reviews along with a note that said, "I know there are things in them which you will hate."

After reading them Hemingway grew sullen; he distracted himself with bear hunting in Wyoming. At first shooting at grizzlies—rather than critics—did not provide the bromide he needed. His companion had killed one, but Hemingway had not. But soon the smell of horsemeat laid as bait drew in a five-hundred-pound black bear. Hemingway reached for his rifle, took aim, and fired. He had his trophy.

If the judgment of critics was the measure of success in the book trade, Dos Passos was back on top for the first time since 1924, the year he helped Hemingway get his first book published. But by the all-important measure of sales, a book with Hemingway's name on the spine found readers no matter what the critics said. *1919* had sold only nine thousand copies, fewer than the first print run for *Death in the Afternoon*. It hardly felt like success when, to make ends meet, Dos Passos had to ask Hemingway for a loan.

Max Perkins, from his perch at Scribner's, offered an explanation for Dos Passos's failure to catch on with readers. "The truth is I do not think his way of writing and his theory make books that people care to read unless they are interested objectively in society or literature for pure sake," Perkins confided to Fitzgerald. "They are fascinating, but they do make you suffer like the deuce, and people cannot want to do that."

Hemingway had fame and fortune; Dos Passos had unremunerated literary praise. For Hemingway the world, its wars, depressions, and politics remained a personal matter. Dos Passos, however, believed writing without a larger purpose was indulgent. In Key West the adulation given to the Provincetown writer for the purity of his principled approach to writing began to grate on his friend's nerves.

21

AS 1933 OPENED, SPAIN WAS ON THE MINDS OF BOTH ERNEST HEMING-
way and John Dos Passos. It had been three years since Dos Passos had
been in the country, two years for Hemingway. The men's love for Spain
was stronger than their affection for Paris—Spain had been their place of
escape and an inspiration for their literature. They were cheered because
dictator Miguel Primo de Rivera, who had ruled for almost a decade, had
been thrown out of power and a shaky republic was in place. Hemingway
told Dos Passos they had to go back.

This urgency grew out of a meeting in New York City Hemingway
had just concluded with film director Lewis Milestone. Born in Moldova,
Milestone had risen to be among the most successful American film directors, winning two successive Best Director awards that the Academy of
Motion Pictures began handing out in 1928. He wanted to film Hemingway's bullfighting book in Spain with amateur actors. Hemingway urged
Dos Passos to come south to work on the logistics of the film. If all went
well, they could go to Spain at the end of the summer for the shooting.

Dos Passos agreed to the plan but first had to accompany Katy to Johns
Hopkins Hospital in Baltimore for a tonsillectomy. Always short of funds,
they had found cheaper medical care there than near Boston. But after
her surgery was completed successfully, John suddenly became the patient. His limbs swelled to such an extent that he could not even move an

arm sufficiently to write. His hands were so swollen that they looked to Katy like boxing gloves. His rheumatic fever was back with a vengeance.

Sitting at her husband's bedside and still sore from the tonsillectomy, Katy took out pen and paper. "Things are very bad. . . . Hellishly painful," John said as she transcribed his faltering dictation into a letter to Hemingway. Putting up a playful front, he continued, "The only thing we could find out about rheumatic fever is that you can't have it in the tropics so you may see two thin and ghostly figures totter off the Ward Line any day." Before sealing the letter in an envelope, Katy added her own postscript. "Oh Wemedge it's awful. Pauline it's awful."

Providentially a doctor with a familiar face came to their rescue. Dr. Horsley Gantt, the American doctor who had worked with Pavlov in Russia and had accompanied Dos Passos on his walk through the Caucasus, was now working at Johns Hopkins Medical School. He secured the needed medical assistance and medicine at greatly reduced rates.

Despite his father's wealth John had not inherited much, as the estate had gone mostly to settle bills and loans. What little cash he received he spent shortly after the war, some of which financed the publication of his first novel. The couple's financial bedrock was Katy's house in Provincetown. The hospitalization put all their plans for the year in jeopardy. "M. Fish says," Katy told Ernest and Pauline, using her husband's nickname of Muttonfish, "he is working on Natural Enemies to finance a trip to Spain." The *natural enemies*—as he and Hemingway liked to call editors—delivered. His new publisher, Harcourt, Brace, advanced $1,000 toward a short book about Spain.

When Katy's letter reached Key West, Hemingway grabbed his copy of *Black's Medical Dictionary*. Only the year before, he had jested about his friend's health. "You can write so damned well it spooks me something might happen to you," he had then said. Now that Dos Passos was actually sick, Hemingway turned serious. "That's a hell of a disease and had me spooked," he wrote.

In his reply Hemingway enclosed a check for $1,000, almost an entire year's salary for many Americans. "Listen this G is off the record," Hemingway said. He explained that Pauline's uncle had given them stock to sell to finance a planned trip to Africa, and he would still have plenty left to pay for the trip after giving Dos Passos the money. "I couldn't make a trip to Coney Island let alone Africa with you, you ignorant Portuguese having some lousy disease that swells the hands and saps the brain," he said. "So cash this before I change it into pennies and pelt you publicly as a hypochondriac—this won't keep you from giving the *pooblishers* hell—nor anything else—just make it simpler to turn around—you can pay a few creditors and re-establish their borrow-ability."

Without telling Dos Passos, Hemingway also contacted Arnold Gingrich, who was launching a new quarterly to be called *Esquire*. Dos Passos had returned $200 to Gingrich because he could not deliver a promised article on the Scottsboro case in which nine black Alabama teenagers had been accused of raping two white women on a train. Gingrich had contracted for the piece from Dos Passos because his business plan was to fill the magazine with work from the nation's best writers. He was trying to persuade Hemingway to write some articles by appealing to his manliness. *Esquire*, said Gingrich, will be for men what *Vogue* is for women. "But it won't be the least damn bit like *Vanity Fair*. It aims to have ample hair on its chest, to say nothing of adequate cojones."

Hemingway agreed to contribute something, perhaps even in time for the first issue. He also asked Gingrich to help Dos Passos out. The editor responded by not only sending the $200 back to Dos Passos but also including an extra $75 for an original painting or drawing to be submitted later.

Friends came calling at the Johns Hopkins Hospital as Dos Passos's confinement to bed lengthened. José Robles, who taught Spanish literature at Johns Hopkins University, stopped in frequently. The two had met in Spain as teenagers and had remained in touch over the years. It had been Robles who translated *Manhattan Transfer* for the Spanish edition published in 1929. He left Spain during the years of the dictatorship but had begun returning to his homeland in the summers since the republic had been established. Like Dos Passos, he was optimistic but nervous about Spain's future.

F. Scott Fitzgerald also stopped in for extended visits. He was living in Baltimore so Zelda could obtain care from psychiatrists at Johns Hopkins in her struggles with mental illness. He was worried that time was running out for Zelda. "If she were an anti-social person who did not want to face life and pull her own weight that would be one story," Scott wrote to her doctor, "but her passionate love of life and her absolute inability to meet it, seems so tragic that sometimes it is scarcely to be endured." Dos Passos found his friend was working hard to control his drinking and write as much as he could to pay for his wife's bills. "He was so much worse off than I was," said Dos Passos, "that I felt I ought to be sitting at his bedside instead of his sitting at mine."

Although Lewis Milestone had abandoned the bullfighting film project, Dos Passos began to recover well enough to make the planned Spanish reunion with Hemingway in the summer. Freed from the clutches of the doctors, on May 25 John and Katy Dos Passos boarded the Europe-bound *Conte di Savoia* in a cabin provided by Gerald and Sara Murphy, who promised a month's rest and recuperation was awaiting their ill friend in Southern France and on their yacht *Weatherbird*. The Dos Passoses carried Hemingway's $1,000 gift and money from *Esquire* and from Harcourt, Brace. "The wily Portuguese shakes down his friends," John Dos Passos quipped to Hemingway.

"Damn Tooting we'll be in Spain, dead or alive," Dos Passos scribbled on a note he penned after boarding he ship. "To attain that situation, haven't I just signed a contract to write a book (a short book) about the Second Republic which will be burned by Hitler, pissed on in the Kremlin, used for toilet paper by the anarchist syndicalists, deplored by the *Nation*, branded by the *New York Times*, derided by the *Daily Worker* and left unread by the Great American Public."

✛

Hemingway had spent the spring working on new short stories for a collection Scribner's wanted to publish that fall. They were a gruesome set of tales about death, shell shock, unfulfilled longing, and degeneration that came with age. If he delivered the stories to Max Perkins, it would be his first book of fiction since *A Farewell to Arms*.

Only his literary—not financial—success hung in the balance. For Hemingway, putting pen to paper was as good as signing a check. He was certainly America's best-known writer. *A Farewell to Arms* was in movie houses starring Helen Hayes and Gary Cooper. The film, directed by Frank Borzage, hardly measured up to the book, and grievously for Hemingway, the despairing nightmarish ending had been altered to one of dreamy hope. Viewers, egged on by the film's publicity agents, made autobiographical connections between the story and its author. A little more than a dozen years since a teenage Hemingway embellished his war exploits to an American press and hometown crowd, the exaggerations now irritated him. He wrote a lengthy notice disclaiming what he deemed to be false military heroism imputed to him in a movie publicity release, and he asked Perkins to send it to the press. He diminished his service in the ambulance corps, saying he chose Italy because it was safer than France, claiming he was never involved in anything heroic, and asking "the motion picture people to leave his private life alone."

At the end of the summer the Hemingway family, including Bumby, who had been staying with them, and Pauline's sister Jinny, sailed for Europe. Disembarking in Santander on the northern Atlantic coast of Spain, they each went their own way. Pauline, Jinny, and children took a train north to Paris to return Bumby to his mother, Hadley, who was now remarried. The marriage was a happy one, making Hadley's meeting with Pauline less off-putting. Ernest, free of wife and children, rushed on to Madrid.

But like the time Hemingway returned to Italy in search of the battlefield, Spain also no longer seemed the same. In Madrid his favorite café had given way to a new office building, and although one could still swim at the swimming hole he had once frequented, the spot was now a natatorium. Even the bulls and their matadors disappointed him.

Soon after Hemingway reached Madrid John and Katy Dos Passos arrived, their health much the better for their stay with the Murphys. They were traveling in a secondhand Fiat they named "the cockroach" that was as unreliable as the Fiat ambulances John had driven in the war. At one point the steering pin fell out and the car came to a stop in a meadow. None of it mattered much to the two, however. Happy together, feeling healthy, and grateful to be in Spain, the lousy vehicle that belonged in a junkyard was their Rocinante. Its end came when a man posing as a would-be buyer stole it. The car was eventually recovered, but by then the Dos Passoses were departing, so it was left behind in a Spanish police impoundment lot.

Dos Passos and Hemingway lunched at Sobrino de Botín, a landmark restaurant that was established in 1725 by a Frenchman. It was the place where, in the closing pages of *The Sun Also Rises*, Barnes and Ashley ate roasted young suckling pig and washed it down with three bottles of wine from Rioja Alta. US ambassador to Spain Claude Bowers joined the men on several occasions. A journalist and historian known for his book defending impeached President Andrew Johnson, Bowers was worried about the new Spanish government. Dos Passos plied him with questions about Spanish politics, but Hemingway would not be drawn into the discussion. "Hem had no stake in it," said Dos Passos. "His partisanship was in various toreros."

But Dos Passos was wrong about Hemingway's silence. What he had seen that summer alarmed him. He believed that those in power in Spain had, in his words, their fingers in the pie. "When they run out of pie there will be another revolution," he wrote to his mother-in-law from Madrid. More ominously, Hemingway was worried about Hitler. "War is the health of the State," he told Mary Pfeiffer, "and anyone with his conception of the state has to have war or the threat of war to keep it going." If he had not signed the letter, one might have thought the words were drawn from a Dos Passos wartime letter.

As the fall of 1933 descended, the Dos Passoses went south to Gibraltar to catch a ship back to the United States. Hemingway returned to Paris where Pauline waited, and the two embarked on the much-delayed African safari.

+

The two couples were together again a few months later in Key West. The Dos Passoses arrived first in February, hoping a lengthy stay in the tropics would chase off the symptoms of John's rheumatic fever that persistently returned. The book Dos Passos had promised his publishers before leaving for Spain was almost ready for publication. Instead of being devoted solely to Spain, the author had padded *In All Countries*, as the finished book was being called, with essays on his travels in the United States, Mexico, and Russia.

Esquire, which had been launched while Dos Passos and Hemingway were out of the country, was a success, the one bright light in publishing during the economic darkness of the 1930s. It gave Dos Passos a modest infusion of cash and Hemingway, who didn't need the money, a platform to expound upon the arts of fishing, bullfighting, and lion hunting as well as to take potshots at his critics. For the $75 that had been advanced to him by the magazine for an illustration, Dos Passos had supplied a brightly colored painting he did in Madrid. The magazine used it to accompany a Hemingway dispatch from Spain. In other issues Dos Passos's art ran adjacent to his fiction, which included an excerpt from the third novel he had begun for his USA trilogy still awaiting completion.

As Dos Passos completed proofing the galleys of *In All Countries* in Key West, Ernest and Pauline Hemingway disembarked from a French liner in New York City. "The lion is a fine animal," Hemingway told awaiting reporters eager to hear about his African hunting trip. "He does not want to fight, but sometimes man makes him, and then it is up to the man to shoot his way out of what he had got himself into." He announced he was heading to Key West to begin work on a new novel about lion and buffalo hunting. But before boarding a train he and Pauline went by taxi to a Brooklyn shipyard. There he purchased a thirty-eight-foot-long fishing boat he planned to name *Pilar*, one of the codenames he used for Pauline when he was still married to Hadley.

The Dos Passoses and the Hemingways were finally together again under the Florida sun in April. For John and Katy the Hemingway children Patrick and Gregory—Gigi and the Mexican Mouse—were cute and fun to see. It was also painful. Katy had been pregnant several times since their marriage five years earlier, but each time she had miscarried. There seemed little hope they would ever have a child of their own.

The reunion had all the elements of previous ones: a boat trip to Havana, swimming, fishing, and intimacies of friendship. When Ernest came down with a sore throat, the gang brought their drinks and suppers on trays in the bedroom. But something was not right, and Dos Passos noticed.

One day he and Katy came across a plaster cast bust of Hemingway decorating the hall of the house. It looked to John as if it was made of soap, and he and Katy laughed upon seeing it. In the days that followed, he treated it as a ring toss, lobbing his panama hat at it upon entering the house. Ernest caught him in the act. With a sour look on his face, Hemingway took the hat off the bust and returned it to his friend. It should have been a small matter, especially for two men whose friendship was laced with arguments about literature, politics, and fishing. "He was grouchy for the rest of the day," said John. "Nobody said anything but after that things were never quite so good."

Hemingway's reaction to what he saw as effrontery regarding the bust caused Dos Passos to pause. He wondered whether their friendship had changed or perhaps it was his friend? In the years after the war, when their wallets had both been empty and staying true to their literary visions animated their conversations over cheap drink in a Paris café, the men had found merriment and pleasure in each other's company. Now that Hemingway had literary success accompanied by money, the laughing seemed to be over.

✛

After the Dos Passoses left, Hemingway finished reading Fitzgerald's long-awaited novel *Tender Is the Night*. As Hemingway had done in *The Sun Also Rises*, Fitzgerald used the people in their circle for his characters. Hemingway had his complaints, but he couldn't be specific when he wrote Fitzgerald because he no longer had a copy of the book. "Godamn it Dos took it with him so I can't refer to it," he said. The problem, Hemingway told Fitzgerald, was that in taking Gerald and Sara Murphy as models for characters, he failed to be consistent in his use of them. "You can take you or me or Zelda or Pauline or Hadley or Sara or Gerald but you have to keep them the same and you can only make them do what they would do."

With the sensitivity of a steamroller, Hemingway went on to dismiss his friend's recent financial and personal calamities that had made the recent years the darkest years in Fitzgerald's life. "Forget your personal tragedy," Hemingway told him. "We are all bitched from the start and you especially have to be hurt like hell before you can write seriously. But when you get the damned hurt use it—don't cheat with it."

The compassion he had shown for Dos Passos the year before when he battled his illness was no longer there. His old friend Archibald MacLeish, who had taken him to the hospital in Paris when glass from the fallen skylight sliced into Hemingway's forehead, was also a target on Hemingway's verbal firing range. On board Hemingway's new boat, a seasick MacLeish fished ineptly and lost a sailfish at the end of the line. Disgusted,

Hemingway picked up his double-barreled shotgun, aimed it at the slender gray birds darting about, and, in MacLeish's words, "taking one with one barrel and the grieving mate with the other."

Hemingway's churlishness was not confined to his friends. William Saroyan, who had burst onto the literary scene in 1934 with a collection of stories called *The Daring Young Man on the Flying Trapeze*, crossed the line when he poked fun at *Death in the Afternoon*. "Even when Hemingway is a fool, he is at least an accurate fool."

Hemingway gave him a verbal pummeling in an article he wrote for *Esquire*. The author of a cruel satire about his mentor Sherwood Anderson years earlier now stooped to the level of a literary schoolyard brawl. "He had it coming," Hemingway wrote. "He started bandying names in a story he wrote. A godamn sight better than any name he'll ever pick. He was talking about Dos, and Joyce and Faulkner. You see he thought using their names put him in their class. Why the poor ignorant *bastid*. He was asking for it wasn't he?"

Hemingway's treatment of their friends bewildered Dos Passos. "Men of letters suffer from conceit more than ordinary men," Dos Passos reflected later. "The bull that was friendly and playful as a calf will gore the guts out of you at the drop of a hat when he's grown."

✦

In July 1934 John Dos Passos was in New York City, having left Katy in Provincetown. The American economy remained mired in the Great Depression, and the Dos Passoses were struggling financially. The cost of trips to Key West to combat rheumatic fever was mounting, and neither of the first two volumes of the *USA* trilogy had produced much in the way of royalties. "Getting in the red and need the money," Dos Passos told his editor.

Dos Passos's agent had good news. Director Josef von Sternberg, who had made Marlene Dietrich into an international star when he cast her in the German-made film *The Blue Angel*, proposed that Dos Passos adapt the 1898 French novel *La Femme et le Pantin* by Pierre Louÿs for his sixth film with her. Money and the glamour of Hollywood proved irresistible. Dos Passos signed the contract and, without as much as letting Katy know, boarded a western-bound plane. "Oh possum," he hastily wrote Katy from Los Angeles, "I'm not sure that it's not a grave tactical error but my feet are in the flypaper now."

It was a turbulent twenty-two-hour trip across the country. "Filled two quart cartoons full of vomit and felt a little groggy," Dos Passos reported to Hemingway. The flight might have been an omen. Within days his rheumatic fever returned, and Dos Passos was confined to bed in the Hollywood Plaza Hotel, where Marlene Dietrich sent him flowers. Screenwriter Francis Faragoh, whom had been part of the radical theater group in New York, offered Dos Passos a bed in his Hollywood house, and there he remained until Katy arrived in late August after burying her father in Columbia, Missouri.

Von Sternberg had in mind creating a sinister tale of love, betrayal, and humiliation, making considerable use of flashbacks to highlight his beautiful femme fatale. He visited Dos Passos each day to discuss the script. The conversations did not go well, and the men found themselves talking at cross-purposes. In the end much of what Dos Passos wrote was ignored. Three other screenwriters put the script in order in time for the filming.

"In some ways," Dos Passos confessed to Edmund Wilson, "I don't quite understand I am still in collaboration with Mr. Von Stern and the walking ghost of Pierre Louÿs on this little drama of Spanish passion and still receive my salary."

By October their checking account was sufficiently recharged so Dos Passos was able to send Hemingway $300 toward a loan he had received from him while last in Key West. Together John and Katy Dos Passos left Hollywood behind and took a recuperative ship ride through the Panama Canal to Havana, where they settled into the Hotel Ambos Mundos in a pair of rooms that overlooked Morro Castle. Katy, however, soon left to see doctors in the United States. She had another pregnancy that was failing.

Hemingway, piloting his new boat, came over to Havana. He was close to finishing a draft of his book about his African adventures. It was another nonfiction book in the style of his one on bullfighting. There was still no new novel in the works. It was almost as if he had lost his touch. When his story collection *Winner Take Nothing* had appeared the previous fall, *New York Times* critic John Chamberlain said in print what some were saying privately: "He has evidently reached a point in writing where the sterile, the hollow, the desiccated emotions of the post-war generation cannot make him feel disgusted; he is simply weary of contemplation," Chamberlain wrote. "He feels sorry for himself, but he has lost something of the old urgency which impelled him to tell the world about it in good prose."

In contrast, Dos Passos was completing the most ambitious work of his life. If he could get his vigor back, he thought, he could finish the climactic volume of his trilogy in 1935. He was approaching the end of his quest to write the Great American Novel. In the years since Hemingway's last novel had appeared, Dos Passos had published the first two highly praised volumes and was now at work on the third. In contrast, all Hemingway had produced at that time was an ill-received collection of stories and a book about bulls. In his envious frustration he decided Dos Passos had sold out to Hollywood. "Poor Dos Passos got rich out there," wrote Hemingway, whose film rights to *Farewell to Arms* had fetched $80,000—more than twice what the Yankees paid Babe Ruth that year. He declared his friend had become a hypocrite. Scribbling on the back of a poem, Hemingway wrote, "Marx the whimpering bourgeois living on the bounty of Engels is exactly as valid as Dos Passos living on a yacht in the Mediterranean while he attacks the capitalist system."

As Dos Passos regained his strength, he had to wonder about the health of his valued friendship with Hemingway.

22

PAINTER LUIS QUINTANILLA, LIKE MANY OTHER POLITICALLY ACTIVE artists, found himself in trouble in his native Spain in the fall of 1934. A friend of Dos Passos and Hemingway since he had worked in Paris in the 1920s, Quintanilla permitted a group opposed to the conservative government to store weapons in his Madrid studio. As an anticipated general strike got underway in October, he and his friends passed the day making paella and awaiting instructions to deliver the guns. When none came, they went to bed. In the middle of the night the police, tipped off by a neighbor who had overheard indiscreet talk of revolution on the studio's terrace, burst in and made what they considered highly prized arrests. Quintanilla was locked up, where he awaited sentencing, which might possibly be execution.

In Key West word of his arrest brought Hemingway and Dos Passos together in a common cause and calmed the roiled waters of their friendship. They convinced the Pierre Matisse Gallery in New York City to mount an exhibit of forty Quintanilla etchings of Madrid street scenes. Hemingway paid to pull prints from the etchings and provided funds to support the show. He and Dos Passos then set about writing the text for the catalog. It was like the days of Paris as the pair of authors wrote, drank, and shared their drafts.

While the men penned their pieces about Quintanilla, *Esquire* editor Arnold Gingrich arrived in Key West. Hemingway's contributions to the magazine were an essential part of its success, and in turn, Hemingway had used his columns to enlarge his public persona as a hunter, fisherman, outdoorsman, and worldly figure. Dos Passos watched in fascination as Hemingway played the editor as if he were a marlin at the end of a fishing line. "Hem would reel in gently letting his prey have plenty of line. The editor was hooked," said Dos Passos.

By then Dos Passos had sent his portion of the Quintanilla catalog copy to his friend Malcolm Cowley at the *New Republic* to run as an article. Hemingway used Gingrich's visit to talk Dos Passos into changing his plans and, instead, publish it with Hemingway's portion in Gingrich's magazine. Dos Passos wired Cowley to retract his offer.

The January 1935 issue of *Esquire* carried Hemingway and Dos Passos's commentaries along with six of Quintanilla's sepia-toned stark etchings of everyday Spanish life. Dos Passos, as was his way, went further than the written page. He wrote letters to friends, circulated a petition, and organized a picket line in front of the New York City Spanish consulate. The consul, who was a friend of Quintanilla, sent telegrams to Madrid greatly exaggerating the turnout.

✛

Sad news greeted Dos Passos and Hemingway after a day of fishing in early March 1935. Sixteen-year-old Baoth Murphy, the eldest child of Gerald and Sara Murphy, had died of meningitis. His death was a shock to his parents because it had been his young brother Patrick who had been battling tuberculosis for years. Dos Passos inarticulately conveyed his condolences in a note with meandering sentences. "Trying to think of some kind of cheerful word to end a letter with I can't find any," he confessed.

The next day Hemingway took his turn. He was surer of his words. "Remember," he wrote to the Murphys, "that he had a very fine time and having it a thousand times makes it no better. And he is spared from learning what sort of a place this world is." Almost as if he were writing a riff in *A Farewell to Arms*, Hemingway continued his meditation on death. We will all die by defeat when our bodies fail and our world is destroyed, he wrote, but Boath got over it while his world still remained intact. He vacillated between providing comfort—"No one you love is ever dead"— to ruminating on his sense of the future—"It seems as though we are all on a boat now together, a good boat still, that we have made but that we know will never reach port."

A few weeks later Dos Passos and Hemingway headed back out onto the Gulf waters in the *Pilar* in the company of a Key West fishing friend of Hemingway's, Henry Strater, a painter whom they both knew from Paris. A Princeton classmate of F. Scott Fitzgerald, Strater had been the model for the character Burne Holiday in *This Side of Paradise.*

They set course for Bimini, 260 miles northeast of Key West and along the rich fishing grounds of the Gulf Stream. They were trawling only a few hours from harbor when they spotted a green turtle and made plans to harpoon it for its meat. But before they could, a dolphin grabbed the bait on Dos Passos's rod. Then another took Strater's bait. In the ensuing battle to reel them in, both Strater and Dos Passos lost their fish.

Sharks appeared, and in an instant Hemingway and Strater had them on the end of their lines. Hemingway managed to reel in his shark to the side of the boat. The boat's cook gaffed the shark, and Hemingway took out his .22-caliber Colt pistol. He shot at the thrashing shark's head, using hollow-point bullets designed to expand and cause deadly damage.

Dos Passos, more than glad to be given a chance not to be holding a pole, watched from the command bridge above, where he had retreated with his eight-millimeter movie camera. Hemingway once again took aim at the shark. Suddenly it convulsed, breaking the gaffing pole that held the shark in place. A broken portion of the pole slammed into Hemingway's right hand, which held the gun. It fired, but no one heard the shot over the loud crack from the breaking of the pole. The bullet struck the brass boat rail and broke into pieces that ricocheted. Looking down, Hemingway found where some of the fragments went. He had two holes just below one knee and lacerations on both legs where scars could still be seen from the battlefield shrapnel of 1918. He sat down.

"Get the iodine, Bread," Hemingway told his pilot.

"What did it, Cap?"

"I got shot when the gaff broke."

They boiled water, scrubbed the wounds with soap, and doused the two holes with the iodine as the *Pilar* made its way back to port and a doctor. Hemingway soon turned the incident into an article for *Esquire*, cleaning up his language so "asshole" became "the outlet of his colon" and "fuck the bastard" appeared as "Fornicate the illegitimate."

One week later the *Pilar* set out for Bimini again with a patched-up Hemingway at the helm. Katy joined her husband this time. On the island the couple occupied an old beachside bungalow, leaving Hemingway to stay on his boat. As usual, the group went fishing. One day Hemingway hooked a large tuna, and sharks attacked, tearing twenty-five- to thirty-pound bits of flesh off the fish at the end of the line. Katy watched as Hemingway brought out a machine gun. "It's terrific to see the bullets ripping into them," she wrote to Gerald Murphy when safely back on land. "The sharks thrashing in blood and foam—the white bellies and fearful jaws—the pale cold eyes—I was really aghast but it's very exciting."

John and Katy Dos Passos walked the beach each day, collecting shells and watching the crabs dart about the fallen coconuts. Hemingway teased them for collecting shells and going out in a rowboat together—people did that before they were married, not after, he told them. Aside from momentary moments of crotchetiness, Hemingway appeared to his old friends as the more playful version of the olden days. "Life still seemed enormously comical to all of us," Dos Passos recalled.

✢

When Hemingway had earlier written his contribution to the Quintanilla exhibit catalog, he suggested that the artist got in trouble because of the Spanish tradition "that a man should be a man as well as an artist." Until this moment Hemingway had chosen to remain exclusively the artist. Unlike Dos Passos, he had steadfastly kept out of politics. He had even refused to lend a hand or, indeed, a signature to Dos Passos in the campaign to save Sacco and Vanzetti.

Hemingway grew defensive by the published—and unpublished—criticism of his preoccupation with hunting, fishing, bullfighting, and travel. He could not, he insisted, be a Communist because of his belief in Liberty. Everyone claims that if one does not become a Communist, one will have no friends and will be alone, Hemingway wrote to Ivan Kashkin in Moscow, who had translated much of Hemingway's work into Russian. But being alone is not so dreadful, nor is a lack of friends, Hemingway concluded.

Hemingway gleefully noted that his books in Russia were outselling Dos Passos, Dreiser, and Sinclair Lewis, but he forgot what Dos Passos told him when he had gone to the worker's paradise. "The great joke about the USSR to foreign writers," Dos Passos had written him when leaving Russia, "is that although you can get jack out of publishers, you can't take it out of the country, but you have to drink it up in vodka and malt herring."

Unbeknownst to Hemingway, the carping about his friend's apolitical approach to writing also irritated Dos Passos. "I don't think it's entirely because he is a good friend of mine that I'm beginning to get thoroughly sick of every little inkshitter who can get his stuff in a pink magazine shying bricks at him," he wrote privately to Cowley, using a dated term for flinging. "I suppose they are all sore at H. because they think he's in on the big money."

Rambling on, Dos Passos told Cowley that "when the little inkshitters are on your side that's the time to start worrying and taking stock of your premises." Dos Passos followed his own prescription.

Growing doubts about his political beliefs, the ones whose certainty seemed unchallengeable a few years earlier, crept into Dos Passos's mind. He became convinced that none of the Marxist groups offered viable solutions. This put him at odds with fellow travelers like his old friend John Lawson. Dos Passos's change of mind surprised Cowley, who was at work establishing the leftish League of American Writers, and he flooded him with questions. "I'm through with writing these lousy statements," Dos Passos replied. "I can't make myself clear. What I meant to imply was that the issue right now is the classic liberties and that the fight had got to be made on them."

"I don't know why I should blurt all this out," Dos Passos told Wilson about confessing his waning support for Communists, "except that since I've been laid up I've been clarifying my ideas about what I would be willing to be shot for and frankly I don't find the Kremlin among the items." He had become convinced that oppression creates more oppression, and the use of inappropriate means resulted in a bad end. "It's the sort of thing you have to grow up and look around for a number of years to see—possibly it's the beginning of adult ossification—but I don't really think so."

As Dos Passos moved to the center, a storm blew Hemingway to the left.

✛

On Saturday, August 31, Hemingway sat on his porch in Key West with a drink and unfurled the evening newspaper. It reported that a tropical disturbance near the Bahamas was traveling toward the Keys and could likely become a hurricane. Hemingway immediately set about securing the *Pilar*, moving the cars out of his rickety garage, and nailing shutters on the house. The preparations turned out to be unnecessary. The storm mostly avoided Key West and caused minimal damage.

Two days later, as boats began to move again, Hemingway crossed over to Lower Matecumbe Key, an island to his north, to see whether he could help after hearing that the hurricane had caused devastating damage there. Of concern to him was the fate of nearly one thousand veterans who were working for the Civilian Conservation Corps and were camping on the island. Hemingway had met many of them at Sloppy Joe's, the bar he favored in Key West.

When his boat reached Lower Matecumbe Key he began to get the answer. Bodies were floating in the ferry slip. Walking on the shore in the company of two men who accompanied him, Hemingway saw that Flagler's railroad bed was gone and that the veterans who had taken cover behind it were lying dead in the mangroves. He and his compatriots became the first to reach the camp where the highway construction crew lived. Only 8 of the 187 had survived. There were more dead bodies than he had seen since working as a Red Cross volunteer along the Piave River in 1918.

Then he spotted the bodies of two women who ran a sandwich shop not far from the ferry. "Max," Hemingway wrote to Perkins upon getting back to his house, "you can't imagine it, two women, naked, tossed up into trees by the water, swollen and stinking, their breasts as big as balloons, flies between their legs."

A cable came from the editor of the *New Masses* asking whether he would write an article about the death of the veterans. Hemingway took to his typewriter and pounded out an account of what he had witnessed. No one yet knows the number who died, he told readers, especially as many bodies had been swept out to sea, but it might exceed one thousand. The civilians had chosen of their free will to live there. The veterans had not. They had been sent there, given no chance to leave, no protection, and no chance to live. They were good men down on their luck and look-ing for a paycheck. "Who sent them there to die?" Hemingway asked.

"But I would like to make whoever sent them there carry just one out through the mangroves, or turn one over that lay in the sun along the fill, or tie five together so they won't float out, or smell that smell again you thought you would never smell again, with luck," he wrote. "But now you know there isn't any luck when rich bastards make a war."

Even Hemingway's *Esquire* articles turned political. Penning what he called "A serious tropical letter," he predicted another world war would erupt soon, describing the economic and political forces at play in Europe in the manner he once had as a *Toronto Star* correspondent.

"They wrote in the old days it is sweet and fitting to die for one's coun-try," he said. "But in modern war there is nothing sweet or fitting in your dying. You will die like a dog for no good reason."

"We were fools to be sucked in once on a European war and we should never be sucked in again," wrote thirty-six-year-old Hemingway, eighteen years after begging his father to permit him to join in the fighting.

✤

As 1935 closed, Hemingway sat at his desk in Key West and wrote a letter to Dos Passos beginning with an apology for his recent rudeness. Hem-ingway said he regretted having accused Dos Passos of having failed to visit their grieving friend Sara Murphy when he had a chance. It had been a typical and ill-thought-out complaint on his part. Indeed, Dos Passos *had* gone to see the Murphys, and Sara Murphy immediately rebuked Hemingway. The apology he sent Dos Passos, however, was meant only to clear the air. Hemingway was lonely. "It is gloomy as hell here without you," he wrote.

Since the romp on Bimini the days had been glum for both men. The Dos Passoses were more broke than ever, having to borrow money from friends just to pay expenses. Gerald Murphy, who had taken over the op-erations of Mark Cross, his family's company, provided a partial rescue when he gave Katy a job. Sara sent several hundred dollars, claiming it came from a recent settlement of her mother's estate that left her with more than she needed. To avoid any sense of charity, she did the same with Hemingway, who hardly needed an infusion of cash.

Whereas Hemingway could write himself out of any financial short-fall, it certainly was not the case for Dos Passos. When his agent sent work to the *New Yorker* the magazine was uninterested. "The Dos Passos doesn't seem at all in his usual powerful and effective manner," wrote back an editor. "Are these old things that have recently come to light, or what?" His hopes for a remunerative revival of his career rested with completing the wishfully titled *The Big Money*, the third volume of the trilogy. Dos Passos was making progress, though slower than he hoped. By this point he was nearing a decade's work on the trilogy, consuming more than one-third of his professional life so far. "This novel business is an awful business," he told Hemingway. "Why the hell did I ever get mixed up in it?"

Ten thousand copies of Hemingway's *Green Hills of Africa* were offered up to readers in October. As with his bullfighting book, his new book about hunting big game puzzled charitable critics and provided fodder to those who had been disappointed with Hemingway since *A Farewell to Arms*. John Chamberlain at the *New York Times* couldn't resist a dig at the author in the first line of his review. "Ernest Hemingway went to Africa to shoot the bounding kudu and the ungainly rhinoceros and to reply to his critics," he wrote.

"Not that one objects to Mr. Hemingway's diversions. He has just as much right to his hunting and fishing as New Yorkers have to dancing and ping pong," Chamberlain continued. "But to offer *Green Hills of Africa* as a profound philosophical experience is something else again. It is simply an overextended book about hunting, with a few incidental felicities and a number of literary wisecracks thrown in."

The fall and winter had not been a good one for either writer. So when John and Katy Dos Passos got into their car on May 10, 1936, to head south for a reunion with the Hemingways, it was with great anticipation of an escape from their woes. Also traveling with them was Sara Murphy.

Dos Passos packed the galleys of *The Big Money*. The book included only four of the dozen or so characters that had inhabited *The 42nd Parallel* and *1919*. The others disappear, almost as how in life one loses contact with acquaintances, never to learn what happened to them. Dos Passos put his character Charley Anderson center stage. Anderson's experience as a flyer in the war convinced him that there was money to be made in manufacturing planes. He is right and makes vast sums of money, only to be done in by women and liquor. Mary Dowling barely survives a violent marriage to a Cuban but goes to Hollywood, where her luscious qualities soon make her a movie star. Mary French uses her Vassar education to work in settlement houses and the labor movement. A series of lovers betray her, leaving French with only the cause as a loyal companion. Richard Ellsworth Savage, whom readers met in 1919 as a young poet on his way to the Paris peace conference, ends up slaving for J. Ward Moorehouse, the agile but unscrupulous public relations pioneer.

Dos Passos treats the women more sympathetically than the men, who seem to design their own fate rather than suffer from one imposed by others. In either case the ending for all his characters is bad. Dos Passos was offering a wide-ranging satire of life in the United States. With each page the story grows darker. Change is constant, but progress of the kind Dos Passos valued is stalled. In his conception those who pursue their dreams are battered senseless, and the survivors sell out. Channeling his two decades of novelistic observation, Dos Passos produced a grim tale in which the war's effects were like a cancer on society, worsened by the myopic pursuit of money, fame, and success.

In Miami John and Katy Dos Passos and Sara Murphy took a Pan American Sikorsky seaplane to Havana, where Hemingway awaited their arrival looking forward to days filled with literary talk and gossip. He didn't get it. Dos Passos hardly looked up from his galleys, even when on the *Pilar*. When he did grab a fishing rod, it was without sufficient skill to keep a marlin on the line. "Dos blew," is how Hemingway recorded the moment in his ship's log. Hemingway was unsympathetic. To Dos Passos the manuscript represented a literary hope; to Hemingway it was robbing him of the pleasures of the old days.

Only at dinner in the restaurant at the Ambos Mundos Hotel did the men talk—that is, until Dos Passos took his leave to work on the galleys in his room. Then Katy, Sara, and Hemingway would remain to listen to rumba-playing Cubans and down drinks, often resulting the next morning in breakfasts of Bromo-Seltzer. Displeased, Hemingway became sullen, especially at having to entertain Sara and Katy while Pauline, who could have helped, was in Arkansas with the children.

Hemingway could not be as he was when he had Dos Passos all to himself. The presence of a friend in grief placed the onerous demand of civility on Hemingway, and this was made worse by seeing Katy, a woman whom he had once wanted and might still. At this point in Hemingway's life she and her brother Bill were his longest-lasting set of steadfast friends, except for a lengthy period when he and Bill had not spoken after a dispute. In short, no one knew Hemingway the way Katy did. But her best friend and lover was now another writer, the one in the room upstairs proofing his next book, not the young Hemingway who had pined for her in the days of Michigan summers. Even in the company of this remarkable group, Hemingway felt alone. He hated being alone.

"Gosh, Hem," Dos Passos wrote immediately after leaving Havana, "it was a tough proposition for you, me bringing all the women folk to Havana, but the trip really did Sara a great deal of good." Hemingway reciprocated with his own apology for his "bellyaching."

He also told him after reading a copy of the galleys Dos Passos had left behind for him, "It's as long as the Bible but I can see why you couldn't cut it more." Hemingway remained mum, however, on what he thought of Dos Passos's book. The silence was telling.

✛

On August 6, 1936, *The Big Money* was published. For the first time in two years and for only the twelfth time in the nearly seven hundred issues *Time* had published since its launch in 1923, the magazine put a writer on the cover. Wearing an open shirt, without his glasses, and tugging on a cigar stub clamped in his teeth, was John Dos Passos striking a pose as a writer on top of his game.

Almost all reviewers joined *Time* in its praise. The trilogy, despite its faults, had come closer than any other book so far in the pursuit of the Great American Novel, said *Time*, which compared the work to Tolstoy's *War and Peace*, Balzac's *Comedie Humaine*, and James Joyce's *Ulysses*—heady company indeed. This list, however, did not include Hemingway's name. Edmund Wilson, Upton Sinclair, F. Scott Fitzgerald, and other writers sent their congratulations to Provincetown.

In Key West Hemingway brooded. Melancholic and lacking in sleep, he was in a touchy, explosive mood. Over the years he had liked to convey the impression he could easily resort to fisticuffs. From the fistfights in his fiction to his entry into a boxing ring in Paris and Bimini, Hemingway exuded the impression of being a fighter. And earlier in the year he had pummeled poet Wallace Stevens who, while in Key West, had disparaged the author before Hemingway's visiting sister. Both victor and loser promised to tell no one about the fight, but Hemingway, of course, had dashed off letters to Murphy and Dos Passos.

Ever since Paris, when he had savaged Sherwood Anderson and Gertrude Stein in *The Torrents of Spring* or later taken revenge on Harold Loeb in *The Sun Also Rises*, Hemingway used his writing to strike back at those who had failed him. It was the way he placed them in his personal ninth circle of hell, the one reserved for treachery. He began with Sara Murphy, who recently had the temerity to suggest he should stick with Pauline now that it became apparent to his friends that his affections for her were growing cold. Hemingway created a character of a wealthy man with the attributes of her husband Gerald. Dying of gangrene on the slopes of Mount Kilimanjaro, he laments how his relationship with a rich woman robbed him of other possible loves.

In a moment when he might have been writing about himself, Hemingway penned, "He remembered the good times with them all, and the quarrels. They always picked the finest places to have the quarrels. And why had they always quarreled when he was feeling best?"

Sara Murphy, toughened by the loss of one son and watching another die of tuberculosis, could charitably ignore Hemingway's tempestuousness. She had stuck with F. Scott Fitzgerald and others through their dark periods. To her mind Hemingway's moods came with the job of being a patron of the arts.

But for others Hemingway's method of seeking revenge with the written word was worrisome. "Difference which, when men and women were still in their twenties, were the subject of cheerful and affectionate arguments brew recrimination and bitterness when they reach their thirties," Dos Passos wrote years later.

By 1936 Hemingway's list of lost friends was lengthy. Dos Passos wondered whether he might soon be on it.

23

THE MONTH PRIOR TO THE PUBLICATION OF *THE BIG MONEY* THE UNITED Press office in London had received a telegram from its bureau in Madrid. To telegraph operators who keyed in the message from Lester Ziffren on July 17, 1936, it seemed a routine domestic matter. "Mothers Everlastingly Lingering Illness Likely Laryngitis," said Ziffren, "Aunt Flora Ought Return Even If Goes North Later Equally Good If Only Night . . . " But to editors in London, the telegram hardly conveyed family news; rather, it signaled war.

Taking the first letter of each word, the editors decoded Ziffren's dispatch. "Melilla foreign legion revolted martial law declared." Disgruntled generals who opposed the democratic left-wing government that had taken power in Madrid were launching a coup in Melilla on the Spanish colonial northern coast of Africa. The rebellion triggered a civil war.

Hitler, Mussolini, and the dictatorship in Portugal all rushed to support the rebellion, which would soon be under the leadership of Francisco Franco, a general whom the Republican government had demoted. The struggle for power on the Iberian Peninsula rapidly became a proxy war pitting European Fascists on one side and a weak Spanish government, whose only allies were the Soviet Union and Mexico along with thousands of untrained international volunteers, on the other. The Nationalists, as the Franco forces were called, engaged in a war of terror. Military squads shot or bayoneted thousands, bodies of dead supporters of the Republican government were left to rot in the open, and priests who protested the brutality faced decapitation.

In Provincetown Dos Passos heard a rumor that the artist Quintanilla had been shot. He immediately contacted Hemingway, who knew nothing. Dos Passos was in a state of agitation. From what he read, the Republic was in its death throes, and the Fascists had the upper hand. "Civilization seems to be going in for one of its richer phases of butchery," Dos Passos told Hemingway. "When they've properly massacred the Spaniards they'll start on the French." Looking for a means to help, Dos Passos agreed to cooperate with an effort to create a news service that would publicize the horrors of Spain and persuade the US government to allow the sale of arms to the embattled Spanish government. The plan did not get off the ground, but he stood ready to do whatever he could.

Hemingway was preoccupied with finishing his novel *To Have and Have Not*, comprising an amalgam of short stories. What he was writing explained the growing silence from Key West. The novel told the tale of a Key West boat captain who had taken up smuggling to survive the Great Depression. Into one corner of the manuscript Hemingway let flow the envy and growing resentment he felt toward Dos Passos.

It had been one thing when *Time* put Dos Passos on the cover, but the continued adulation from the literary world for his principled approach to novel writing, particularly from the left, galled Hemingway. During the 1920s Dos Passos's radical politics had made him an exception among his literary friends. But now, during the Great Depression, a writer was presumed to be part of the left. Artistic sensitivity would leave one no other choice. At least that is how it seemed, and Hemingway felt the pressure and lashed out at his friend's supposed purity.

In the book Hemingway created a character named Richard Gordon, a balding author of proletarian novels, in a childless marriage, with a penchant for travel to spots like Cap d'Antibes, the Swiss Alps, or Key West.

Because he is incorruptible his rich friends loan him money. They're proud to back him . . .

Always tells the truth about the interest too. Attack Hearst, Morgan, anyone. Fearless you know. In a year he'll borrow about what the average writer makes. When he started he always paid every one back and he was really incorruptible. Then he began to work at it. Of course every once in a while he has a book out but he never pays anyone any more. He doesn't have to. He has such a reputation for incorruptibility that it's like a trust fund.

His literary knock at Dos Passos included the lowest blow Hemingway could devise—impotence. Hemingway described as useless the "disproportionally large equipment that had once been his pride" under Gordon's pajamas, giving Gordon the infirmity Jake Barnes had in *The Sun Also Rises*, the book Dos Passos had publicly criticized.

As for Gordon's wife, Helen, who was quite Katy-like, Hemingway took up his pencil again.

You know I really think he was honest until he married her. She's handsome and she's charming and she's very good to him but she has just one little defect. She likes to steal as much as the monkey does. More I guess. . . . She's raised incorruptibility in him from a characteristic of making a living.

The accusation that Katy was manipulative and used her husband's principled stance for monetary gain had been on Hemingway's mind for years. Seven years earlier he had jokingly warned Dos Passos to keep money away from his wife because for writers, money and women were trouble. By this time he was convinced that what he perceived as Dos Passos's dishonest pursuit of wealth from rich friends and Katy's domination of him meant his friend's ruin as a writer.

✦

Hemingway shared the manuscript *To Have and Have Not* with Arnold Gingrich, the editor of *Esquire*. Upon reading it Gingrich telephoned Hemingway. From his reading, three of the characters in the book were clearly based on Dos Passos and Hemingway's friend Grant Mason and his wife, Jane, who may have had an affair with Hemingway or at least friends widely suspected it. Gingrich told Hemingway his use of them was libelous.

Hemingway protested. He insisted that if he was going to take the trouble to alter the text, Gingrich had to come to Key West and he would invite his lawyer Maurice Speiser to join them. "It isn't that I don't respect your experience," Hemingway said over the telephone, "on this subject I'm sure you are as great an expert as the burnt monkey on the subject of hot soup, but after all you're not a lawyer and he is, and I'd like the added security of somebody to check the checker."

Gingrich flew down from New York City, and the two men, along with Pauline, listened to the editor's complaint about the book. Hemingway did not take it well. "He began behaving like a stuck pig, squealing its head off," recalled Gingrich. But Hemingway came up with a plan to fix the parts concerning Dos Passos. "You know all I have to do to get Dos to okay everything in here that you object about him?" Hemingway asked. "All I have to do is tell him *you* don't like it! That shakes *you* up a little, doesn't it? Moe, you can draw up the tightest-ass release you can dream up, and I'll get it signed."

"You know what Dos thinks of you?" Hemingway asked Gingrich. "He thinks you're a shit, that's what he thinks of you. Who had to get Dos into your magazine in the first place? Who had to get Dos to let you have the piece about the Quintanilla exhibition that he and I did together— when Dos had promised his part to the *New Republic*? For chris'sake, you come down here and try to tell me how to write about one of my oldest friends!"

"But Ernest," interjected Speiser. "I thought your defense of that part was that it *isn't* about Dos Passos. I frankly don't see how I can draw up a release for a man to sign that isn't *about* him."

With Hemingway at the wheel of the *Pilar* the three men continued their discussions on waters off Key West. Hemingway told Gingrich that people should feel flattered for being used in his books the same way one should be happy if Cézanne included one in a painting.

"You aren't mixing your métiers, by any chance?"

"Not really," Hemingway replied. "After all, what I can't get through your Pennsylvanian Dutch skull is that you're not dealing with some little penny-a-liner from the sports department of the Chicago *Daily News*. You're asking for changes in the copy of a man who *has* been likened to Cézanne, for bringing 'a new way of seeing' into American literature."

In the end the Cézanne of literature cut the passages.

✛

After Gingrich took his leave, Hemingway was spending an afternoon at his favorite post in Sloppy Joe's bar down the street from his Key West house. A mother and her two adult children, a son and a daughter, entered the dim cool barroom. Dressed in a one-piece black dress and high heels, the blond-haired daughter came over to Hemingway and introduced herself as Martha Gellhorn. Twenty-eight years old, she knew whom she was meeting. His photo had been tacked on the wall of her Bryn Mawr dorm room. Her collection of Depression stories, *The Trouble I've Seen*, had just been published, and the two writers filled the remainder of the afternoon in literary talk over Papa Dobles made with rum, lime, and grapefruit juice.

During the next few weeks Hemingway escorted Martha, her brother, and mother around Key West and spent hours talking with her about writing when she remained behind on the island on her own. Pauline watched as this woman, thirteen years her junior, moved in on her husband as she had done to Hadley eleven years before. A month later Gellhorn returned to her hometown of St. Louis, the same city in which Hadley and Pauline grew up. Hemingway escorted her as far as Jacksonville, Florida, and then went on to New York City.

Dos Passos was also in the city. He had come from visiting the Murphys, whose son Patrick's battle with tuberculosis was nearing its end. They already had lost one child two years earlier and now prepared to lose another one. "Gerald and Sara both behaving so well in their separate ways that it's heartbreaking," Dos Passos reported to Hemingway.

Both men had a fondness for Patrick, whom they had known practically since birth. The month before, Hemingway had visited the Murphys at their Saranac Lake home. He stood by Patrick's bedside in the company of his mother and sister and talked with the young boy about fishing. "I think I can come back later to say good night, Patrick," Hemingway said as his voice cracked. In the hall he seemed on the verge of tears. "Goddamn it," he said, "why does that boy have to be so sick?" Patrick died on January 30. "Fate can't have any more arrows in its quiver for you that will wound like these," wrote F. Scott Fitzgerald on hearing the news.

Dos Passos was in New York City to try to raise money for a documentary to be made about the war. An earlier film called *Spain in Flames* had gained Hemingway and Dos Passos's support and assistance but had been perceived as too propagandist. Dos Passos's new idea was to make a documentary on what was happening to everyday Spaniards caught up in the Civil War. In this effort he worked with Archibald MacLeish and Lillian Hellman, among others, to form a film company they called the Contemporary Historians Company.

Hemingway agreed to join the effort. As he had felt when the Great War broke out, he did not want to miss the one in Spain. The North American Newspaper Alliance agreed to pay Hemingway a handsome sum for any dispatches he could send from Spain. He also helped raise money to send ambulances to Spain, telling the press that the old ambulance driver himself might go and drive one.

But from the start he and Dos Passos squabbled over the content of the proposed film. Hemingway wanted to emphasize the fighting, not the troubles of ordinary Spaniards. He was unconcerned about reports of atrocities committed by the Communists and others supporting the embattled Republican government. More than their differing vision for the film provoked Hemingway's quarrelsomeness; Dos Passos had just been elected to the National Institute of Arts and Letters, an honor not yet bestowed on Hemingway, and the unpaid loans to Dos Passos now amounted to about $1,400. "Damn sorry about not being able to pay you back any dough," Dos Passos told him.

The New York meetings ended with agreement that they would all meet in Spain along with Joris Ivens, who would direct the film, and John Ferno, who would act as cameraman, both of whom were Communists. The fractious talks had been complicated, made more so by the presence of Martha Gellhorn, who had come from St. Louis at Hemingway's invitation. The mood changed when she accompanied Hemingway to dinner with John and Katy Dos Passos. Katy, who counted both Hadley and Pauline among her oldest friends, was wary of the young woman who could have doubled as a magazine fashion model. Gellhorn took her exit from the city and returned to St. Louis. Once there she wrote to a friend, "Me, I am going to Spain with the boys. I don't know who the boys are, but I am going with them."

✢

Hemingway left for Europe first, boarding a ship in late February in the company of friends—but not Pauline, who had chosen to remain in Key West with the children. From Paris he went to Toulouse, where he found the border to Spain was now so hard to cross that people without press credentials could not get through. Even a former Red Cross nurse from the war was barred from bringing canned milk for refugee children fleeing from the fighting in Madrid.

As the Dos Passoses got ready to take their ship, John ate dinner with Carlo Tresca, whom he had known for years. An old-time radical with a pedigree that included membership in the Industrial Workers of the World and prison time for publishing an advertisement for birth control, Tresca was an outspoken critic of Soviet Communism. Dos Passos explained their plans to make a documentary with Ivens and Ferno.

"John," Tresca said over their plates of pasta, "they goin' make a monkey outa you . . . a beeg monkey."

Dos Passos protested, saying the Contemporary Historians Company backing the film would have complete control over its contents.

"How can you?" Tresca asked while laughing and reminding Dos Passos that his director was a member of the Communist Party. "Everywhere you go you will be supervised by Party members. Everybody you see will be chosen by the Party. Everything you do will be for the interest of the Communist Party. If the communists don't like a man in Spain right away they shoot him."

✦

A few weeks later Dos Passos was running up the steps to the street from the Place de Clichy metro in Paris. The moment brought back memories of the city he saw in the summer of 1917, two decades earlier. For a young man in uniform it had been a place of noisy bars, late nights at sidewalk cafés, and prostitutes. Only now they—not the bars or cafés—seemed to have diminished in number. "But twenty years from war to war," he wrote in his first dispatch, "have somewhat eroded the venereal mount of martyrs of bidet and makeupbox, and taken the glitter out of the last lingering tinsel of nineteenth century whoopee."

Katy and Dos spent three weeks in Paris as he interviewed French politicians for his freelance articles while at the same time urging them to support the Spanish Republic. The officials all displayed the same reluctance to take any steps—the identical refrain he had heard from American politicians. It was discouraging.

Publicly Dos Passos allegiance to the Republicans was unshaken, but he had nagging doubts about their conduct in the war and the dominance of Communists in their leadership. Their presence could make the costly defense of the government a pyrrhic victory if in the end the political liberties the Republican government secured were ultimately lost. Hemingway had no such doubts. So great was his desire to be near combat that he had become an unquestioning supporter of the Republicans.

The time had come for Dos Passos to see the war for himself. He left Katy in Paris and rode a train south to Perpignan along the Mediterranean coast a few miles from the Spanish border. There, under the burning sun, he made his way through the narrow streets, by the medieval walls, and past clusters of bedraggled Spanish refugees until he found the Café Continental. He had been told Republicans used the café as a meeting place and could arrange transportation to Valencia, which now served as the capital. The Republican government had fled Madrid for the safer confines of the northeastern seaside city only to find it being shelled by naval ships from Italy, whose government was supporting Franco.

Dos Passos secured passage in a caravan of southbound trucks, cleared the French side of the border with difficulty—the truck carrying gasmasks was not permitted to go on—and sailed through Spanish customs. After several days' drive under the blue Catalonian sky and past green fields, orange groves, and white villages with blue-tiled church domes, they reached Valencia. The city looked much as it had on his last visit four years earlier.

Dos Passos's first goal was to find his friend José Robles and invite him to work on the documentary. Locating him proved difficult. Robles's family had been evicted from their apartment. They now lodged in a small flat off one of Valencia's backstreets. Upon being admitted, Dos Passos found José's wife, Mágara Fernández de Villegas, in a haggard state. Her husband, she said, had been taken from their former apartment in December by a group of men in plain clothes. After making inquiries, she had learned that Robles was imprisoned in a building near the Túria River that runs through Valencia. She told Dos Passos she had been able to visit him, and he had reassured her that he would be freed when—what he called—the misunderstanding that had led to his arrest was cleared up.

Alarmed, Dos Passos went to the press office. But when he asked about Robles, the faces of the officials took on a look of embarrassment that Dos Passos believed included fear. A visit to the foreign ministry, where he met with minister Julio Álvarez del Vayo, left Dos Passos more confused. The minister told him he knew nothing but promised to look further into the matter. But Dos Passos believed Robles had been assigned to the Ministry of War, where he used his knowledge of Russian to work with Soviet advisers. It was a position of importance, and the government was small. So it hardly seemed likely to Dos Passos that del Vayo was telling the truth.

The obfuscation may have been because Robles's job had not been to be an interpreter, as many assumed. The paranoid Soviet commanders would have been reluctant to use a Spaniard in this capacity. It was more likely that Robles had been serving in a sensitive post of liaison officer between the war department and the Soviet military attaché, making everyone reluctant to speak about him.

Robles's seventeen-year-old son was the first to learn anything. An American Communist working in the propaganda office told him he had heard that Robles was dead. The family discounted the news, and officials continued to claim it was merely a rumor. "The general impression that the higherups in Valencia tried to give us," Dos Passos said, "was that if Robles was dead he had been kidnapped and shot by anarchist 'uncontrollables.'" It was the same story the officials provided members of the US Embassy who made inquiries on Dos Passos's behalf.

✤

Dos Passos grew worried and wanted to continue his search for Robles, but he was scheduled to be in Madrid to start work on the documentary. Two French journalists with a Hispano-Suiza automobile offered him a ride to Madrid. The two-hundred-mile drive took the greater part of a day. Their nervous driver, eager to get the expensive car into a garage for the night, took them down through the center of Madrid on the Gran Vía. Wartime precautions darkened the expansive and ornate street.

When they reached Hotel Florida, the grandiose hotel on the Plaza de Callao, they found the normally bustling square deserted. The car's engine silent, Dos Passos heard machine gun fire in the distance. "We listen. It's not very near, but up the street from the front the night pours into the city shattered and dented with gunfire." Everything Dos Passos saw and heard brought back memories of his service as an ambulance driver.

In the hotel Dos Passos found Hemingway, who had been in the city for several weeks, and Gellhorn, who had come later and was planning on doing her own reporting. He followed them to Hemingway's sixth-floor suite. Nineteen years earlier, during the Great War, the two men had met for the first time while sharing a meal close to the Italian front. They were once again within earshot of falling shells, and it should have been a moment of remembrances. But food, which had brought them together the first time, now served as a wedge in their fractured friendship. Hemingway turned icy when he learned that Dos Passos had brought only a few chocolate bars and oranges with him. How could he not know that everyone who came brought with them cans of sardines, pâté, or other food items unavailable in wartime Spain?

Hemingway's mood, already soured by Dos Passos's failure on this score, worsened when Dos Passos brought up his concerns about Robles.

"I absolutely guarantee him," Dos Passos said. "I know he is absolutely loyal to the government and I guarantee him personally. Absolutely and without reservations."

"When did you last seem him?" Hemingway asked.

"Not for over a year."

"Have you tried to see him since the revolt started?"

"No."

"How do you know he is still loyal to the government? How do you know something might not have happened to change his belief? Or that he might not have shifted over to Franco's side at the start of the rebellion?"

"I tell you I know this man," said Dos Passos. "He is my friend and I absolutely guarantee his honesty."

Hemingway's irritation flared. This line of questioning, he told Dos Passos, would antagonize the government they were trying to defend by making the documentary. It was a shock for Dos Passos. Here he was telling Hemingway about the disappearance of his friend, not some theoretical matter about war. Robles was missing and might be dead, and all Hemingway could say was: don't ask questions.

There was a reason. Hemingway was withholding information. "This all made me feel rather badly," he said later, "because I happened to know this man had been shot two weeks before as a spy after a long and careful trial in which all the charges against him had been proven."

Hemingway had learned about Robles's execution from Josephine Herbst, a radical sympathetic to the Communists who had been a friend of both Hemingway and Dos Passos since meeting them in Paris in the 1920s. She had filled him in on what her source in Valencia had told her. Robles, whose family had supported the monarch and whose brother had refused to join the Republican army, had been executed for giving away military secrets. The lawlessness of Spain made the story credible, even if Robles weren't a Fascist spy. The Soviets had helped create the ruthless *Brigadas Especial* that regularly executed anyone simply suspected to be a fifth columnist. Robles could have easily been one of their many victims.

Over glasses of brandy in his room Hemingway discussed with Herbst the dangers to the Republican cause if Dos Passos did not desist from making his inquiries. Hemingway told her that their friend's investigations would throw suspicion on all of them. He would have to be the one to tell Dos Passos the news.

He was too late. Since Dos Passos's first meeting with Hemingway Carlos Posada, the man in charge of counterespionage in the Republican government, had confirmed what Dos Passos had learned from Robles's son while in Valencia. But he had not been told why Robles had been executed, only that Posada, whom he had known for more than twenty years, was of the opinion the execution had been a mistake.

A saddened Dos Passos retreated to his room on the ninth floor overlooking the city. For the reporters and writers at Hotel Florida, it was an odd mix of luxury and war. From his bed in the morning Dos Passos could hear the shrieks of incoming shells followed by the loud boom as fighting resumed. On the Gran Vía Dos Passos found that everyone walked at a fast pace, pausing only to glance at the new shell holes in the buildings. Further down the grand avenue he came across barracks housing members of the International Brigades. "The dictators have stolen their world from them; they have lost their homes, their families, their hopes of a living or a career; they are fighting back," Dos Passos wrote in one of his dispatches.

Back in his room Dos Passos removed his clothes, took a bath, and lay down in the bed made by the chambermaid who came every day without fail. Lying there, he wondered what would happen if she were hit by a shell and reduced to a "mashedout mess of blood and guts to be scooped into a new pine coffin and hurried away." He decided that "they'd slosh some water over the cobbles and the death of Madrid would go on."

✢

At a lunch for foreign correspondents on April 22 Hemingway sat with Dos Passos. He told Dos Passos the news he already knew. To Herbst, looking at them from across the room, the friction between the two men was easily discerned. Robles's death was not the only cause. Dos Passos's presence was an uncomfortable reminder to Hemingway of his betrayal of Pauline now that he was sleeping with Gellhorn. Dos Passos was, after all, married to Pauline's friend Katy, who knew Hemingway longer than any of them. Other matters like Dos Passos's unpaid debts and his failure to have brought food supplies with him only added to Hemingway's vexation with his friend.

But underlining the tension was a deep and fundamental difference that stretched back twenty years to the Great War. Dos Passos had come away from the experience with the belief that war was a macabre and purposeless dance of death. For Hemingway the first war and now this one had provided the love of a woman. More important, the closeness to death made him feel alive. It was like the days of watching bullfighting in Pamplona. Then, as now, he hungered to be in the ring. "He wanted to feel he was one of the fighters, and one of the best," said one member of the International Brigades.

In Dos Passos's novel *Three Soldiers* the injustices of the oppressive military triggered the death of the sergeant at the hand of one of his soldiers. Not justifiable but understandable. In *A Farewell to Arms* Hemingway portrayed a similar death when an Italian soldier is summarily executed for failing to obey orders. Justifiable and to be expected in combat. To Hemingway the death was a consequence of war. To Dos Passos it was the loss of an old trusted friend.

Dos Passos's weakening allegiance to Communists made Hemingway's petulance worse. For as many years as he could remember, Hemingway had rebuffed Dos Passos's pleas that he become politically active and join the left. Now that, at long last, he had done so, it was only to discover that his friend was running away from the left. It was a bitter moment for a man who five years earlier had defended Dos Passos as man whose political views were unwavering. Hemingway felt betrayed.

Dos Passos was running because he saw a new enemy. In the Great War Dos Passos had fixed the blame for the season of death on militarism and the crushing cogs of modern society. But the death of his longtime friend and translator was an example of the untrustworthiness of Communists for whom there was no distinction between means and ends. Hemingway's callous response to Robles's death convinced Dos Passos that his friend was taking the Communist line. Desperate to be loved by the left and wanting to be on a battlefield, Hemingway was blind to the dangers the Communists posed.

Dos Passos saw no point in remaining much longer in Spain. It was clear he would have little role in the film as long as Hemingway, who had taken over the project, remained hostile. Dos Passos's idea that the film focus on the life of Spaniards, specifically on the struggle of farmers to build an irrigation system in Fuentidueña de Tajo, a poverty-stricken small village in Old Castile where only rich landowners had water, had been dismissed. It remained visible only in the opening and closing shots. Director Joris Ivens was giving Hemingway the war movie he wanted by filming the fighting in Madrid on the vague narrative thread that the road from Madrid to Valencia must remain open in order to save the capital. When the Republicans prevail over the Fascists, the film would close with scenes of water flowing to the fields in Fuentidueña de Tajo.

Dos Passos packed and left for Fuentidueña de Tajo to meet with the farmers and tour their irrigation project. If they weren't going to make a film about it, at least he could still write about it. He found what he had hoped for. The irrigation project built by the collective he had wanted to show in the film now brought water to the fields. "Everybody felt very good about it," he wrote, "so good that they almost forgot the hollow popping beyond the hills that they could hear from the Jarama River front fifteen miles away, and the truckloads of soldiers and munitions going through the village up the road to Madrid and the fear they felt whenever they saw an airplane in the sky."

From Fuentidueña de Tajo Dos Passos traveled to Valencia in a vain effort to get documents to prove Robles's death so his wife could collect on an insurance policy. He then left Spain but not before helping the young Communist volunteer who had told Robles's son about his father's death get across the border. In Paris John was reunited with a worried Katy.

In mid-May 1937 John and Katy left their Paris hotel and took a taxi to the Gard du Nord. As they prepared to board one of the boat trains that would take them to England where they were to take a ship home, Hemingway emerged from the crowd on the platform. He'd been back from Spain two days, and from the anger on his face it seemed unlikely he was coming to bid bon voyage to his old friend; rather, he had come to demand that Dos Passos tell him what he intended to say publicly about Robles. Dos Passos replied he would tell the truth as he saw it.

With those words the two men fell back into their Madrid quarrel about war and liberty. What's the use of fighting for the Republicans if it meant that civil liberties in Spain would be extinguished? asked Dos Passos. Hemingway refused to be drawn in. He told Dos Passos either he was for the Republicans or against them. In the nineteen years they had known each other many an argument had animated their conversation from Paris cafés to Key West boats. But they had been good-spirited disagreements, usually over their craft. This was different. The two ambulance drivers were at loggerheads.

Deciding further talk was futile, as it had been in the Hotel Florida, Dos Passos shrugged and made as if to leave. Hemingway balled up his fists and glared at him. If Dos Passos didn't incontestably side with the Republicans, he threatened that New York reviewers would crush him.

"Why Ernest," Katy interjected, "I've never heard anything so despicably opportunistic in my life."

The couple stepped into the train. Like losing Robles to the firing squad, the friendship between John Dos Passos and Ernest Hemingway had become a casualty of war.

EPILOGUE

DOS PASSOS RETURNED TO THE UNITED STATES IN MAY 1937 BEREFT OF his treasured friendship with Hemingway and racked with doubts about the beliefs that had animated his life since he set off to the Great War in the summer of 1917. Three events shattered the remaining sympathies he held for Communists: the slowly emerging but now undeniable reports of the barbarous rule of Joseph Stalin in Russia, which prompted many American Communists and fellow travelers to lose faith in Communism; what he had learned while in Spain; and the death of his friend Robles. On this score Hemingway turned out to have been wrong when, five years earlier, he said that Dos Passos was the exception of most left-wing writers who eventually moved to the right. Incongruously it was now the previously apolitical Hemingway who was the darling of the American left.

Among the first to whom Dos Passos confessed he was moving from the political left to the right was John Lawson, the friend he had made on the troopship twenty-one years earlier. The two had then pledged to turn the world upside down, but now it was only Lawson who remained on the far left. "Dear Jack," Dos Passos wrote, "you must have patience with the unbelievers—the real difference between your attitude and mine about politics is that you think the ends justify the means and I think that all you have in politics is means; ends are always illusionary."

Done with this confession to his old friend, he nevertheless accepted a $200 loan from Lawson. As usual, John and Katy Dos Passos were broke and applied the funds to overdue bills. "The sheriff and the banker are temporarily out of the living room," John wrote to Lawson in thanks. Some modest financial relief also came when *Redbook*, a popular general-interest magazine, paid Dos Passos for an article about a visit with members of the International Brigade celebrating a fiesta in a town about thirty miles north of Madrid. But what seemed to Dos Passos like a straightforward journalistic account of a parade, speeches, and meals rekindled Hemingway's wrath.

From Paris Hemingway let loose a tirade that began in a cable and ended in a letter to Dos Passos. He accused him of accepting money to give readers of *Redbook* the wrong impression that the Spanish conflict was a Communist-led war with Russians in charge. After pointedly reminding Dos Passos of his unpaid debts, Hemingway charged that money had corrupted his friend of two decades and he no longer wanted anything to do with him.

"So long, Dos. Hope you are always happy. Imagine you will be. Must be a dandy life. Used to be happy myself. Will be again. Good old friends. Always happy with the good old friends. Got them that will knife you in the back for a dime. Regular price two for a quarter. Two for a quarter, hell. Honest Jack Passos'll knife you three times in the back for fifteen cents and sing Giovinezza free," he wrote, referring to the official hymn of the Italian National Fascist Party.

Not content with a private rebuke, Hemingway published one for the world to see. Just as he had done with Sherwood Anderson and Gertrude Stein when he wrote *The Torrents of Spring* in the early 1920s, Hemingway wanted a public break with Dos Passos. He turned to Arnold Gingrich, editor of *Esquire*, who a few months earlier had launched *Ken*, a biweekly political magazine that resembled the large format of *Life*. Gingrich was glad to oblige, knowing that any article by the highly visible and popular Hemingway would attract attention to his fledgling magazine.

Although Hemingway did not name Dos Passos in the article he sent to Gingrich, only one person fit the description of an American writer who was a good friend and in Madrid trying to locate the translator of his work. "When my American friend heard that this man had been shot he felt that he was a martyr," Hemingway wrote, referring to Robles. "The fact that the man might have been a spy and a traitor was impossible for him to face." Dos Passos was blinded by his friendship with Robles, said Hemingway, and could not believe he could be guilty of treachery, despite not knowing what his friend had done for more than a year. "This is as good an example of any of the good hearted naïveté of a typical American liberal attitude." Hemingway concluded, adding snidely, "Perhaps it is just old Harvard loyalty."

Several months later John and Katy Dos Passos lunched with *Redbook* editor Edwin Balmer, who had been a Chicago friend of both Katy and Ernest in the years right after the war. Seeing Balmer caused Katy to write Ernest. "Oh Wemedge," she said, "how did we all get where we are?" No answer came. Then she wrote to Pauline. "I often wish our husbands were pals as nature intended—and feel bitter about all forms of politics and international warfare, also peace, fascism, democracy and the Kraft-cheese evil," Katy said with a quip, adding to the list of abominations the once-tiny cheese company they had known as children whose national headquarters now took up a block of Chicago.

For Pauline the plea from her old friend may have seemed ironically timed. She too was losing Ernest.

✛

Dos Passos's three books *The 42nd Parallel*, *1919*, and *The Big Money* were republished in 1938 as one volume under the title *USA*, garnering more critical praise but few sales. Money woes for the Dos Passoses persisted while Hemingway's fortunes continued to rise, especially after the publication of *For Whom the Bell Tolls* in 1940. Set in the Spanish Civil War, the novel told the story of a young American member of the International Brigades and included, as had *A Farewell to Arms*, a romance. For Hemingway war was still the handmaid of love. In the Great War it had been Agnes von Kurowsky, and in Spain, Martha Gellhorn. Hemingway divorced Pauline, gave her custody of their children, and in 1940 he married Gellhorn.

In the third year of the American participation in World War II Dos Passos and Hemingway both took up war correspondent assignments for *Life* and *Collier's*, respectively. Dos Passos began by reporting within the

United States and then traveled across the Pacific in late 1944 and early 1945 on warships. He witnessed the shelling of Iwo Jima, prior to the US invasion of the island, flew on a plane that had an engine shot out and barely landed safely, and was in Manila when the troops under General MacArthur landed. Eventually he went to Europe after the end of the fighting to cover the opening of the Nuremberg trials.

Unlike Dos Passos, who retained a sense of war's danger from his time in Verdun, Hemingway vied to reach a war front. On D-Day, June 6, 1944, Hemingway was allowed to ride in a landing craft but not alight on Normandy until twelve days later. When troops approached Paris, he accompanied a regiment of American troops and briefly removed his correspondent's insignia and took an active role among resistance fighters, violating the Geneva Convention's prohibition on members of the press taking part in combat. He reached Paris shortly after it was liberated and reported on combat to the north. For his work in describing the work of frontline soldiers he was later awarded a Bronze Star in 1947.

During the war Hemingway's marriage to Gellhorn grew contentious. She had her own reportorial ambitions to cover the war that conflicted with Hemingway's desires. "Are you a war correspondent or wife in my bed?" he cabled her. But war provided once again a suitable lover. In London he met correspondent Mary Welsh, who became his fourth wife in March 1946 after he secured a divorce from Gellhorn. "Funny," he told Max Perkins, "how it should take one war to start a woman in your damn heart and another to finish her."

+

After World War II the wounds of the spoiled friendship still festered in the two men. Hemingway in particular continued to bristle when Dos Passos's name surfaced. In the summer of 1947 the *Los Angeles Times* asked the director general of the National Library in Paris to list the most influential American novelists in France. John Dos Passos, William Faulkner, and Erskine Caldwell, he replied. Only a few months before, English students at the University of Mississippi put a similar question to William Faulkner. He listed Thomas Wolfe, Dos Passos, Hemingway, Willa Cather, and John Steinbeck as the five most important contemporary writers.

"If you don't think it too personal," asked a student, "how do you rank yourself with contemporary writers?"

Faulkner said he was second to Wolfe and above Dos Passos, leaving Hemingway now fourth on his list. "Ernest Hemingway," he said, "has no courage, has never crawled out on a limb. He has never been known to use a word that might cause a reader to check with a dictionary to see if it is properly used."

When Hemingway read about Faulkner's comment in a story running on the Associated Press wire, he sprung to action. He asked a general he had known during World War II to send Faulkner an account of the danger he had seen as a correspondent, proving he had "crawled out on a limb." Faulkner rushed an apology to Hemingway in Havana, where he now mostly lived.

In his reply Hemingway used the moment to once again lash out at Dos Passos. He called him a second-rate writer who had no ear, comparing him to a boxer deprived of a left hand and is thus pummeled. "This happened to Dos with every book." But following that dig Hemingway resurrected a long-rumored accusation that Dos Passos had African American lineage. "Also terrible snob (on acct. of being a bastard) (which I would welcome) and very worried about his Negro blood when could have been our best Negro writer if would have just been a Negro as hope *we* would have."

There seemed little hope for peace between Hemingway and Dos Passos. Events, however, changed the odds.

Two months later, on the afternoon of September 12, 1947, John and Katy Dos Passos departed from Provincetown on a trip. Leaving the Cape and heading west on Route 28, John drove toward the setting sun while Katy slept. As the sun reached the horizon directly in front of him, John squinted. His eyesight, poor as it already was, failed him in the brightness. He let the car drift to the right. Ahead, on the side of the road, a truck was parked with its tailgate open. At full speed the Dos Passos's car ran into it. The top of their automobile was sheared off.

Bleeding profusely, his body pressed against the steering wheel and the car's horn blaring, John turned to see Katy. In order to do so, he had to turn his head completely to the right because he could not see out of his right eye. The police arrived on the scene and extricated John from the car. Holding his hand to his injured eye, he walked to a pay phone at a nearby garage and called Katy's best friend, Edith Shay, in Provincetown. "Look, Edie," he said, "Katy's dead."

Dos Passos was hospitalized, and except for losing his right eye, he recovered from his injuries. Among the cables that poured into the hospital was a condolence telegraph from Hemingway to which Dos Passos sent a warm thank-you note. It was the first civil contact between the two in ten years. Katy's death triggered deep sadness and anger in Hemingway. At first he found himself incapable of even writing a letter to her brother Bill, whom he had known since the carefree summer days of youth in Michigan. "But he knows I loved Katy almost as much as Bill and Dos did," he wrote to Bill's wife. "As much as anybody could without being her brother or her husband." Private notes betrayed deep-seated rage. "Katy Dos Passos," Hemingway explained to Charles Scribner, "was an old girl of mine, had known her since she was eight years old, and Dos drove her into a parked truck and killed her last Saturday."

Dos Passos was unaware of Hemingway's private sentiments, and the short exchange of a telegraph and letter delivered an armistice between the two writers.

+

In September 1948 Dos Passos and Hemingway crossed paths for the first time in more than a decade. Dos Passos was heading to Brazil and stopped in Havana, where he saw Ernest and Mary Hemingway briefly on board a ship they were taking to Italy. The two men had an unalloyed good time. Referring to Hemingway as "the old Monster," Dos Passos reported to Sara Murphy that he "seemed in splendid fettle." Much champagne was drunk on board the liner before it departed. Hemingway's oldest son, whom Dos Passos had helped bathe in Paris when Bumby was a baby, was present. "Papa was so pleased to see him," he said. "They were as happy as bedbugs."

The renewed ties between Dos Passos and Hemingway prompted friendly correspondence. Several months later Dos Passos, who was financially more stable than he had been in a long time, wrote to Hemingway, offering to repay the money he owed to him. Hemingway declined the offer and instead suggested Dos Passos send the repayment in French francs to Georges Scheuer, the well-known bartender at the Paris Ritz Hotel who had loaned money to Hemingway when he arrived in Paris during the liberation short of cash. Dos Passos's gesture touched Hemingway. "I wish we could have spent them together in Paris like in the old days."

The renewed contact grew warmer. In the fall of 1949 Hemingway sent congratulations to Dos Passos upon hearing his friend had remarried. "If you are married to a new wife you ought to be happy," said Hemingway dictating into a wire recorder in Havana when he heard the news of the marriage. "I had a lot of luck the last time I drew cards and I am not trading in Miss Mary on any new models of any kind. But still, a new wife is a good thing for any old Portuguese to have."

Dos Passos had met Elizabeth Holdridge while working on a series of articles for *Reader's Digest*. Holdridge, who worked for the magazine, had also lost a spouse in a car accident. She offered to help Dos Passos organize the mass of unruly material he had assembled for his articles. They worked together over a holiday weekend in New York City's Fifth Avenue Hotel. On the last day of work Dos Passos took Holdridge to dinner. At the table in the restaurant he put his hand on hers and asked, "Is it one for all and all for one?" They were married in 1949. The two found much happiness. The marriage gave John, who had been raised as an only child and for many years without two parents, a family. He became a stepfather to Elizabeth's son, Christopher, and, to his joy, a father when Lucy Hamlin Dos Passos was born not long after.

The rapprochement between the writers, however, ended two years later when Hemingway picked up a copy of *Chosen Country*, the first novel by Dos Passos to earn extensive praise from critics in years. "*Chosen Country* may well be John Dos Passos's best novel," proclaimed the *New York Times*. "It is good news that Dos Passos, after years of indirection, seems at last to have recovered his strength and purposefulness as a novelist," said the *Washington Post*.

Good news, that is, except for Ernest Hemingway. Reading it, he saw at once that Dos Passos had populated his novel, set in Katy and Ernest's Michigan countryside and Chicago, with real people just as Hemingway had done with *The Sun Also Rises*. The main character, the illegitimate son of an attorney, a Harvard graduate, and ambulance driver was clearly

Dos Passos. His love, Lulie Harrington, was Katy, and the unappealing George Elbert was Hemingway. The Elbert portrait was unflattering and included a suggestion that the Hemingway-like character had benefited as a reporter from a scandal connected to Lulie's brother and his wife. To Hemingway it was a painful but private reminder. Readers would not have known the details, but Hemingway's 1921 quarrel with Katy's brother resulted in an extended loss for years of friendship with Bill Smith.

Hemingway explained his wrath to a writer working on a book about his life. Dos Passos knew nothing about Michigan until he met, married, and killed Katy. "The windshield cuts her throat and Honest John loses an eye," Hemingway said. He told Edmund Wilson that reading *Chosen Country* had sickened him. "Dos fooled us all," he said. "Have you ever seen the possession of money corrupt a man as it has Dos?" Hemingway had first put this accusation to words in 1936 in the portions of his novel *To Have and Have Not* that were aborted prior to publication. Yet there was nothing in Dos Passos's life that lent credence to it. It was almost as if Hemingway, in his anger, had contrived the one accusation that could batter down the perceived wall of literary integrity surrounding Dos Passos's work among critics.

Oddly, in writing the novel as a remembrance of Katy, Dos Passos seemed blithely unaware of the slights that Hemingway might perceive upon reading the book. As a matter of fact, he continued his correspondence with his friend. The death of Pauline in October 1951 prompted Dos Passos to write. "It's hard to think of Pauline gone," he said. "I was very fond of her. Lord it seems longer than a half a lifetime ago, when I first met the dark-haired Pfeiffer girls with you in Paris." If Dos Passos had intended literary revenge, he could have gone for the jugular as he had in his portraits of enemies during his radical years; rather, Dos Passos seems to have accidently walked into the Hemingway buzz saw.

✢

In 1956 managers of the Ritz Hotel in Paris decided that the time had come for Hemingway to retrieve two steamer trunks he had stored in the hotel three decades earlier. In them were notes, bits of writing, newspaper clippings, and even some old clothes. Ernest and Mary packed the contents into a new Louis Vuitton trunk and brought it to the United

States. The newly discovered archaeological fragments of his early Parisian life inspired Hemingway to work on a memoir of those days. It also gave him the opportunity to even the score with Dos Passos.

As he wrote his account of the Paris years, Hemingway said that the rich he knew then were always accompanied by a pilot fish. In the ocean the foot-long striped fish keep company with sharks, eating harmful parasites and even cleaning up bits of excess food from the shark's teeth. In Hemingway's Paris the pilot fish was Dos Passos.

As Hemingway recalled those years he said it was his friendship with and trust in the pilot fish—Dos Passos—that corrupted him as an artist when he was led into the world of the rich. "I wagged my tail with pleasure," Hemingway wrote, "and plunged into the fiesta concept of life to see if I could not bring some fine attractive stick back, instead of thinking, 'If these bastards like it, what is wrong with it?'" By implication Hemingway even suggested that Dos Passos's action led to what Ernest described as his seduction by Pauline and abandonment of Hadley. "Maybe the rich were fine and good and the pilot fish was a friend," he wrote.

Written so only the few could follow some of the references, such as one to John Dos Passos's car accident in which Katy died, Hemingway closed this section of the book with a remembrance of the time they all skied with the Murphys in Austria and with an elegy for the Paris of an earlier time "when we were very poor and very happy."

The revengeful words reached Dos Passos from beyond the grave, as *A Moveable Feast* was not published until 1964, three years following the morning on July 2, 1961, when Ernest Hemingway unlocked his gun cabinet and ended his life with a twelve-gauge, double-barreled shotgun.

Dos Passos kept his reaction to *A Moveable Feast* private, but in 1968, while on vacation in Upper Michigan, he and friends attended a church service at which a memorial to Hemingway was read aloud. Dos Passos rose from his pew and walked out of the church. Two years later, on September 28, 1970, John Dos Passos died of congestive heart failure.

✦

In history Hemingway surpassed his friend and rival in all respects. Today few people recognize Dos Passos's name and even fewer read his books. Writing in the *New Yorker* in 2005, George Packer said, "It's hard now to remember that, several generations ago, the trio of great novelists born around the turn of the century—Hemingway, Fitzgerald, Faulkner—was a quartet, with the fourth chair occupied by Dos Passos."

In 1998 Random House's Modern Library published a list of what, in the estimation of its editors, were the one hundred best novels. Dos Passos's *USA* appeared as number twenty-three, while Hemingway's *The Sun Also Rises* was forty-seven and his *A Farewell to Arms* was seventy-four. A concurrent list assembled from 217,520 votes cast by readers included no titles by Dos Passos but retained the two Hemingway books on the original list. Following publication of the lists, the Radcliffe Publishing Course released its own list of the century's top one hundred novels. It included three Hemingway books but none by Dos Passos. Once again Dos Passos was admired by critics but shunned by readers.

It's not surprising. To read his trilogy today is hard work. One comes away from it with admiration of a kind similar to seeing a work in a museum that is important for what it attempted to do rather than for the pleasures it imparts. *Three Soldiers*, however, remains an important and highly readable novel of war. But it too is neglected while Hemingway's *A Farewell to Arms* and *For Whom the Bell Tolls* is in the literary diet of English classes. Hemingway's view of war as an inevitability of life, how it tests one's mettle, and how it brings with it the possibility of glorious love accompanied a century of almost continuous war. Dos Passos's impassioned warning against war fell on deaf ears.

Dos Passos's friend John Lawson tried to explain the difference between the two men in his unpublished autobiography. "Dos Passos and I were, I think, typical of certain young intellectuals. Hemingway was different," he wrote, "Hemingway found an emotional meaning in the war. But for many of us it was senseless."

The Great War, the damage it left on its survivors, and a pursuit of an appropriate literary response were a key part of the artistic lives of Dos Passos and Hemingway. "These novelists who afterward wrote about the war underscored its disjunctive role," said critic Malcolm Cowley, a veteran of the ambulance corps. "War changed men in such a way that they could never be made whole." War's lasting effect on Hemingway and Dos Passos distinguished them from other members of the Lost Generation. It forged their friendship, but in the end another war took it from them.

Sadly, this kind of loss was one of the unchanging tragic aspects of Hemingway's life. Whether it was fame, money, his mother, or shell shock that are to be blamed, Hemingway destroyed every friendship, every love affair, and, ultimately, himself.

In 1949 Hemingway sent Dos Passos a report from Italy that he had been studying the life of Dante. "Seems to be one of the worst jerks that ever lived but how well he could write," Hem wrote to Dos. "This may be a lesson to us all."

POSTSCRIPT

WE MIGHT NEVER HAVE HEARD OF ERNEST HEMINGWAY HAD IT NOT been for an Italian soldier who was killed taking the brunt of the exploding mortar on the July night in 1918. But it seems little or no effort has been made to identify the soldier, whose death made possible the life of a young man who would eventually become one of the major writers of the twentieth century.

According to Italian military records, these are the names of the eighteen men who died or went missing in combat along the Piave River on July 8 or 9, 1918. If the records are correct, one of the names listed below is that of the soldier who lost his life and, in doing so, preserved that of Ernest Hemingway.

Soldier Michele Nudo
Soldier Giuseppe Artosi Ippolito
Soldier Luigi Sangalli
Soldier Pietro Boselli
Soldier Alfredo Fontanesi
Soldier Lorenzo Caprile
Soldier Giulio Chiesa
Soldier Domenico Quaglia
Soldier Fedele Temperini
Soldier Umberto Bicchieraro

Soldier Sebastiano Ravera
Corporal Tomaso Dognini
Corporal Luigi Riccobono
Corporal Giuseppe Giambrone
Major General Alessandro Fadini Umberto
Sergeant Santino Barba
Lieutenant Doctor Corrado Varvaro
Sailor Domenico Nodari

Scholars or researchers interested in trying to identify the actual sol-dier's name may contact the author for a copy of his research notes, which contain more details.

ACKNOWLEDGMENTS

WHEN I FINISH A BOOK AND APPROACH THE TASK OF WRITING AN AC-knowledgments section I grow anxious. So many people play a role in the writing a book, and the time span of these projects may easily lead one to omit a person to whom thanks are owed.

From the start I want to thank my agent, Alan Nevins. My books certainly don't keep the lights on in his office, yet he has remained loyal to my ideas and to me for more than a dozen years. Robert Pigeon, executive editor at Da Capo Books (part of Perseus Books now owned by the Hachette Book Group), took enormous care of the project from the day he acquired it. Our editorial meetings, in person and by phone, always improved the manuscript and included jollification. Michael Clark, project editor at Perseus, and copy editor Josephine Moore did a lovely job of guiding the book through production. Working with them was a pleasure.

Dale Rice, director of the journalism program at Texas A&M, made it possible for me to spend a memorable spring on his campus teaching a course in narrative nonfiction. Rice and his husband, Antonio La Pastina, also accommodated me in their home, a debt that will be hard to repay. During my stay I became good friends with Watson and Holmes. I only mention this because most dogs never get to see their names in print.

During my time at Texas A&M I made use extensive use of the university's library receiving wonderful assistance from Stephen Bales, associate professor and humanities and social sciences librarian, in procuring hard-to-find items. Professor Raffaele Montuoro, along with La Pastina, helped me evaluate material found in an Italian World War I book.

Others who helped with matters of war include novelist J. Howard Shannon, who spent more than twenty-five years in the military, including two tours in Afghanistan, and helped me greatly in writing the section of my book regarding Hemingway's wounds in World War I; Gordon A. Blaker, author of *Iron Knights: The United States 66th Armored Regiment* and curator of the US Army Field Artillery Museum, was immensely helpful in sorting out the details of the mortar attack that wounded Hemingway; Pierre Purseigle with the International Society for First World War Studies connected me with Michele Bellelli, an archivist at Istoreco, Institute for Contemporary History in Reggio Emilia, Italy, who helped me compile a list of Italian war dead in hopes of determining whose life saved that of Hemingway's. Robbie Hutto let me use her grandfather's World War I diaries, which were an immense help. Professor Alexander Watson of the University of London also provided me with insights in fragging.

Rendering long-distance research assistance were Lelia Troiano at the University of Virginia; Lynn Farnell at the JFK Presidential Library and Museum; Rebecca Baumann at the Lilly Library at Indiana University in Bloomington; Pam Lyons, executive director of the Ernest Hemingway Foundation of Oak Park; Emily Reiher, archivist, Oak Park Public Library; Pat Burdick, assistant director for special collections, Colby College; and Laurie Austin and her colleagues in the audio visual archives of the JFK Presidential Library and Museum.

As he has done with many of my recent books, author David Stewart read every portion of my manuscript as it was being written and provided great advice. My best friend, Dean Sagar, who read the completed manuscript, gave me an excellent suggestion for the final chapters. David Morrell, a novelist perhaps best known for *First Blood* that served as the basis for the *Rambo* films, shared his expertise as a Hemingway scholar by reading my manuscript and making valuable comments. The Women of the Gym Lofts, a remarkable gathering of writers in Albuquerque that, yes, includes men, read and discussed the work at our biweekly meeting. Their suggestions strengthened it greatly. Linda DiPaolo Love proofed the manuscript and saved me from countless errors.

Lucy Dos Passos Coggin and John Dos Passos Coggin helped from the earliest days of this project. I will long remember my visit to John Dos Passos's Virginia house. Joan Clickner, the granddaughter of Crystal Ross, gave generously of her time.

Authors Patricia O'Toole and the late Chip Bishop answered my questions regarding Theodore Roosevelt and his children. Author Will Swift helped me solve a puzzle regarding an alleged meeting between Dos Passos and Joseph Kennedy.

Each year the JFK Library, in consultation with the Hemingway Society Board, grants awards to scholars seeking to work with the manuscripts in the Hemingway Collection. I was honored by my selection as one of the grant recipients in 2015. I also need to thank Kirk Curnutt of the Hemingway Society for his assistance in securing permissions to quote from unpublished Hemingway letters.

Once again, thanks are also owed to E/TL&DS for its support of this work. Its assistance, as that it provided my previous two books, was of immeasurable value. Its director, J. Revell Carr, also lent a hand with useful nautical information regarding my subjects' many sea passages.

Jan Constantine of the Constantine Cannon law firm helped me as she has continuously assisted authors for years.

Finally, thanks are owed but inadequately expressed to Patty Morris. She brought Rummy to the fore and her careful reading saved me from embarrassing errors. This work would not exist without her support, not to mention how dull my life would be without her.

NOTES

It is difficult enough to write an accurate account of an individual's life, but novelists can be particularly challenging. The fiction they write is often based on their lives, but the reverse is not necessarily true. Yet many authors freely use material from fiction as if it were an account of an event in the author's life. In the case of Hemingway and Dos Passos this is a frequent occurrence. To give only one example, several biographers and writers describe a meeting on board the *Berengaria* in March 1937 between Dos Passos and Joseph P. Kennedy, who is described as the US ambassador to Great Britain. In fact, it would be another nine months before President Franklin Roosevelt would nominate Kennedy to serve as ambassador to the Court of St. James. In March 1937 Kennedy was in Washington being appointed to the Maritime Commission. The erroneous account comes from the fact that Dos Passos created such an encounter in his novel *Century's Ebb*.

So in the rare instance, if a description of a place or event taken from Hemingway or Dos Passos fiction appears in this work, it does so only with confirmation from other sources as to its accuracy.

There is no lack of sources when it comes to Hemingway. His papers are extensive, and the scholarship devoted to him and his writings almost endless. But remarkably, after so many years of scholarship, the first complete biography of Ernest Hemingway remains the best. Later works corrected errors, but Carlos Baker's *Ernest Hemingway: A Life Story* is still the single-most authoritative and dependable work on the writer.

That said, the hero of Hemingway scholarship is Michael S. Reynolds, the author of a five-volume biography. Anyone who reads his books will be impressed by his diligence and the undeniable charm of his writing. The subsequent major biographies, listed here, are each valuable. In particular, the works of Philip Young and the later work by Kenneth S. Lynn offer helpful psychological approaches to this complicated man. The two books by Peter Griffin, *Along with Youth: Hemingway, the*

Early Years and *Less than a Treason: Hemingway in Paris*, offered new material and were captivatingly well written. However, my research found the books to be factually unreliable at times.

Stephen Koch's *The Breaking Point: Hemingway, Dos Passos, and the Murder of José Robles* is an intriguing book and enjoyable to read. His approach, however, lessens the book's reliability when it comes to determining the facts of what happened in Spain in 1937.

The work of two scholars was also deeply helpful in understanding Dos Passos and Hemingway. Books and articles by Donald Pizer and Scott Donaldson provided enormously helpful accounts and analysis of the two men and the relationship between them.

Dos Passos was fortunate to have his life carefully reconstructed in two major even-handed biographies, each offering differing takes on his life. His letters, though not as voluminous as those of Hemingway, provide candid insights into his thinking and emotions. Hemingway's letters make for fascinating reading, but as he gained fame it became increasingly clear that he knew others, aside from the recipient, would eventually read his letters.

I gained valuable insights that one can only obtain from spending time with a subject's papers. I found this to be especially true in researching Hemingway. Portrayals of him in popular culture have reduced him into a stereotype when, as scholars well know, he is quite the enigmatic fellow. By the end of my visits to the Ernest Hemingway Collection at the John F. Kennedy Library in Boston I felt a closer and more sympathetic connection to him.

It's hard to explain, but permit me an anecdote. A well-known journalist recounted how when he was a cub reporter in the 1950s, he wrote a piece with all kinds of flourishes about a divorce trial. The wife came into the small-town newspaper, flung the paper down on his desk, and asked the reporter how dare he use her misery for his own literary advancement. I've always thought of that woman when writing biographies.

Biographers must remain true to the story wherever it takes us, but we have an ethical obligation to remember we are writing stories about the lives of real people, their joys and sadness, their triumphs and failures, and their place in history. Touching and spending time with the papers that were once in Hemingway's hands helped me in holding up that ethical obligation.

✤

Writing about two highly documented lives creates choices in assembling endnotes. I have decided to design the notes for the ease of readers wanting to learn more. So whenever possible I include a reference to a published version of the material. Also, because the depositories of Hemingway and Dos Passos's papers maintain detailed finding aids, I have dispensed with listing the box and file numbers.

The names of newspapers, archives, and the titles of books and persons cited frequently appear in abbreviated form in the endnotes. Readers wanting the full bibliographical information for these sources will find it here or in the bibliography.

Archival Collections of Repositories Cited

AAA&L   American Academy of Arts and Letters, New York, NY
CBPUL   Carlos Baker collection of Ernest Hemingway. Department of Rare Books and Special Collections, Princeton University Library, Princeton, NJ
HEMJFK   Ernest Hemingway Collection, John F. Kennedy Presidential Library and Museum, Boston, MA
JDPUVA   John Dos Passos Collection, Albert and Shirley Small Special Collections Library, University of Virginia, Charlottesville, VA
RANRC   Records of the American National Red Cross, National Archives, College Park, MD
RWBP   Robert W. Bates, papers, private collection retained by family, Santa Barbara, CA
SIU   Special Collections Research Center, Southern Illinois University, Carbondale, IL
WDHPUL   William Dodge Horne collection of Ernest Hemingway. Department of Rare Books and Special Collections, Princeton University Library, Princeton, NJ
WPP   Waldo Peirce Papers, Archives of American Art, Smithsonian Institute, Washington, DC

Personal Names

AKM   Arthur K. McComb
AVK   Agnes von Kurowsky
EEC   E. E. Cummings
EH   Ernest Hemingway
EP   Ezra Pound
EW   Edmund Wilson
FSF   F. Scott Fitzgerald
HR   Hadley Richardson (This acronym is retained in the notes even after she married Hemingway.)
JDP   John Dos Passos
JL   John Lawson
KDP   Katy Dos Passos
KS   Katy Smith (This acronym is retained in the notes even after she married Dos Passos.)
MC   Malcolm Cowley
MH   Marcelline Hemingway
MP   Max Perkins
WRM   Walter Rumsey "Rummy" Marvin

Frequently Cited Books or Manuscripts

AMF   Hemingway, Ernest. *A Moveable Feast*. New York: Scribner, 2009.

ATH   Sanford, Marcelline Hemingway. *At the Hemingways*. Moscow, ID: University of Idaho Press, 1999. (Originally published in 1962.)

BSoL   Stewart, Donald Ogden. *By a Stroke of Luck: An Autobiography*. New York: Paddington Press, 1975.

DPToLu   Ludington, Townsend. *Dos Passos: A Twentieth Century Odyssey*. New York: Carroll & Graf Publishers, 1998. (Originally published in 1988.)

DPViCa   Carr, Virginia. *Dos Passos: A Life*. New York: Doubleday, 1984.

ErHeARe   Young, Philip. *Ernest Hemingway: A Reconsideration*. University Park: Pennsylvania State University Press, 1966.

EWSY   Vaill, Amanda. *Everybody Was So Young: Gerald and Sara Murphy, A Lost Generation Love Story*. New York: Houghton Mifflin Co, 1998.

FoCh   Ludington, Townsend, ed. *The Fourteenth Chronicle: Letters and Diaries of John Dos Passos*. Boston: Gambit, 1973.

GeVo   Hansen, Arlen J. *Gentlemen Volunteers: The Story of American Ambulance Drivers in the Great War, August 1914–September 1918*. New York: Arcade Publishing, 1996.

Hem30s   Reynolds, Michael. *Hemingway: The 1930s*. New York: W. W. Norton & Company, 1997.

HemCaBa   Baker, Carlos. *Ernest Hemingway: A Life Story*. New York: Scribner's Sons, 1969.

HemJaMe   Mellow, James R. *Hemingway: A Life Without Consequences*. New York: Houghton Mifflin, 1992.

HemJeMe   Meyers, Jeffrey. *Hemingway: A Biography*. Boston: Da Capo Press, 1998. (Originally published in 1985.)

HemKeLy   Lynn, Kenneth Schuyler. *Hemingway*. New York: Simon and Schuster, 1987.

HemLtrs   Spanier, Sandra, and Robert W. Trogdon, *The Letters of Ernest Hemingway*. 3 vols. New York: Cambridge University Press, 2011–2015.

HemPaYe   Reynolds, Michael S. *Hemingway: The Paris Years*. Oxford: Basil Blackwell, 1989.

HemSeLtrs Baker, Carlos, ed. *Ernest Hemingway: Selected Letters, 1917–1961*. New York: Scribner, 1981.

HemTAH   Reynolds, Michael, *Hemingway: The American Homecoming*. Cambridge, MA: Blackwell, 1992.

HemTPY   Reynolds, Michael. *The Paris Years*. New York: W. W. Norton and Company, 1989.

HLW   Villard, Henry S., and James Nagel. *Hemingway in Love and War*. New York: Hyperion, 1989.

HoFl   Vaill, Amanda. *Hotel Florida: Truth, Love, and Death in the Spanish Civil War*. New York: Farrar, Straus and Giroux, 2014.

HTFMHem   Sokoloff, Alice Hunt. *Hadley: The First Mrs. Hemingway*. New York: Dodd, Mead & Company, 1973.

JDPCAKM   Landsberg, Melvin. *John Dos Passos' Correspondence with Arthur K. McComb of "Learn to Sing the Carmagnole."* Niwot: University Press of Colorado, 1991.

JDPR   "John Dos Passos: The Art of Fiction No. 44." *Paris Review* no. 46 (Spring 1969). www.theparisreview.org/interviews/4202/the-art-of-fiction-no-44-john-dos-passos.

PWE   Diliberto, Gioia. *Paris Without End: The True Story of Hemingway's Wife.* New York: HarperCollins, 2011. (Originally published in 1992.)

TTG   Brian, Denis. *The True Gen: An Intimate Portrait of Ernest Hemingway by Those Who Knew Him.* New York: Grove Press, 1988.

TYH   Reynolds, Michael. *The Young Hemingway.* New York: W. W. Norton and Company, 1986.

Works by Hemingway

ComShSt   *The Complete Short Stories of Ernest Hemingway: The Finca Vigia Edition.* New York: Simon and Schuster, 2014.

DITA   *Death in the Afternoon.* New York: Charles Scribner's Sons, 1932.

DT   *Dateline: Toronto.* New York: Scribner, 2002.

FTA   *A Farewell to Arms.* New York: Scribner, 2014. (Originally published in 1929.)

iot1924   *in our time: The 1924 Text.* Edited by James Gifford. Victoria, BC: The Modernist Versions Press, 2015.

MoFe   *A Moveable Feast: The Restored Edition.* New York: Scribner, 2003. (Originally published in 1964.)

NAS   *Nick Adams Stories.* New York: Charles Scribner, 1972.

SAR   *The Sun Also Rises.* New York: Scribner, 2006. (Originally published in 1926.)

ShStEH   *The Short Stories of Ernest Hemingway.* New York: Simon & Schuster, 2002.

SoK   *The Snows of Kilimanjaro and Other Stories.* New York: Simon & Schuster, 1995. (Originally published in 1961.)

THaHN   *To Have and Have Not.* New York: Scribner, 1987. (Originally published in 1937.)

ToS   *The Torrents of Spring.* Middlesex, UK: Penguin Books, 1966. (Originally published in 1926.)

Works by Dos Passos

CeEb   *Century's Ebb: The Thirteen Chronicle.* Boston: Gambit, 1975.

FtC   *Facing the Chair: Story of the Americanization of Two Foreignborn Workmen.* New York: Da Capo, 1970.

JBW   *Journeys Between Wars.* New York: Harcourt, Brace and Company, 1938.

MT   *Manhattan Transfer.* New York: Houghton Mifflin Harcourt, 1953. (Originally published in 1925.)

OMICUP	*One Man's Initiation: 1917.* Ithaca, NY: Cornell University Press, 1969.
TBT	*The Best Times: An Informal Memoir.* New York: New American Library, 1966.
TS	*Three Soldiers.* New York: George H. Doran Company, 1921.
TTiF	*The Theme Is Freedom.* New York: Dodd, Mead & Company, 1956.

Newspapers

BoGl	*Boston Globe*
ChTr	*Chicago Tribune*
LAT	*Los Angeles Times*
NYT	*New York Times*
NYTBR	*New York Times Book Review*
WaPo	*Washington Post*

Notes

Prologue

1 **tentative fashion with a mild stammer:** Malcolm Cowley, "John Dos Passos: 1896–1970." *Proceedings,* AAA&L, 1971, 73.

2 **"characteristic, worships the lovely creature":** *WaPo,* October 5, 1924, SM2.

3 **"take away from you that was important":** Cowley, *Exile's Return,* 102; *HemPaYe,* 236; Stein, *What Are Masterpieces,* 70.

3 **Europe like crows to a cornfield:** Eastman, *Love and Revolution,* 141; EH, "Living on a $1,000 a Year in Paris," *Toronto Star Weekly,* February 4, 1922, reprinted in *DT,* 88. "Exchange," noted Hemingway, "is a wonderful thing." For more on Paris in the 1920s, see the masterful John Baxter, *The Golden Moments of Paris: A Guide to the Paris of the 1920s* (New York: Museyon, 2014).

3 **students, artists, teachers, and tourists:** *NYT,* May 11, 1924, XX10; Maxtone-Graham, *Liners to the Sun,* 55; Levenstein, *Seductive Journey,* 235.

3 **"whom Ernest could really talk to":** *TTG,* 49.

3 **not one that imitated another from the past:** Reynolds, *The Sun Also Rises,* 6.

4 **pursuit for a new means of expression:** *AMF,* 22.

4 **"not suffered for a cause but courted for itself":** Cowley, *Exile's Return,* 41.

1

5 **passengers had canceled their reservation:** *NYT,* October 15, 1916, 1, 21, and October 14, 1916, 1.

5 **"I was frantic to be gone":** *TBT,* 24.

6 **named the Norton-Harjes Ambulance Corps:** *GeVo,* 28. Hansen's work is a remarkable account of the service of the drivers. Hansen died before the book was published, but his friends and family brought the work to publication.

6 **France, 348 from Harvard alone:** Hansen, *Gentlemen Volunteers,* vi.

6   **"hook or crook," he confided to a friend:** JDP to AMcM, undated, 1916, *DPViCa*, 99.

6   **son out of New York City's harbor:** JRDP to Mrs. Harris, undated, *DPToLu*, 6.

7   **"many men's feelings for their fathers":** *FoCh*, 6; *TBT*, 4.

7   **childhood devoid of genuine family life:** 1911 diary entry quoted in *JDP-CAKM*, 1–2. It was a ruse so successful that later obituaries of the senior Dos Passos would refer to his first son, Louis, as his only child. For an example of an obituary that makes no mention of John Dos Passos the son, see Henry Wollman, "Memorial of John E. Dos Passos," *Yearbook* (New York: New York County Lawyers' Association: 1917), 276.

8   **reading these in Latin, of course:** *TBT*, 17; *DPViCa*, 56.

8   **without finding the Dos Passos byline:** The scholar Richard Layman assembled a fascinating collection of Dos Passos's undergraduate writings, including a novel called *Afterglow*. Reading it, one can see the emergence of some of the themes and style found in his later professional writings. See Richard Layman, *John Dos Passos: Afterglow and Other Undergraduate Writings* (Detroit: Omnigraphics, 1990).

8   **She died a few days later:** *DPViCa*, 72.

8   **made to remain in touch:** *DPViCa*, 76–77; *DPToLu*, 67–68.

9   **death now sparkled with renewal:** JDP to WRM, August 28, 1915, *FoCh*, 24; JDP to WRM, November 12, 1915, JDPUVA.

9   **an ample supply of alcohol:** *TBT*, 23.

9   **his studies, and full of life:** "Dos did more in a week with more gusto than any of us," recalled his friend Poore. "Yet when he came to see you it was never in haste to leave unless, the hour growing late, it were to carry you along with others to a French restaurant called the Bourse or an Italian one somewhere on Hanover street." (*DPToLu*, 73).

9   **"hating the Huns became a mania":** *TBT*, 23.

10   **the great power of a writer:** Sawyer-Lauçanno, *E. E. Cummings*, 85.

10   **"The world was the war":** *TBT*, 25–26.

11   **put the car in reverse:** *GeVo*, 112–114.

11   **an avant-garde dance recital:** *DPToLu*, 122–123.

11   **"no good will come out of Cambridge":** *DPToLu*, 123; JDP to AKM, date unclear, but internal evidence suggests his comments were written in May or June 1917, AAA&L.

11   **bring American troops to war:** OMICUP, 6; Bonsor, *North Atlantic Seaway*, 2:660.

12   **troops were being called into battle:** A third son, Quentin Roosevelt, was killed in the war. Thompson, *Never Call Retreat*, 190; Theodore Roosevelt to General John Pershing, May 20, 1917, reproduced in Walker, *The Namesake*, 72–73.

12   **graduating from Harvard a year earlier:** JDP to WRM, June 20, 1917, *FoCh*, 75.

2

15   **seventeen-year-old son, Ernest:** Description of the drive drawn from Morris Buske, "Dad, Are We There Yet?" *Michigan History Magazine*, March–April 1991, 17–26.

16   **his graduation from high school:** *HemKeLy*, 19; *HemJeMe*, 4.

16   **visited frequently, and a pair of servants:** *HemJaMe*, 18; *HemCaBa*, 7.

16   **outside the New York Metropolitan Opera:** *HemCaBa*, 8–9; *HemJaMe*, 9; *HemJeMe*, 6–7.

17   **"he was tired and sleeping heavily":** EH, "Remembering Shooting-Flying," *Esquire*, February 1935, 21 and 134.

17   **"was maddeningly condescending":** *HemJaMe*, 36–37; *HemJeMe*, 16. Katy Smith was born October 26, 1894.

17   **University of Chicago to the region's students:** Fenton, *The Apprenticeship of Ernest Hemingway*, 4.

18   **literature was placed on narrative:** Hemingway's transcript, reproduced in Reynolds, *Hemingway's Reading*; *HemCaBa*, 21.

18   **after leaving Oak Park High:** Rhodes, *Old Testament Narratives*, 13; *ErHeARe*, 173. At home he and his sister Marcelline entered a Bible reading competition. They failed to win but passed a detailed test (Hemingway, *At the Hemingways*, 134–135).

18   **could quote Kipling passages verbatim:** *ApErHe*, 6; *HemKeLy*, 61. See EH to Emily Goetzmann, July 13, 1916, *HemLtrs*, 1:33.

18   **he wrote, "removed all the traces":** *HemJaMe*, 26–27.

19   **heard of his writing ability from other students:** Fenton, *The Apprenticeship of Ernest Hemingway*, 21.

19   **"he unquestionably had 'personality plus'":** *HemJeMe*, 18.

19   **serve as soldiers and Red Cross nurses:** *HemCaBa*, 28.

19   **the course of his grisly battlefield work:** *HemJeMe*, 1 and 22; *HemJaMe*, 35.

3

21   **"we're going to see the damn show through":** *TBT*, 48.

21   **"were not strong enough to risk prison":** John Lawson, *A Haystack in France*, unpublished autobiography, SIU, 40A; *TBT*, 47.

22   **make the world safe for democracy:** *TBT*, 48. JDP to AKM, June 28, 1917, on board *Chicago*, AAA&L.

22   **"picture out of a book of old fairy tales":** *TBT*, 48.

23   **walking into a mystery melodrama:** *TBT*, 49.

23   **fire engines hurried up and down streets:** *JBW*, 330–331.

23   **"duty in our excitement at meeting":** JDP to WRM, July 12, 1917, *FoCh*, 88.

24   **would soon be booming in his ears:** *DPViCa*, 129–130; JDP to WRM, July 12, 1917, *FoCh*, 88. Dos Passos's complaints, however, were muted when he learned he could have been drilling as a soldier. A letter from the States reported that his name had been among those drawn in the first draft lottery.

25   **"literally stuffed with corpses":** Ellis, *Eye-Deep in Hell*, 48, 55, and 59. Other general descriptions of the trenches in this chapter are also drawn from this excellent book.

25   **"of mustard gas in its early stages":** Ibid, 67.

25   **"the comfortable stillness of night":** OMICUP, introduction, 11. It's interesting that Dos Passos chose the term *charnel*. "Soldiers often referred to Verdun as a "charnel house," according to Ousby, *The Road to Verdun*, 268.

25   **fields or woods to lie about and read:** OMICUP, introduction, 17.

26   **"they are going to their deaths":** JDP to WRM, August 29, 1917, *FoCh*, 97.

26   **abundance, anesthetized the men:** *TBT*, 52; Barthas, *Poilu*, 174.

26   **"is forming gradually in my mind":** DPToLu, 131. See also introduction by Dos Passos to the OMICUP; Diary, August 24, 1917, *FoCh*, 93–94.

27   **razzed for their literary pretentiousness:** *Dark Forest*, JDP told to his friend Arthur McComb, "seems to me confoundedly good." JDP to AKM, September or October 1916, JDPCAKM, 26. *TBT*, 44–45; OMICUP, footnote, 18.

27   **"scavenger crows," said Dos Passos:** *JDPR*.

27   **white handkerchief draped from an epaulet:** *DPViCa*, 134.

27   **one location to another during the interludes:** JDP to WRM, August 23, 1917, *FoCh*, 92; *DPViCa*, 136.

28   **"groaned horribly," said Dos Passos:** *TBT*, 54.

28   **"and laid it over the dugout":** Lawson, *A Haystack*, 41; *DPViCa*, 136–137.

28   **"a more hellish experience":** *TBT*, 54; DP to AKM, August 27, 1917, AAA&L; JDP to WRM, August 23, 1917, *FoCh*, 92.

28   **from the dorms of Choate and Harvard:** *DPViCa*, 136.

28   **their lights seemed like shooting stars:** *DPViCa*, 137–138.

29   **"possible to us, by putting words on paper":** Lawson, *A Haystack*, 41a.

29   **list possessed by a gambler's exhilaration:** Diary, August 26, 1917, *FoCh*, 95.

30   **"the aims of this ridiculous affair":** JDP to WRM, August 23, 1917, *FoCh*, 92.

30   **being either freed or charged with treason:** GeVo, 156–157.

30   **"the resignation of despair":** *FoCh*, 98.

30   **briefly considered fleeing to Spain:** JDP to AKM, September 12, 1917, AAA&L; *TBT*, 56; JDP to Dudley Poore, August 25, 1917, Yale Collection of American Literature, Beinecke Rare Book and Manuscript Library, New Haven, CT.

31   **and now Italy's warfront awaited:** George Buchanon Fife, "Section One, Italy: The Chronicle of an Eventful Run Through France," 1, Box 881, folder 954.11/08, RANRC.

4

33   **job on the *Kansas City Star*:** HemCaBa, 32, and see in particular the notes on 570.

34   **"edition," an awestruck Hemingway said:** "Lionel Moise was a great rewrite man." HEMJFK.

35   **Hemingway recalled years later:** "Back to His First Field," *Kansas City Times*, November 26, 1940, 1–2, reprinted in H. Bruccoli, *Conversations with Ernest Hemingway*, 21.

35   **up with tales of his work:** EH to Clarence Hemingway, October 25, 1917, *HemLtrs*, 1:54–55. EH to Hugh Walpole, April 14, 1927, *HemLtrs*, 3:227.

36   **"finish paying for that home of yours":** EH, "At the End of the Ambulance Run," *Kansas City Star*, January 20, 1918, 7C, reprinted in Bruccoli, *Ernest Hemingway, Cub Reporter*, 27.

36   **let his father believe something not true:** The clipping was included in EH to MH, January 8, 1918, *HemLtrs* 1:73–75. It is extremely unlikely that Hemingway wrote the article, according to researchers and a reporter who worked at the paper at the time. See Bruccoli, *Ernest Hemingway, Cub Reporter*, 21.

36   **"war retains something of its old glamour":** Florczyk, *Hemingway, The Red Cross, and the Great War*, 6.

36   **"any body after the war and not have been in it":** EH to Clarence and Grace Hall Hemingway, November 15, 1917, *HemLtrs*, 1:60–61; EH to Marceline Hemingway, *HemLtrs*, 1:58–59. Hemingway also told his family and friends that the army had rejected him because of his poor eyesight in his left eye. Yet he functioned fine as a reporter without glasses, and men with far worse vision were in uniform, including the bespectacled and future president Harry S Truman, who fooled the Kansas City draft board by memorizing the eye chart. There is no record of Hemingway trying to join the military, according to biographer Kenneth S. Lynn. In fact, he points to Truman's service as an example of men who were willing to serve being able to do so despite poor eyesight. But some reports suggest that as many as one out of five men were classified unfit to serve in World War I because of poor eyesight. "During World War 1 military doctors were reportedly very rigid about vision, rejecting many recruits for defects that were correctible," according to Segrave, *Vision Aids in America*, 26.

36   **the new man at the adjacent desk:** Theodore Brumback, "With Hemingway Before *A Farewell to Arms*," *Kansas City Star*, December 6, 1936, reprinted in Bruccoli, *Ernest Hemingway, Cub Reporter*, 3–11.

37   **Brumback's plan could:** According to biographer Kenneth S. Lynn, Hemingway was untruthful about trying to join the army and was likely put off by the prospect of trench warfare. See *HemKeLy*, 73. If he did have such reluctance, the idea of ambulance work that Brumback extolled may have been more appealing.

38   **"non coms must salute us smartly":** *HemKeLy*, 73; EH to family, May 14, 1918, *HemLtrs*, 1:97.

38   **reviewed by President Wilson:** *NYT*, May 19, 1918, 8; EH to family, May 1918, *HemLtrs*, 1:101.

38   **to restore familial calm:** For more on this episode, see *HemKeLy*, 74–75.

38   **cheated by the evasive maneuvers:** Brumback, "With Hemingway Before *A Farewell to Arms*," 8.

39   **a large recessed statue of St. Luke:** Several years later Ernest brought Hadley to see the statue that had not been repaired and instead was marked with a sign that dated the damage to May 30, 1918.

39   **He got his wish:** *HemCaBa*, 40.

40   **many of whom were women:** William Horne Chronology, WDHPUL.

40   **"laid the thing on the stretcher":** Milford Baker Diary, CBPUL, also quoted
      in *HemJaMe*, 57. The comparison of Hemingway's experience as a hunter and
      now facing human bodies was suggested to me by Carlos Baker's work.

40   **"Oh, Boy!!! I'm glad I'm in it":** EH to friend at *Kansas City Star*, June 9, 1919,
      HemLtrs, 1:112.

41   **where wool had once been stored:** Description of sites drawn from *Hem-
      CaBa*, 41.

41   **along with large quantities of wine:** Milford Baker Diary, CBPUL; *Hem-
      CaBa*, 41. JDP to Carlos Baker, January 13, 1965, and Carlos Baker to JDP,
      January 17, 1964, CBPUL. There was debate among Hemingway and Dos
      Passos scholars whether this meeting actually occurred. Several of Heming-
      way's biographers concluded that Dos Passos had left the area by the time
      Hemingway arrived. But the diaries kept by Captain Robert Bates, which
      these authors did not consult, reveal that Dos Passos's unit was kept past the
      end of its service, such that the two men were in the same place at the same
      time. Dos Passos's own letters and diaries don't prove that he was in Hem-
      ingway's unit nor do they prove he could not have been there. Thus the late-
      in-life remembrances of Dos Passos, along with those of Sydney Fairbanks,
      who was present in Schio, cannot be dismissed as wishful thinking on the part
      of aging men. In fact, only a year prior to his death Dos Passos told a French
      filmmaker of his wartime meeting with Hemingway. See "John Dos Passos:
      La Collection des *Archive du xxe siècle*," par Jean José Marchand (Paris: Edition
      Montparnasse, 2000).

5

43   **while awaiting repairs in Milan:** Reproduced in *DPViCa*, 142.

43   **their memories until years later:** *DPToLu*, 159.

44   **and other irresistible distractions:** JDP to WRM, December 9, 1917, *FoCh*,
      105; *TBT*, 59.

44   **"seen it every day of one's life":** JDP, diary entry, November 28, 1917, *FoCh*,
      103; *DPViCa*, 143. There are accounts of sailors witnessing a similar act at a
      bar in Subic Bay in the 1960s, but it also seems that Dos Passos's ribald tale in-
      spired accounts of the act in fiction, such as in Yuriy Tarnawsky's *Three Blondes
      and Death: A Novel* (Tuscaloosa: University of Alabama Press, 1993) and Nina
      Graboi's *One Foot in the Future: A Woman's Spiritual Journey* (Santa Cruz, CA:
      Aerial Press, 1991).

44   **"tragedy of lust," Dos Passos wrote:** JDP, diary entry, December 7, 1917,
      FoCh, 103; JDP, diary entry, November 14, 1917, *FoCh*, 103. "Sexual relations
      ought to involve 'a human relation,' not be only a matter of a casual piece of
      tale," *DPToLu*, 171.

45   **"Graved inside of it, 'Italy'":** *NYT*, December 17, 1917, 12, and January 4,
      1918, 18; *Independent*, February 28, 1920, 319; *American Poets' Ambulances in Italy;*

Report of the Chairman to Contributors, to the General Committee, and to the Public, 1918 (copy in Library of Congress).

45 **American troops were on their way:** Box 44, Folder 041, American Poets, Ambulances in Italy, RANRC. Later, when an Austrian was captured and he saw the insignia denoting the Red Cross ambulance had been donated by poets, an officer told the prisoner, "So you see, you have the entire world against you, even the American poets." Florczyk. *Hemingway, the Red Cross, and the Great War*, 2.

45 **"distressed humanity is heir":** Translated from Italian newspaper of February 6, 1918; RANRC, Box 881, Folder 954.102, Commission to Italy W.W.I Officers Their Duties. "The newspapers tried to give the impression that our little Section I was the vanguard of a great American army," Dos Passos wrote. *TBT*, 59.

46 **"colossal asininity," he wrote:** JDP, diary entry, January 1, 1918, *FoCh*, 115–116; *DPViCa*, 143.

46 **"that it isn't done successful":** JDP, diary entry, January 21, 1918, *FoCh*, 129.

46 **"cock against the rocks of fact":** *DPToLu*, 147; JDP, diary entry, January 28, 1918, *FoCh*, 134.

47 **"the censor evidently didn't notice me":** JDP to Mrs. Cummings, December 16, 1917, *FoCh*, 108.

47 **but was forced to resign:** *DPViCa*, 145.

47 **"war—I mean modern war—is death":** *FoCh*, 151; the French and translated versions of the letter appear on pages 150–152.

48 **"it is always in terms of admiration":** Bates, letter to "Dear Harry," February 28, 1918, RWBP.

48 **"I have no sympathy for him":** Robert W. Bates to Guy Lowell, attached to JDP to José Giner Pantoja, SIU.

48 **together in the midst of the war:** This dating of events was done by using Bates's journal. *RWBP*; *DPToLu*, 154.

49 **a black mark on his record:** JDP to AKM, *JDPCAKM*, 101.

49 **admissions as compounding the offense:** *TBT*, 68–69.

50 **Rendezvous des Mariners on the Île Saint-Louis:** JDP to WRM, July 27, 1918, *FoCh*, 194.

50 **"good time in a quiet mournful way":** JDP to AKM, undated, American Academy of Arts and Letters, quoted in *DPViCa*, 149; DP to WRM, July 27, 1918, *FoCh*, 194.

6

51 **"what a bum prophet I was":** EH to Ruth Morrison, June or July 1918, *HemLtrs*, 1:113.

51 **"I can't find out where the war is":** *HemCaBa*, 42.

52 **with soldiers in the trenches:** EH to Ruth Morrison, June or July 1918, *HemLtrs*, 1:113–114; Brumback to Clarence and Grace Hall Hemingway, July 14, 1918, *HemLtrs*, 1:115.

52   **a mortar's slow, lofting arc:** "The Voice of the Gun" by T. J. Slamon, *The Cornhill Magazine*, London, reprinted in the *Lotus Magazine*, October 1916. Many authors describing the wounding of Hemingway confuse the "chuh-chuh-chuh" sound he referred to in his novel *A Farewell to Arms*, wrongly assuming it is what he heard on the night he was wounded. It was not, as one author wrote, the sound "as it arched and descended." Rather, the sound is only that of the mortar's launch. I consulted with several military experts, and mortars do not make sound in flight.

53   **first aid station close to the front:** Over the years there has been considerable debate about Hemingway's actions following the mortar explosion. The various Hemingway biographers have offered different versions of the events, some diminishing the possibility that Hemingway was wounded by a machine gun or was capable of carrying a wounded soldier to safety. The account offered here is based on some later discoveries, such as the X-ray of Hemingway's leg. More important than each fact, I have let Hemingway tell as much of the story as possible because his view of events will shape his later writing and his exaggeration of what occurred demonstrates the fuzziness in his mind between reality and fiction.

53   **being treated for war wounds:** *HLW*, 224–225.

53   **"valor medal for the act":** Theodore Brumback to Clarence and Grace Hall Hemingway, July 14, 1918, *HemLtrs*, 1:114–116.

53   **whether he would keep them:** The vast and unprecedented use of airborne projectiles delivering this death had also added a new word to the vocabulary. Within six months of the start of the war a British doctor had noted a similar traumatic neurosis appearing among three soldiers who had survived a blast. He called it *shell shock*. See Caroline Alexander, "The Shock of War," *Smithsonian*, September 2010.

54   **McKey's death the previous month:** Edward Michael McKey, a member of the canteen service, was killed on June 16, 1918, by an Austrian shell near the site where Hemingway was wounded. Hemingway certainly knew of the death, but he may not have known that Richard Cutts Fairfield was killed while on duty as an ambulance driver on the Italian front in late January.

56   **"attention by American nurses":** *HLW*, 11; Theodore Brumback to Clarence and Grace Hall Hemingway, July 14, 1918, *HemLtrs*, 1:114–116.

56   **"and played the Victrola":** *HLW*, 62.

57   **"she radiated zest and energy":** Kert, *The Hemingway Women*, 53; *HLW*, 28.

7

59   **for the remainder of his life:** *DPViCa*, 149.

59   **home for early August 1918:** JDP to Jack Lawson, August 11, 1918, *FoCh*, 196; *TBT*, 70.

60   **soldiers poured into the Paris hospital:** *Annual Report of the Surgeon General, U.S. Army*, part I (Washington, DC: U.S. Government Printing Office, 1920), 3744.

60   **"ambulance driver in disgrace," he said:** *TBT*, 71; *OMICUP*, 4. "When you are in wrong with the authorities always travel first class," Dos Passos wrote in the 1968 edition of *One Man's Initiation.*

60   **"heard that summer on the** ***Voie Sacrée***": *TBT*, 66. The ballad came from *Robinson Crusoe, Jr.*, an extravagant and immensely popular 1916 Schubert Broadway production that was essentially a plot-free vehicle to showcase Al Jolson in his customary blackface.

61   *At last things have come to pass:* *OMICUP*, 45.

61   *where the nose should have been:* *OMICUP*, 54–55.

61   **war destroyed everything of value:** Rohrkemper, "Mr. Dos Passos' War," 41.

62   *half buried in the mud of the ditches:* *OMICUP*, 122.

62   **"He won't last long":** *OMICUP*, 124–125.

62   **the angry members of the draft board:** "I have but finished part four," Dos Passos wrote to Lawson while on board the ship, August 18, 1918. *FoCh*, 197.

62   **"Also, Mom I'm in love again":** EH to Grace Hall Hemingway, August 29, 1918, *HemLtrs*, 1:134. He quickly reassured his mother that it was not a repeat of the moment when he falsely claimed to be engaged.

63   **"I don't know how I'll end up":** "The Lost Diary of Agnes von Kurowsky," August 26, 1918, 72; August 27, 1918, *HLW*, 73.

63   **"that was developing between them":** "The Lost Diary of Agnes von Kurowsky," August 31, 1918, 74–75; September 7, 1918, *HLW*, 77.

63   **horses at the racetrack of San Siro:** Kert, *The Hemingway Women*, 58–59.

64   **"haunted me so I could not stay in it":** AVK to EH, September 25, 1918, *HLW*, 92–93; AVK to EH, September 11, 1918, *HLW*, 78.

64   **"go to sleep with your arm around me":** *HemCaBa*, 51; AVK to EH, October 16, 1918, *HLW*, 99.

64   **"hold out your brawny arms":** AVK to EH, October 17, 1918, *HLW*, 101.

64   **"any more—at least not to you":** AVK to EH, October 20–21, 1918, *HLW*, 106, and October 25, 1918, *HLW*, 113.

65   **he would cease to love her:** AVK to EH, October 17, 1918, *HLW*, 102–103.

65   **so dear and necessary to me:** AVK to EH, October 29, 1918, *HLW*, 119.

65   **mustard and skin tinted yellow:** *HemCaBa*, 53.

65   **when she joined the Red Cross:** AVK to EH, November 2, 1918, *HLW*, 124–125.

65   **after the signing of an armistice:** AVK to EH, November 4, 1918, *HLW*, 125; October 20–21, 1918, 105–106, and November 5–6, 1918, *HLW*, 126–127.

66   **"I must try and not think of it":** AVK to EH, December 1, 1918, *HLW*, 135.

66   **"So that shows I've changed some":** EH to MH, November 23, 1918, *HemLtrs*, 1:156–157.

66   *by the shell of trench mortar:* Unpublished manuscript, HEMJFK, quoted in *HEMJaMe*, 81. See also Benson, *New Critical Approaches to the Short Stories of Ernest Hemingway*, 142.

67   **"looked at death, and really I know":** EH to family, November 18, 1918, *HemLtrs*, 1:146–148.

67   **"I'm away from that Kid is wasted":** EH to William B. Smith, December 13, 1918, *HemLtrs*, 1:163–164.

67   **in Genoa bound for home:** AVK to EH, December 20, 1918, *HLW*, 145.

8

69   **treasure trove of war stories:** Manifest is available online from the Statue of Liberty-Ellis Island Foundation records.

70   **in the shoulder and right leg:** *The Sun*, January 22, 1919, 8; *New York Evening World*, January 21, 1919, 3, and January 22, 19, 6.

70   **leg of his journey home:** *HemCaBa*, 56.

70   **steps of the station toward the car:** *ATH*, 176–177.

70   **"who saw him in that light":** L. Hemingway, *My Brother, Ernest Hemingway*, 52–53.

71   *we have been such dupes*: OMICUP, 120–121.

71   *the waxen look of death*: OMICUP, 173–174.

72   **enter the belly of the beast:** JDP, diary, September 17, 1918, *FoCh*, 211.

72   **"The band played on":** JDP, diary, September 30, 1918, *FoCh*, 212.

72   **"stupidity hardly shared by animals":** JDP to WRM, October 20, 1918, *FoCh*, 226. In the letter Dos Passos talks at length about his views on sex, including the American disparaging hatred of prostitutes.

72   **"here you are—drowned in it":** *DPToLu*, 169; JDP, diary, October 1, 1918, *FoCh*, 213.

73   **"the windows there is no end":** JDP, diary, October 1, 1918, *FoCh*, 212.

73   **beginning of Rome's domination:** JDP, diary, October 4, 1919, and October 1, 1918, *FoCh*, 217; *DPViCa*, 157–158.

73   **Dos Passos was not yet free:** JDP to WRM, January 22–25, 1919, *FoCh*, 242.

73   **"forty-eight?" he wrote Rummy:** JDP to WRM, March 17, 1919, *FoCh*, 244.

74   **not issued revolvers to its men:** *Oak Parker* (school newspaper), March 14, 1919. Quoted in *TYH*, 57.

74   **side so he would not wake alone:** EH to Arthur Mizener, June 2, 1950, *HemSeLtrs*, 697.

74   **she was marrying another man:** AVK to EH, March 7, 1919, *HLW*, 163–164. For a perceptive account of Hemingway's breakup with Kurowsky, see Donaldson, "The Jilting of Ernest Hemingway."

75   **Ernest told her the news:** *ATH*, 188.

75   **"develop into some kind of writer":** L. Hemingway, *My Brother, Ernest Hemingway*, 60.

76   **he had failed to die in battle:** "The Woppian Way," HEMJFK.

76   **who promptly rejected them:** The description "rapturous nostalgia" is taken from *HemKeLy*, 120.

76   **asleep in the seat by his side:** EH to Grace Quinlan, September 30, 1920, *HemLtrs*, 1:244.

9

77   **shared campfires with shepherds:** Dos Passos and his friend were likely to be walking along the Camino del Norte, one of the Camino de Santiago routes.

77   **one of the finest months of his life:** Sawyer-Laućanno, *E. E. Cummings: A Biography*, 79; *TBT*, 79–80; JDP to Thomas P. Cope, September 1919, *FoCh*, 262.

77   **documents to a disbelieving commander:** "Gièvres may not have been hell but it made me understand the concept of limbo," said Dos Passos, *TBT*, 78.

78   **"I am a free man":** JDP to WRM, July 13, 1919, *FoCh*, 254.

78   **"but it won't come":** JDP to WRM, September 20, 1919, *FoCh*, 259.

79   **help him get others published:** JDP to Stewart Mitchell, December 8, 1919, *FoCh*, 271.

79   **while at the French warfront:** Two excellent scholarly articles helped guide my presentation of *Three Soldiers* in this chapter: Hughson, "Dos Passos' World War"; and Rohrkemper, "Mr. Dos Passos' War."

79   *merely an expendable cog:* TS, 63.

80   *the German had shot himself:* TS, 149.

80   *make their flesh tingle with it:* TS, 22.

81   *among the new-fallen leaves:* TS, 188.

81   *He would do as the others did:* TS, 189.

82   *This was his last run with the pack:* TS, 211.

82   *"becoming slaves again in their turn":* TS, 421.

83   *the floor was littered with them:* TS, 433.

83   **"raw humanity," he wrote Rummy:** JDP to WRM, April 30, 1920, quoted in *DPViCa*, 171.

83   **"the shackles close definitely":** JDP to Stewart Mitchell, February 17, 1920, *FoCh*, 281.

84   **"it would never be worth while":** Hughson, "Dos Passos's World War," 53; *TS*, 269.

84   **"smoke in social intercourse":** Eastman, *Love and Revolution*, 141.

84   **"The publisher had other ideas":** *TBT*, 85.

85   **"last part," Dos Passos told a friend":** JDP to Stewart Mitchell, December 8, 1919, *FoCh*, 271.

85   **"they goddamn pleased with it":** *DPToLu*, 176; *TBT*, 85.

85   **"You order tea and find it's gin":** JDP to JL, November 2, 1920, *FoCh*, 305.

10

87   **"plenty of spare time to really write":** William D. Horne to EH, October 13, 1920, *HemJaMe*, 126.

89   **she thought she might be in love:** *PWE*, 15; *HemLtrs*, 1:249.

89   **notice the woman who wore it:** *Bulletin of the United States Bureau of Labor Statistics*, no. 315 (Washington, DC: U.S. Government Printing Office, 1923), 63.

89   **made Richardson more appealing:** *HTFMHem*, 17.

89   **"I'd do anything your eyes said":** *PWE*, 41; *Hemingway's Women*, 88.

90   **doubt remained in her mind:** EH to Ursula Hemingway, December 1919, *HemLtrs*, 1:217.

90   **"the nicest lover a person ever had":** *PWE*, 46; Kert, *Hemingway's Women*, 88. The lack of a more substantial embrace set Richardson to worry and complain. Hemingway wrote, "I didn't want to kiss you goodbye—that was the trouble—I wanted to kiss you good night—and there's the difference. 'couldn't bear the thought of you going away when you were so very dear and necessary and pervading." EH to HR, December 23, 1919, *HemLtrs*, 1:259.

90   **"your *litry* name later on," she said:** *PWE*, 47; The society eventually went bankrupt. See Colston E. Warne, "The Co-operative Society of America—A Common Law Trust," *The University Journal of Business* 1, no. 4 (August 1923): 373–392.

90   **"certain look came into your eyes":** EH to HR, December 23, 1920, *HemLtrs*, 1:259; *PWE*, 78.

91   **"keep close to me in every way":** *PWE*, 51.

91   **replaced it with psychological insights:** Ray Lewis White, "Introduction," *Sherwood Anderson's Secret Love Letters: For Eleanor, a Letter a Day* (Baton Rouge: Louisiana State University Press, 1991), 4.

92   **expectation of readers won them over:** Rideout, *Sherwood Anderson*, 319.

92   **five-month odyssey across Asia Minor:** Howe, *Sherwood Anderson*, 132; JDP to Sherwood Anderson, January 7, 1922, *FoCh*, 345.

93   **"goodbye to them," he wrote Rummy:** *TBT*, 112; JDP to WRM, January 10, 1922, *FoCh*, 347.

93   **Dos Passos discovered he was famous:** Dos Passos told his friend Robert Hillyer that it took three hot baths, four large meals, and a quart of pomade to restore himself after his ride across the desert. See JDP to Robert Hillyer, January 10, 1922, *FoCh*, 346.

94   **their fears were well founded:** *NYT*, October 2, 1921, 55.

94   **"a seething mass of putridity":** *NYT*, October 9, 1921, 87, October 30, 1921, 89.

94   **"have been sung instead of whined":** *NYT*, October 16, 1921, 37; "Harold Norman Denny," *Annals of Iowa* 27 (1945), 165–166.

95   **wrote one of the magazine's editors:** *LAT*, October 30, 1921, III30; *NYT*, October 23, 1921, 89; *New Republic*, October 5, 1921, 163.

95   **"the food he had to abandon":** Anderson, *Sherwood Anderson's Memoirs*, 473.

11

97   **"Paris and Switzerland and Italy":** EH to KS, January 27, 1923, *HemLtrs*, 1:325.

98   **woman resists the man's advances:** Sherwood Anderson to Gertrude Stein, December 3, 1921 quoted in *HemJaMe*, 149; *HemCaBa*, 87.

98   **"Oh, Jim. Jim. Oh":** *ComShSt*, 62; *ShStEH*, 87.

98   **had been so nice to him:** *AMF*, 31.

99   **"gained any degree of recognition":** EH, "The Mecca of Fakers," *Toronto Daily Star*, March 25, 1922, reprinted in *DT*, 154–156; EH, "American Bohemians in Paris," *Toronto Star Weekly*, March 25, 1922, reprinted in White, *By-Line*, 23–25; Reynolds points out Hemingway's repeated use of satire in *HemPaYe*, 192.

99   **remained skeletal at best:** EH to Howell G. Jenkins, March 20, 1922, *HemLtrs*, 1:334; *HemPaYe*, 23.

99   **the average American in 1922:** *DPViCa*, 192; *Statistics of Income from Returns of Net Income for 1922* (Washington, DC: U.S. Treasury Department, U.S Government Printing Office, 1925).

99   **"business and government maintained":** *ChTr*, March 13, 1922, 10.

100   **"I wrote it to get it off my chest":** *LAT*, May 21, 1922, III40.

100   **"very small part of the truth":** *NYT*, May 29, 1922, 8.

100   **a cozy affair in the 1920s:** Lewis M. Dabney offers a number of insights into the friendship between Dos Passos and Wilson in his *Edmund Wilson: A Life in Literature*. Fascinatingly, Dabney's mother was Crystal Ross, whom Dos Passos almost marries. See page 107 in Chapter 12 of this edition.

101   **Dos Passos's poems in *Vanity Fair*:** *TBT*, 139.

101   **he wanted to meet Dos Passos:** FSF to EW, May 30, 1922; *St. Paul Daily News*, September 25, 1921.

101   **with his fellow ambulance drivers:** EH, "A Veteran Visits an Old Front," *Toronto Star*, July 22, 1922, reprinted in *DT*, 176.

102   **"You were inhibited about sex":** *TBT*, 127–130; Mary Jo Murphy, "Eyeing the Unreal Estate of Gatsby Esq.," *NYT*, October 1, 2010, C35; Matthew J. Bruccoli, "A Literary Friendship," *NYT*, November 7, 1976, L13.

104   **"not the monster he has been pictured":** *Toronto Star*, June 24, 1922, quoted in *HemJaMe*, 184.

104   **menstrual cycle on a calendar:** EH to HR, November 28, 1922, *HemLtrs*, 1:373.

105   **she said. "I could see that":** Alice Sokoloff interview Hadley Hemingway, quoted in *PWE*, 130. Unlike what he wrote in *A Moveable Feast*, Hemingway did not return immediately to Paris. One book claims Hemingway did return right away but uses Hemingway's fiction to support the claim. See Lesley M. M. Blume, *Everybody Behaves Badly: The True Story Behind Hemingway's Masterpiece* The Sun Also Rises (New York: Houghton Mifflin Harcourt, 2016).

105   **"3 years on the damn stuff":** EH to Edward J. O'Brien, May 21, 1923, *HemLtrs*, Vol. 2:20; EH to EP, January 23, 1923, *HemLtrs*, 2:6.

12

107   **correspondents across the Atlantic:** *Harvard Alumni Bulletin*, 25:52; *NYT*, August 29, 1922, 1. Much of the correspondence between Dos Passos and Crystal Ross are among the JDPUVA papers. Also see Ross Dabney, *The Good Fight*.

107   **through Spain a few years earlier:** *DPToLu*, 205–206; Sawyer-Lauçanno, *E. E. Cummings*, 188.

108   **Italian resort in the Southern Alps:** *HemPaYe*, 120.

108   **would be used to buy alcohol:** *ComShSt*, 136–137.

109   **"dimensions I was trying to put in them":** EH, *AMF*, 23.

110   **"now that you have Hadley":** *HemKeLy*, 190.

110   **join the soldier in the United States:** *iot1924*, 14–15.

111   **Giverny to the west of Paris:** Crystal Ross to JDP, September 21, 1923, JDPUVA.

111   *Outline of History* **that became a hit:** *NYT*, August 3, 1980, 32.

111   **"fortunate enough to be their friends":** *EWSY*, 114.

111   **"porcupine," said Dos Passos:** *TBT*, 145–147.

112   **"more than they understood":** *AMF*, 71.

113   **"thing on them immediately after cover":** EH to Robert McAlmon, August 5, 1923, *HemLtrs*, 2:39.

114   **descent from commercial success:** Pizer, "John Dos Passos' 'Rosinante to the Road Again.'" The book of poetry was entitled *A Pushcart at the Curb*.

114   **"effects and inferred the causes":** *Spectator*, January 26, 1924, 129; FSF to John Peale Bishop, April 1925, in Bruccoli, *F. Scott Fitzgerald*, 104.

115   **from Hadley's trust fund:** The Spanish portion of his name was inspired by Ernest's admiration of matador Nicanor Vilata, whom they had met in Pamplona the previous summer; EH to EP, December 9, 1923, *HemLtrs*, 2:83.

115   **"drink and enjoy the show":** *TBT*, 143.

115   **"first great American stylist":** *TBT*, 142.

13

117   **"I'm trying hard not to count on you":** *DPViCa*, 206; letters are at UVA. Her thesis is entitled "Le Conteur américain O Henry et l'art de Maupassant."

117   **"It is a naturalism":** Crystal Ross, "Ernest Hemingway, Expatriate," *Dallas Morning News*, January 16, 1927.

118   **"all in a tangle together":** EH to William D. Horne, July 17–18, 1923, *HemLtrs*, 2:36; Pizer, *Toward a Modernist Style*, 11; JDP to WRM, December 4, 1916, *FoCh*, 57.

118   **experienced Spanish hand than he:** Ludington, "Spain and the Hemingway-Dos Passos Relationship," 273; EH, "American Bohemians in Paris," *Toronto Star Weekly*, March 25, 1922, reprinted in *DT*, 114.

118   **considered him a member of the family:** *BSoL*, 115; *TBT*, 58.

119   **Ernest as he followed the boys:** *HemPaYe*, 211.

119   **she recovered, resting by a stream:** Ross, "Ernest Hemingway, Expatriate"; *DPToLu*, 232.

119   **Kingdom of Navarre:** In the summer of 2016 my wife and I made the same walk and grew very sympathetic to Ross as we made the arduous climb up the pass. "The independence of a kingdom builds an imposing architecture against the hills, not without delicate ornaments upon its front," noted Gertrude Bone in *Days in Old Spain*, 230–231.

120   **double room with Dos Passos:** EH to Donald Ogden Stewart, July 1924, *HemLtrs*, 2:127; *DPToLu*, 232; *DPViCa*, 201.

120   **lined with wooden barricades:** Michener, *Iberia: Spanish Travels and Reflections*, 502–505.

120   **the notebook he carried with him:** One may read about the accident at "A Tragic History," Sanfermin.com, www.sanfermin.com/index.php/en/encierro/historia/historia-tragica.

120   **"wars were over, was in the bull ring":** *DITA*, 2.

121   **"Hemingway shamed me into it":** Sarason, *Hemingway and the Sun Set*, 193.

121   **evening of dancing and drinking:** *BSoL*, 132.

121   **wounded on the Italian front:** *ChTr*, July 29, 1924, 1.

121   **"spot to make sketches from":** *TBT*, 155; Sarason, *Hemingway and the Sun Set*, 193.

122   **"goings on, in them but not of them":** Pizer, "Hemingway in Action"; *TBT*, 156.

123   **The crisis had passed:** McAlmon and Boyle, *Being Geniuses Together*, 246–247.

123   **"shock troops, wave after wave":** EH to Grace Hall Hemingway, July 18, 1924, *HemLtrs*, 2:134; *TBT*, 156–157.

123   **red-plush carpeted room:** JDP to JL, undated, SIU, *DPViCa*, 203.

124   **"utterly fantastic and New Yorkish":** *EWSY*, 148; JDP to Germaine Lucas-Championnière, quoted in *DPToLu*, 228.

124   **wage slaves of the citizenry:** See Pizer, "John Dos Passos in the 1920s"; *MT*, 216.

125   **"call me another of his imitators":** EH to EP, July 19, 1924, *HemLtrs*, 2:135.

125   **he did not have in real life:** Donald Pizer's perceptive article "The Hemingway-Dos Passos Relationship" should be credited for making this observation.

125   **and the action begins:** EH, *NAS*, 227.

126   **"better than anything I've done":** EH to Gertrude Stein and Alice B. Toklas, August 28–31, 1924; *HemLtrs*, 2:151; EH to Edward J. O'Brien, September 12, 1924, *HemLtrs*, 2:154.

126   **until she finished her thesis:** JDP to WRM, September 1924, *FoCh*, 359.

127   **onto the bookstore shelves:** *HemPaYe*, 235.

14

129   **"immediately," Dos Passos told Rummy:** EH to George Breaker, August 27, 1924, *HemLtrs*, 2:148: JDP to WRM, Winter 1925, *FoCh*, 360.

129   **crippled him with caisson disease:** Quoted in Mariani, *The Broken Tower*, 151–152; McCullough, *The Great Bridge*, 387. *Caisson disease* is today called the bends or nitrogen narcosis and is caused by dissolved gases turning into bubbles inside the body upon depressurization.

130   **walks on the Brooklyn Bridge:** Seed, *Cinematic Fictions*, 131–132; O'Connell, *Remarkable, Unspeakable New York*, 140–141.

130   **turn into "hungry tongues":** See Spindler, "John Dos Passos and the Visual Arts."

131   **"immovable painful vegetable":** JDP to Robert Hillyer, quoted in *DPViCa*, 208.

131   **she had her own ambitions:** *DPViCa*, 208–209; *DPToLu*, 238–239.

131   **earned Hemingway any money:** EH to JDP, April 22, 1925, *HemLtrs*, 2:322–323.

131   **"friends expect him to go far":** Wilson, "Paris for Young Art," 8.

132   **he was not yet ready:** *HemCaBa*, 147.

133   **the leader of the pack:** *BSoL*, 142; *HemCaBa*, 150.

133   **"a dangerous friend to have":** From Sarason, *Hemingway and the Sun Set*, quoted in *HemJaMe*, 299.

134   **"I'm tearing those bastards apart":** Cannell, "Scenes with a Hero," 149–150; Svoboda, *Hemingway & The Sun Also Rises*, 8; *EHDoBa*, 154.

134   **channel into the harbor:** *TBT*, 150–151.

135   **along with some other titles:** *NYTBR*, October 18, 1925, BR8; *The Bookman*, December 1925, 482–483; Reynolds, *HemTPY*, 324.

135   **parody of Anderson's *Dark Laughter*:** EH to Sherwood Anderson, May 21, 1926, *HemLtrs*, 3:81.

136   **"you have wrought a masterpiece":** By log-rolling, Hemingway was referring to exchanging favors, usually in politics, by supporting each other's proposals. *ToS*, 83–84.

136   **only barriers to his eventual success:** *TBT*, 157–158.

136   **talked his friend out of publishing it:** Hemingway insisted when writing to his publisher that he had not submitted *The Torrents of Spring*, in hopes it would be turned down. "I consider it a good book and John Dos Passos, Louis Bromfield and Scott Fitzgerald, who are people of different tastes are enthusiastic about it." EH to Horace Liveright, January 19, 1926, *HemLtrs*, 3:21.

137   **remind Cannell of Japanese dolls:** Cannell, "Scenes with a Hero," 145–146.

137   **Smith chose to remain stateside:** *PWE*, 183; *DPViCa*, 210.

138   **"You are an expatriate, see":** *HemTPY*, 327; *SAR*, 120.

138   **experience made him different:** EH to EP, November 1925, *HemLtrs*, 2:415.

139   **"trying to grow young ever since":** Livengood, "Psychological Trauma: Shell Shock During WWI."

139   **writing about the trauma:** Siegfried Sasson and Wilfred Owen, two of the most famous poets of the conflict, were both patients of his during the war.

139   **"damn out of the whole show":** EH to FSF, December 15, 1925, *HemLtrs*, 2:446.

140   **"never far from their shoulders":** FSF to MP, December 30, 1925, *The Sons of Maxwell Perkins: Letters of F. Scott Fitzgerald, Ernest Hemingway, Thomas Wolfe and Their Editor* (Columbia: University of South Carolina Press, 2004), 57; *NYTBR*, November 29, 1925, BR5.

140   **"great whiteboard, Mr. Joyce's *Ulysses*":** Sinclair Lewis, *Saturday Review of Literature*, December 5, 1925, 361.

141   **"naturalistic fiction of the age":** Alan Tate, "Good Prose," *The Nation*, February 10, 1926, 160–162.

141   **hole in the back of his pants:** *EWSY*, 172–173.

141   **"mistake coupling the words":** EH to MP, April 8, 1926, *HemLtrs*, 3:53; *MT*, 12.

15

143   **"She's a swell girl":** *SAR*, 14.

144   **"when we parted company":** *AMF*, 215; *EWSY*, 173; *TBT*, 158–159.

144   **"Isn't it pretty to think so":** Svoboda, *Hemingway & The Sun Also Rises*, 94–95.

145   **seemed largely beyond its control:** FSF, *The Great Gatsby*, 115.

145   **playwriting were on his mind:** *Harvard Crimson*, October 18, 1926. The New York version of the play was entitled *The Garbage Man*.

145   **1917, also joined the effort:** *DPViCa*, 220; JDP to Daniel Aaron, April 9, 1959, *FoCh*, 619.

146   **case for readers of the *New Masses*:** *TBT*, 166–168.

147   **together for the Braintree robbery:** JDP, "The Pit and the Pendulum," *New Masses*, August 1926, 10–11 and 30; *TBT*, 167.

148   **"Save Sacco and Vanzetti":** *FtC*, 127.

148   **breakup with Crystal Ross:** *FoCh*, 341.

148   **"get along awfully well together":** *HTFMHem*, 173; 86; *PWE*, 211.

149   **material reward of passion:** *HemTAH*, 14.

149   **women remained a mystery to him:** EH to William B. Smith, December 3, 1925, *HemLtrs*, 2:429.

149   **"She's taking my husband":** Cannell, "Scenes with a Hero," 146.

150   **"getting very cock eyed drunk":** EH to Fitzgerald, May 4, 1926, *HemLtrs*, 3:70–71.

150   **matronly mother of Ernest's child:** *PWE*, 217–219; *HTFMHem*, 88–89. The time spent with his two women companions may have prompted Hemingway's novel *The Garden of Eden*, published posthumously, the title of which may have been inspired by a comment Dos Passos made.

16

153   **"season so crowded with good fiction":** *NYT*, October 23, 1926; *NYTBR*, October 24, 1926, BR37. For an excellent account of how the book was received, see Reynolds, *The Sun Also Rises*, and Hays, *Critical Reception of Hemingway's "The Sun Also Rises."*

153   **"literary English to shame":** *NYT*, October 31, 1926, BR7.

153   **"direct, natural, colloquial speech":** *New York Herald Tribune*, October 1, 1926, 4; *New York Sun*, November 6, 1916, 10.

154   **"time on the bibulous shadows":** *The Observer* (UK), June 12, 1927, 8.

154   **pitched the book into the fire:** *ChTr*, November 17, 1926, 13; Grace Hall Hemingway quoted in TYH, 53.

154   **"the article of writing himself":** *The Atlantic*, April 1927, 12.

154   **"dough-headed for not getting it":** *New Masses*, December 1926, 26.

155   **"god damn it and them":** Typewritten review with annotations, November 11, 1926; HEMJFK; JDP to EH, November 10, 1926 (probably mailed November 11, 1926), HEMJFK.

155   **"What a relief":** JDP to Robert Hillyer, Spring 1925, *FoCh*, 361; *TBT*, 170; *DPToLu*, 249.

156   **"The thing is perfectly done":** *Dallas Morning News*, January 16, 1927.

156   **and they parted as friends:** JDP to WRM, April 1916, *FoCh*, 364. According to Dos Passos's daughter, Lucy Coggin, Ross would occasionally telephone him late in life.

157   **their three-year-old son:** *PWE*, 227.

157   **"Mormon?" he suggested:** JDP to EH, November 10, 1926, HEMJFK. *Garden of Eden* is the name Hemingway used for a novel that was published

posthumously probably based on the time when he, Hadley, and Pauline were together in the Riviera.

157 **"and is rising steadily":** *HemCaBa*, 182.

158 **"reader that one tries to write for":** EH to MP, December 21, 1926, *HemLtrs*, 3:183.

158 **airs of the protagonist Jake Barnes:** JDP to EH, January 16, 1927, HEMJFK; also quoted in *DPViCa*, 224; *LAT*, April 17, 1927, 20.

158 **"those bastards apart," were furious:** The passage may be found in Book 1, Folder 194, p. 13, *The Sun Also Rises* manuscript, HEMJFK. Fitzgerald was also mentioned on p. 39 of the manuscript, but Hemingway eliminated references to both Dos Passos and Fitzgerald in subsequent drafts.

159 **"you anywhere from descriptions":** Cannell, "Scenes with a Hero," 150.

159 **slept with the "bloody bullfighter":** *TTG*, 56–57; *HemCaBa*, 179; *HemKeLy*, 371.

159 **to consider living elsewhere:** *BoGl*, December 18, 1927, B3. Smyth was a fine fellow to complain about Hemingway's ethics. In 1942 he was sent to prison for seven years for accepting Japanese money to publish pro-Japanese articles in a publication they purchased with the funds. *NYT*, November 13, 1942, 25.

159 **"Lay off and it always comes back":** EH to JDP, February 16, 1927, *HemLtrs*, 3:209.

160 **cashing in on his newfound fame:** Gallagher, "Waldo Peirce and Ernest Hemingway," 31.

160 **her disapproval of his writing:** EH to Clarence Hemingway, September 9–14, 1927, *HemLtrs*, 3:283–285.

160 **"Geezus I hate mighthabeens":** JDP to EH, March 27, 1927, *FoCh*, 368.

161 **"conspiracy to overturn the Government":** *FtC*, 53.

161 **"the drinking down here is amazing":** *DPViCa*, 225. I could not find any information about "Barbadian enfuriators" but learned that "Green Swizzles" are made primarily with white rum, crème de menthe, lime juice, bitters, and sugar.

161 **"execration of the civilized world":** *NYT*, August 8, 1927, 2.

161 **"effectually silenced the 'best minds'":** *Daily Worker*, August 16, 1927, 5.

161 **"in which to disperse. Move on":** *BoGF*, August 11, 1927, 1; *NYT*, August 11, 1927, 1.

162 **Only John Lawson came:** JDP to EW, August 19, 1927, *FoCh*, 371.

162 **took the group into custody:** *TBT*, 173. In the police wagon Dos Passos sat next to Millay. Examining her tiny frame, eyes that to him seemed violet colored and to others sea green, and the waves of bobbed copper hair, he was smitten. "Outside of being a passable poet," Dos Passos said, "Edna Millay was one of the most attractive women who ever put pen to paper."

163 **police attempting to restore order:** *NYT*, August 24, 1927, 1.

163 **"against a stone wall sometime":** JDP to EW, September 19, 1927, *FoCh*, 371.

163 **Make poem of that if you dare:** "They Are Dead Now—," *New Masses*, October 1927, 228–229.

164 **"as the public press can push it":** JDP to EH, Fall 1927, *FoCh*, 371–372.

17

165 **To Key West, he replied:** *TBT*, 198.

166 **"Atlantic Ocean looks in a gale":** Standiford, *Last Train to Paradise*, 148–149.

166 **"smallness of the beds":** *HemTAH*, 169.

166 **"I shall try to reach Cuba":** EH to Pauline Pfeiffer Hemingway, March 28, 1928, *HemLtrs*, 3:376–377.

167 **Pamplona the previous summer:** EH to MP, April 7, 1928, *HemLtrs*, 3:377–378; EH to Waldo Peirce, April 13, 1928, *HemLtrs*, 3:378–380.

167 **books to prove them wrong:** EH to MP, April 21, 1928, *HemLtrs*, 3:382–383.

168 **"one must first know the conditions":** *HemTH*, 173; JDP to EH. Remark made in "John Dos Passos: La Collection des *Archive du xxe siècle*." Translation by author.

168 **demands on the casual reader:** See Seed, "Media and Newsreels in Dos Passos' U.S.A."

168 **commonality to the group:** Peirce had also been the other artist along with Eben Given, whom Dos Passos had met in Provincetown, who had been given permission to make drawings of the front during the war.

169 **On some days the wait could be long:** Materials contained in the Waldo Peirce papers (WPP) confirm the date of these events; *HemCaBa*, 193.

169 **"like the Garden of Eden":** *TBT*, 201.

169 **best time he ever had in his life:** *TBT*, 199; EH to MP, June 7, 1928, *HemLtrs*, 3:393.

169 **often under a pseudonym:** A file containing the stories as well as a logbook recording her submissions may be seen at *JDPUVA*.

169 **Key West, avoiding its own kind:** *TBT*, 202.

170 **one day to be Mrs. Dos Passos:** The postcard has been preserved in JDPUVA. Hemingway Journals, August 13, 1928, HEMJFK.

170 **"this next book *has* to be good":** EH to MP, March 17, 1928, *HemLtrs*, 3:375.

170 **where doctors stitched him up:** EH to MP, March 17, 1928, *HemLtrs*, 3:373.

171 **combat shaped the narrative:** *HemTAH*, 166–167. Reynolds believes the accident and the blood triggered Hemingway's decision to write about the war at this point. In his biography, Baker concludes the same, though less directly.

171 *time bodily in the wind:* *FTA*, 47, The use of *chu-chu-chu-chu* in the passage led scholars to believe Hemingway was describing the sound of falling mortars rather than the noise they made when fired. Mortars do not make sound when falling.

171 **more than two hundred pages long:** EH to MP, May 31, 1928, *HemLtrs*, 3:387.

171 *inside a tent or behind a falls:* *FTA*, 98.

172 **"kill time while *woiking* on a novel":** EH to Waldo Peirce, July 6, 1928, *HemLtrs*, 3:405.

172 **pulls the trigger, it fails to fire:** *FTA*, 177.

173 **"Give it to me," she says:** *FTA*, 276.

18

175 **her ability to irritate him:** The trip to Oak Park is described in detail in *Hem-TAH*, 198–203.

175 **Oak Park that his father had died:** *HemTAH*, 207.

176 **a growing paranoia:** See *HemCaBa*, 199 and *HemTAH*, 212.

176 **"my father is the one I cared about":** EH to MP, December 9, 1928, *HemLtrs*, 3:479.

176 **"I want like hell to see you":** JDP to EH, December 20, 1928, HEMJFK; EH to JDP, January 4, 1929, *HemLtrs*, 3:491–492.

177 **"has attempted to confront it":** Edmund Wilson, "Dos Passos and the Social Revolution," *New Republic*, April 17, 1929, 256–257.

177 **"somewhat shattered by the encounter":** JDP to EW, March 1929, *FoCh*, 391. I'm not sure what Dos Passos meant about the reference to eating wild herons. I could not find evidence that the birds were hunted for food.

177 **Americans were welcomed:** While Dos Passos was in Russia the Murphys took care of his mail. Gerald arranged for incoming royalty checks to be processed through his bank and made available to Dos Passos in rubles. See Miller, *Letters from the Lost Generation*, 33.

177 *Battleship Potemkin* **had attracted wide attention:** *TBT*, 174–196.

178 **Hemingway during a stop in Dagestan:** JDP to EH, September 1928, *FoCh*, 387.

178 **Dos Passos wrote to E. E. Cummings:** JDP to EEC, September 1928, *FoCh*, 387.

178 **necessity to brush one's teeth:** *TBT*, 70.

179 **"like being let out of jail":** *TBT*, 196.

179 *white except for the leaves:* *FTA*, 3.

180 *that is all I can promise you:* Transcript for *A Farewell to Arms* Alternative Endings—Sean Hemingway, www.ttbook.org/book/transcript/farewell-arms-alternative-endings-sean-hemingway.

180 **Hemingway told Perkins:** EH to MP, March 11, 1929, *HemLtrs*, 3:550.

181 **off-putting to the shy Dos Passos:** Some accounts make it seem as if it were a coincidence Katy Smith showed up in Key West a second time during a Dos Passos visit. As she made clear to Pauline in 1928, the two were becoming romantic, and the 1929 trip was certainly a planned rendezvous.

181 **"really hated his mother," he said:** *HemCaBa*, 200; *TBT*, 210.

182 **"first job was to think and do":** *DPViCa*, 257–258.

182 **"reminds me a lot of Wemedge":** KDP to JDP, dated Sunday, written while John Dos Passos was in Chicago in July 1929, *JDPUVA*.

183 **Hemingway a few days later:** JDP to EH, August 22, 1929, HEMJFK, quoted in *DPViCa*, 261.

183 **"I'm happy as hell about it":** EH to JDP, September 4, 1929, *HemSeLtrs*, 303.

19

185 **"family journal in Boston":** EH to MP, June 7, 1919, *HemSeLtrs*, 297; *Hem-KeLy*, 382; JDP to EH, July 1, 1929, HEMJFK, quoted in *HemJaMe*, 388.

186 **"beautiful book," Hutchison concluded:** *NYT*, September 29, 1929, BR3.

186 **wrote an ecstatic letter of praise:** *ChTr*, September 28, 1929, 11; *HemJaMe*, 390.

186 **"since there was an English language":** *New Masses*, December 1929, 16.

186 **"King of the fiction racket":** JDP to EH, October 24, 1929, HEMJFK, quoted in *DPViCa*, 263.

187 **"Nothing's gone much bigger than that":** JDP to EH, August 22, 1929, HEMJFK; EH to JDP, September 4, 1929, *HemSeLtrs*, 303.

188 **"could hardly have sold less anyway":** *NYT*, January 6, 1930, 55; *TBT*, 205.

188 **"formal French way," said Dos Passos:** *TBT*, 202–203; Cook, *Guide to Paris*, 107.

189 **"heartbreaking to be with them":** EH to FSF, December 12, 1929, *HemSeLtrs*, 314; *TBT*, 203.

189 **was also found dead at the scene:** *NYT*, December 11, 1929, 1.

189 **"Bohemian resorts of Montparnasse":** "Hemingway Gives Up Old Life with Literary Success," *New York Evening Post*, November 18, 1929, 6.

190 **"For a while it worked":** *TBT*, 203.

190 **"models for the Happy Life":** *BSoL*, 186–187.

190 **"sweeping view of the whole country":** *Time*, March 3, 1930, 78.

191 **"I have read since the War":** Edmund Wilson, "Dahlberg, Dos Passos, and Wilder," *New Republic*, March 26, 1930, 157.

191 **"sometimes envies Mr. Dos Passos":** EH to FSF, October 9, 1928, *HemSeLtrs*, 288.

192 **liked an appreciative audience:** EH to Henry Strater, September 10, 1930, *HemSeLtrs*, 328.

192 **"smell him," said Dos Passos:** *TBT*, 204–205.

193 **arm hanging limp and askew:** *HemCaBa*, 216–221; *Hem30s*, 32; *NYT*, November 3, 1930, 29; *Billings Gazette*, November 2, 1930.

194 **"come out to see him die":** Archibald MacLeish to Carlos Baker, August 9, 1963, quoted in *HemSeLtrs*, 332.

20

195 **It pleased him enormously:** EH to MP, December 26, 1931, *HemSeLtrs*, 347.

195 **birth of their second child:** EH to WP, December 31, 1931, *HemSeLtrs*, 344.

196 *I have found true about it:* DITA, 1.

196 **dust with Spanish brandy:** *DITA*, 266.

196 **Unknown Soldier at Arlington Cemetery:** *USA*, 756 and 761.

197 **"weather for the House of Morgan":** *USA*, 648.

198 **"Hell it's only a book after all":** *DPToLu*, 296; JDP to Eugene Saxton, November 1931, *FoCh*, 400.

198 **"ought to be done," he wrote:** JDP to EH, February 1932, *FoCh*, 402–403.

198 **his take on Dos Passos's 1919:** EH to JDP, March 26, 1932, *HemSeLtrs*, 355; EH to JDP, May 30, 1932, *HemSeLtrs*, 360.

199 **"don't let them get to be symbols":** Unlike the advice Dos Passos had provided for *Death in the Afternoon*, much of which Hemingway had followed, Dos

Passos did not see this letter until after he returned from Mexico and the book was out.

199 **The case never went to court:** Members of the National Committee for the Defense, *Harlan Miners Speak*, 2.

200 **"tidied up for the visitors":** Ibid., 278.

200 **nothing came of it:** *TBT*, 207.

200 **"There is only good and bad writing":** EH to JDP, May 30, 1932, *HemSeLtrs*, 360; EH to Paul Romaine, July 6, 1932, *HemSeLtrs*, 363.

201 **"goodbye to Martin Arrowsmith":** *NYT*, April 13, 1932, BR2.

201 **Dos Passos's most recent work:** *NYT*, September 25, 1932, BR5.

201 **"with an art which is supreme":** *ChTr*, September 29, 1932, 13.

202 **He had his trophy:** EH to JDP, October 14, 1932, *HemSeLtrs*, 374; *HemCaBa*, 222–223.

202 **ask Hemingway for a loan:** EH to JDP, October 14, 1932, *HemSeLtrs*, 373.

202 **"people cannot want to do that":** MP to FSF, quoted in *DPViCa*, 309–310.

21

203 **summer for the shooting:** *DPToLu*, 315; *LAT*, May 26, 1932, A9.

204 **"Pauline it's awful":** JDP to EH, April 24, 1933, *FoCh*, 425.

204 **"had me spooked," he wrote:** EH to JDP, March 26, 1932, *HemSeLtrs*, 354; EH to JDP, April 15, 1933, *HemSeLtrs*, 389.

205 **"nothing of adequate cojones":** *Hem30s*, 115.

205 **drawing to be submitted later:** EH to Arnold Gingrich, June 7, 1933, *HemSeLtrs*, 393.

205 **nervous about Spain's future:** See Cordero, "The Spanish Translation of *Manhattan Transfer* and Censorship."

206 **"instead of his sitting at mine":** FSF to Dr. C. Jonathan Slocum, April 8, 1934, reprinted in *NYT Magazine*, December 1, 1996; *TBT*, 209–210.

206 **Dos Passos quipped to Hemingway:** *DPViCa*, 313.

206 **"by the Great American Public":** JDP to EH, May 25, 1933, *FoCh*, 431.

207 **"leave his private life alone":** EH to MP, December 7, 1932, *HemSeLtrs*, 379.

207 **matadors disappointed him:** EH, "The Friend of Spain," *Esquire*, January 1934, 139.

207 **Spanish police impoundment lot:** *TBT*, 226–228.

208 **"His partisanship was in various toreros":** *SAR*, 249–250; *TBT*, 220.

208 **a Dos Passos wartime letter:** EH to Mary Pfeiffer, October 16, 1933, *HemSeLtrs*, 398.

209 **trilogy still awaiting completion:** *Esquire*, January 1934, 27.

209 **he was still married to Hadley:** *NYT*, April 4, 1934, 18.

210 **"things were never quite so good":** *TBT*, 220.

210 **"make them do what they would do":** EH to FSF, May 28, 1934, *HemSeLtrs*, 407–408.

211 **"grieving mate with the other":** *HemCaBa*, 261–262; Hendrickson, *Hemingway's Boat*, 158.

211 **"he is at least an accurate fool":** Saroyan, *The Daring Young Man on the Flying Trapeze*, 34.

211 **"He was asking for it wasn't he":** EH, "Notes on Life and Letters," *Esquire*, January 1935, 21.

211 **"drop of a hat when he's grown":** *TBT*, 219.

211 **Dos Passos told his editor:** JDP to Charles A. Pearce, April 1934, *FoCh*, 437.

212 **"my feet are in the flypaper now":** JDP to KDP, quoted in *DPViCa*, 329.

212 **father in Columbia, Missouri:** JDP to EH, July 27, 1934, *FoCh*, 437.

212 **order in time for the filming:** Apparently writers Baxter Sam Winston, David Hertz, and Oran Schee were mostly responsible for the script in the end.

212 **"and still receive my salary":** JDP to Edmund Wilson, August 24, 1934, *FoCh*, 440.

212 **another pregnancy that was failing:** Many of John Dos Passos's letters speak cryptically of Katy's visits to doctors that required, as he once wrote, "skillful handling." See JDP to EH, May 1935, *FoCh*, 473.

213 **"world about it in good prose":** *NYT*, October 27, 1993, 17.

213 **"attacks the capitalist system":** Comment contained in *HemCaBa*, endnote, 612.

22

215 **might possibly be execution:** Quintanilla, *Waiting at the Shore*, 121.

215 **wrote, drank, and shared their drafts:** EH to Arnold Gingrich, November 16, 1934, *HemSeLtrs*, 411.

216 **"hooked," said Dos Passos:** *TBT*, 216.

216 **wired Cowley to retract his offer:** Telegraph cited in JDP to MC, December 1934, *FoCh*, 457. At this moment Dos Passos was also in the midst of a squabble with Cowley over a letter he had sent that he considered private and Cowley had published. They made up, particularly after Dos Passos apologized for losing his temper and remained good friends.

216 **greatly exaggerating the turnout:** Quintanilla, *Waiting at the Shore*, 122.

216 **"I can't find any," he confessed:** JDP to Gerald and Sara Murphy, March 18, 1932, *FoCh*, 467.

217 **"we know will never reach port":** EH to Gerald and Sara Murphy, March 19, 1935, *HemSeLtrs*, 412.

217 **Dos Passos lost their fish:** EH, "On Being Shot Again," *Esquire*, June 1935, 25, 156–157; JDP to Patrick Murphy, April 1935, Miller, *Letters from the Lost Generation*, 129. Also see Hendrickson, *Hemingway's Boat*, 201–219.

218 **"aghast but it's very exciting":** KDP to Gerald Murphy, June 20, 1935, Miller, *Letters from the Lost Generation*, 132.

218 **"all of us," Dos Passos recalled:** *TBT*, 211.

218 **lack of friends, Hemingway concluded:** EH to Ivan Kashkin, August 19, 1935, *HemSeLtrs*, 418–419.

219 **"vodka and malt herring":** JDP to EH, December 24, 1928, HEMJFK.

219 **"he's in on the big money":** JDP to MC, December 1, 1934, *FoCh*, 456.

219 **"fight had got to be made on them":** JDP to MC, May 28, 1935, *FoCh*, 477.

219   "but I don't really think so": JDP to EW, January 1935, *FoCh*, 462.

220   "balloons, flies between their legs": EH to MP, September 7, 1935, *HemSeLtrs*, 422.

221   "there to die?" Hemingway asked: *New Masses*, September 17, 1935.

221   "die like a dog for no good reason": EH, "Notes on the Next War," *Esquire*, September 1935, 19 and 156.

221   here without you," he wrote: EH to JDP, December 17, 1935, *HemSeLtrs*, 425–426.

221   hardly needed an infusion of cash: *DPViCa*, 344.

222   "did I ever get mixed up in it?": *DPViCa*, 342; JDP to EH, February 7, 1936, *FoCh*, 483.

222   "to reply to his critics," he wrote: *NYT*, October 25, 1935, 19.

223   the pleasures of old days: *EWSY*, 272; *Hem30s*, 220.

224   The silence was telling: *DPViCa*, 348.

225   letters to Murphy and Dos Passos: *Hem30s*, 214–215. Dos Passos was not present on Key West when the fight occurred.

225   "quarreled when he was feeling best": EH, "The Snows of Kilimanjaro," *SoK*, 17.

225   he might soon be on it: *TBT*, 219.

23

227   rather, it signaled war: *WaPo*, November 20, 2007.

228   the brutality faced decapitation: For an excellent account of the war, see Hochschild, *Spain in Our Hearts*.

228   stood ready to do whatever he could: JDP to EH, August 1936, *FoCh*, 486–487.

228   his friend's supposed purity: Malcolm Cowley perceptively points out that Dos Passos's "chief point of exception was to be a radical in the 1920s, when most of his friends were indifferent to politics, and to become increasingly conservative in the following decade, when most of his friends were becoming radical." See Cowley, *Exile's Return*, 292.

228   the Swiss Alps, or Key West: Sections that were eventually cut from the book are quoted in Robert E. Fleming, "The Libel of Dos Passos in *To Have and Have Not*." Information about this incident is also drawn from Pizer, "The Hemingway-Dos Passos Relationship."

229   Dos Passos had publicly criticized: *THaHN*, 186.

229   meant his friend's ruin as a writer: EH to JDP, September 4, 1929, *HemSeLtrs*, 303–304. "You can trace the moral decay of his [Edmund Wilson] criticism on a parallel line with the decline of Dos Passos' writing through their increasing dishonesty about money and other things, mostly their being dominated by women." EH to MP, February 25, 1944, *HemSeLtrs*, 557.

229   his use of them was libelous: *Esquire*, December 1966, 189 and 316–317.

230   "'seeing' into American literature": Unknowingly—or, more likely, knowingly—Hemingway was quoting Gingrich.

231   rum, lime, and grapefruit juice: Rollyson, *Nothing Ever Happens to the Brave*, 90.

231 **then went on to New York City:** Moorehead, *Gellhorn: A Twentieth Century Life*, 105.

231 **Dos Passos reported to Hemingway:** JDP to EH, January 9, 1937, *FoCh*, 504.

231 **F. Scott Fitzgerald on hearing the news:** Donnelly, *Sara & Gerald*, 114; Miller, *Letters from the Lost Generation*, 72.

232 **himself might go and drive one:** *NYT*, January 12, 1937, 4.

232 **"any dough," Dos Passos told him:** Harry Sylvester, a young aspiring Catholic novelist, contacted Hemingway after having felt put off by Dos Passos's muted reaction to news about the execution of priests in Spain. "Dos doesn't know or understand you nor has he the respect for your faith that I have," Hemingway continued. "That is ignorance. There is no snobbishness like radical snobbishness and when it is working in Dos he is not natural nor much fun." But Dos Passos was more circumspect than Sylvester thought. He was growing worried about what he was hearing about atrocities being committed by both parties at war in Spain. EH to Harry Sylvester, February 5, 1937, *HemSeLtrs*, 456. JDP to EH, January 9, 1937, *FoCh*, 503.

232 **"but I am going with them":** Moorehead, *Gellhorn: A Twentieth-Century Life*, 107.

233 **fleeing from the fighting in Madrid:** *NYT*, March 17.1937, 12.

233 **documentary with Ivens and Ferno:** *TTiF*, 116.

233 **"tinsel of nineteenth century whoopee":** *JBW*, 330.

234 **government was supporting Franco:** *JBW*, 345–346.

234 **led to his arrest was cleared up:** Preston, *We Saw Spain Die*, 69 and 73.

235 **reluctant to speak about him:** *TTiF*, 128. The theory that Robles was a liaison officer is convincingly explained in Preston, *We Saw Spain Die*, 65.

235 **inquiries on Dos Passos's behalf:** JDP to editors of the *New Republic*, July 1939, *FoCh*, 527–528.

235 **expansive and ornate street:** *JBW*, 361. Accounts sometimes mention that Dos Passos procured a ride with André Malraux, whom he knew. However, Amanda Vaill's assiduous research properly identifies the two journalists as Lucien Vogel and Philippe Lamour. See *HoFl*, 159.

236 **his service as an ambulance driver:** JDP, "The Road to Madrid," *Esquire*, 243. Typos introduced into the version of this article published in *JBW* wrecks the beauty of the sentence.

236 **items unavailable in wartime Spain:** *DPToLu*, 368.

236 **"Absolutely and without reservations":** *Ken* (a biweekly political magazine), June 30, 1938, 26, Harry Ransom Center, University of Texas, Austin, TX.

237 **been one of their many victims:** Preston, *We Saw Spain Die*, 79 and 67.

237 **the execution had been a mistake:** JDP to editors of the *New Republic*, July 1939, *FoCh*, 527–528.

237 **Dos Passos wrote in one of his dispatches:** *JBW*, 374.

239 **"they saw an airplane in the sky":** *JBW*, 388.

240 **tell the truth as he saw it:** This account is based on Dos Passos's fictional rendering of the moment on pages 98 and 99 in *CeEb*, which is supported by his biographers. See *DPToLu*, 374, and *DPViCa*, 372.

Epilogue

241 **"ends are always illusionary":** JDP to JL, Fall 1937, *FoCh*, 514.

242 **meals rekindled Hemingway's wrath:** JDP to JL, November 4, 1937, *FoCh*, 513; *Redbook*, February 1938.

242 **wanted anything to do with him:** "If with your hatred of communists," Hemingway wrote, "you feel justified in attacking, for money, the people who are still fighting that war I think you should at least try to get your facts right." EH to JDP, March 26, 1938, *HemSeLtrs*, 464.

243 **"Perhaps it is just old Harvard loyalty":** *Ken* (a biweekly political magazine), June 30, 1938, 26.

243 **now took up a block of Chicago:** KDP to EH, September 17, 1938, and KDP to Pauline Hemingway, October 31, 1938, HEMJFK, quoted in *DPViCa*, 390.

244 **later awarded a Bronze Star in 1947:** *HemJaMe*, 535. A hearing was held after complaints about Hemingway's behavior were filed. He was cleared of any charges.

244 **"damn heart and another to finish her":** *HemJaMe*, 529; Bruccoli, *The Only Thing That Counts*, 333.

244 **most important contemporary writers:** *LAT*, June 27, 1947, A12; "An Interview with William Faulkner: 1947," ed. Lavon Rascoe, republished in Inge, *Conversations with William Faulkner*, 71.

245 **"a Negro as hope we would have":** EH to William Faulkner, July 23, 1947, *HemSeLtrs*, 623–624.

245 **their automobile was sheared off:** Account of accident drawn from *DPToLu*, 431–433, and *DPViCa*, 454–455, as well as news articles such as *NYT*, September 14, 1947, 9. Katy was laid to rest in a Cape Cod cemetery. The slate headstone reads:

KATHARINE SMITH
BELOVED WIFE OF JOHN DOS PASSOS
MY SWEET MY LOST LOVE

246 **"killed her last Saturday":** EH to Marion Smith, May 31, 1948, *HemSeLtrs*, 635; EH to Charles Scribner, September 18, 1947, *HemSeLtrs*, 628. Hemingway had the day of the week wrong.

246 **"They were as happy as bedbugs":** JDP to Sara Murphy, September 8, 1948, *FoCh*, 585; *TTG*, 127.

247 **"together in Paris like in the old days":** EH to JDP, May 29, 1949, HEMJFK; JDP to EH, June 23, 1949, *FoCh*, 588.

247 **"any old Portuguese to have":** EH to JDP, September 17, 1949, HEMJFK.

247 **was born not long after:** *DPToLu*, 448.

247 **"novelist," said the *Washington Post*:** *NYT*, December 2, 1951, 245; *WaPo*, December 2, 1951, F7.

248 **Dos Passos's work among critics:** EH to JDP, November 8, 1952, *HemSeLtrs*, 793.

248 **walked into the Hemingway buzz saw:** JDP to EH, October 23, 1951, *FoCh*, 597.

249   **Paris the pilot fish was Dos Passos:** *MoFe*, 213.

249   **"pilot fish was a friend," he wrote:** *MoFe*, 215.

249   **died of congestive heart failure:** *DPToLu*, 499.

250   **"fourth chair occupied by Dos Passos":** *New Yorker*, October 31, 2005, 82.

250   **"But for many of us it was senseless":** Lawson, *Haystack in France*, 46A.

250   **another war took it from them:** Cowley, *Exile's Return*, 38.

251   **love affair, and, ultimately, himself:** Donald Ogden Stewart told author Bertram Sarason that Hemingway had a need to destroy the love of his friends. He listed Dos Passos, Fitzgerald, Gerald Murphy, and himself of the victims. In the end, Stewart said, there was no one left to obliterate but himself. Sarason, *Hemingway and the Sun Set*, note, 107.

251   **"This may be a lesson to us all":** EH to JDP, September 17, 1949, HEMJFK.

BIBLIOGRAPHY

In addition to the books listed above, here is a selected listing of works consulted in the preparation of this book. Still other sources used only once may be found in the endnotes.

Books

Anderson, Sherwood. *Sherwood Anderson's Memoirs*. New York: Harcourt, Brace and Company, 1942.

Barthas, Louis. *Poilu: The World War I Notebooks of Corporal Louis Barthas, Barrelmaker, 1914–1918*. New Haven, Yale University Press, 2014.

Baxter, John. *The Golden Moments of Paris: A Guide to the Paris of the 1920s*. New York: Museyon, 2014.

Benson, Jackson H. *New Critical Approaches to the Short Stories of Ernest Hemingway*. Durham, NC: Duke University Press, 1990.

Berman, Ronald. *Fitzgerald, Hemingway, and the Twenties*. Tuscaloosa: University of Alabama Press, 2001.

Bone, Gertrude. *Days in Old Spain*. London: MacMillan & Co, 1938.

Bonsor, N. R. P. *North Atlantic Seaway: An Illustrated History of the Passenger Services Linking the Old World with the New*, Vol. 2. Newton Abbot, UK: David & Charles, 1956.

Bouvet, Vincent, and Gérard Durozoi. *Paris: Between the Wars, 1919–1939, Art, Life & Culture*. New York: Vendome Press, 2010.

Bowerman, Guy Emerson Jr. *The Compensations of War: The Diary of an Ambulance Driver During the Great War*. Austin: University of Texas Press, 1983.

Bruccoli, Matthew J., ed. *Conversations with Ernest Hemingway*. Jackson, MS: University of Mississippi Press, 1986.

————, ed. *Ernest Hemingway, Cub Reporter: Kansas City Star Stories*. Pittsburgh: University of Pittsburgh Press, 1970.

————, ed. *Fitzgerald and Hemingway: A Dangerous Friendship*. New York: Carroll & Graf, 1994.

————, ed. *F. Scott Fitzgerald: A Life in Letters*. New York: Charles Scribner's Sons, 1994.

————. *The Only Thing That Counts: The Ernest Hemingway/Maxwell Perkins Correspondence, 1925–1947*. New York: Scribner, 1996.

Castillo-Puche, José Luis. *Hemingway in Spain: A Personal Reminiscence of Hemingway's Years in Spain by His Friend*. New York: Doubleday, 1974.

Cecchin, Giovanni. *Con Hemingway e Dos Passos: Sui Campi di Battaglia Italiani Della Grande Guerra*. Milano: Mursia, 1980.

Cook, Stephen S. *Guide to Paris: With Specially Engraved Map, and Vocabulary of French Phrases*. T. Cook & Son, 1900.

Cowley, Malcolm. *Exile's Return: A Literary Odyssey of the 1920's*. New York: Viking Press, 1951.

————. *The Long Voyage: Selected Letters of Malcolm Cowley*. Edited by Hans Bak. Cambridge, MA: Harvard University Press, 2014.

Dabney, Lewis M. *Edmund Wilson: A Life in Literature*. New York: Farrar, Straus & Giroux, 2005.

Dabney, Ross. *The Good Fight*. Privately published.

Donaldson, Scott. *By Force of Will: The Life and Art of Ernest Hemingway*. New York: Viking Press, 1977.

Donnelly, Honoria Murphy, with Richard N. Billings. *Sara & Gerald: Villa America and After*. New York: Times Books, 1982.

Eastman, Max. *Love and Revolution: My Journey Through an Epoch*. New York: Random House, 1964.

Ellis, John. *Eye-Deep in Hell: Trench Warfare in World War I*. Baltimore: Johns Hopkins University Press, 1976.

Fenton, Charles A. *The Apprenticeship of Ernest Hemingway: The Early Years*. New York: Farrar, Straus & Young, 1954.

Fitzgerald, F. Scott. *The Great Gatsby*. New York, Wordsworth Editions, 1993.

Flanner, Janet. *Paris Was Yesterday, 1925–1939*. New York: Viking Press, 1972.

Florczyk, Steven. *Hemingway, The Red Cross, and the Great War*. Kent, OH: Kent State University, 2014.

Griffin, Peter. *Along with Youth: Hemingway, the Early Years*. New York: Oxford University Press, 1985.

Hays, Peter L. *Critical Reception of Hemingway's "The Sun Also Rises."* Rochester, NY: Camden House, 2011.

Hemingway, Leicester. *My Brother, Ernest Hemingway*. Cleveland, OH: World Pub. Co., 1962.

Hendrickson, Paul. *Hemingway's Boat: Everything He Loved in Life, and Lost, 1924–1961*. New York: Knopf, 2011.

Herbst, Josephine. *Starched Blue Sky of Spain*. New York: HarperCollins, 1991.

Hochschild, Adam. *Spain in Our Hearts: Americans in the Spanish Civil War, 1936–1939*. Boston: Houghton Mifflin Harcourt, 2016.

Hook, Andrew, ed. *Dos Passos: A Collection of Critical Essays*. Englewood Cliffs, NJ: Prentice-Hall, 1974.

Howe, Irving. *Sherwood Anderson*. Palo Alto, CA: Stanford University Press, 1951.

Inge, M. Thomas, ed. *Conversations with William Faulkner*. Jackson: University Press of Mississippi, 1999.

Kert, Bernice. *The Hemingway Women*. New York: W. W. Norton, 1983.

Koch, Stephen. *The Breaking Point: Hemingway, Dos Passos, and the Murder of José Robles*. Berkeley, CA: Counterpoint, 2005.

Landsberg, Melvin. *Dos Passos' Path to U.S.A.: A Political Biography, 1912–1936*. Boulder: Colorado Associated University Press, 1972.

———. *John Dos Passos' Correspondence with Arthur K. McComb of "Learn to Sing the Carmagnole*. Niwot: University Press of Colorado, 1991.

Langer, Elinor. *Josephine Herbst*. Boston: Little, Brown and Company, 1984.

Levenstein, Harvey. *Seductive Journey: American Tourists in France from Jefferson to the Jazz Age*. Chicago: University of Chicago Press, 2000.

Mariani, Paul. *The Broken Tower: A Life of Hart Crane*. New York: W.W. Norton, 1999.

Maxtone-Graham, John. *Liners to the Sun*. Lanham, MD: Sheridan House, 2000.

McAlmon, Robert, and Kay Boyle. *Being Geniuses Together*. London: Hogarth Press, 1984.

McCullough, David. *The Great Bridge: The Epic Story of the Building of the Brooklyn Bridge*. New York: Simon & Schuster, 1972.

Members of the National Committee for the Defense. *Harlan Miners Speak: Report on Terrorism in the Kentucky Coal Fields*. Lexington: University Press of Kentucky, 2008.

Michener, James. *Iberia: Spanish Travels and Reflections*. New York: Fawcett Crest, 1982.

Miller, Linda Patterson, ed. *Letters from the Lost Generation*. New Brunswick, NJ: Rutgers University Press, 1991.

Moorehead, Caroline. *Gellhorn: A Twentieth-Century Life*. New York: Henry Holt and Company, 2003.

Morton, Brian N. *Americans in Paris: An Anecdotal Street Guide*. Ann Arbor, MI: Olivia & Hill Press, 1984.

O'Connell, Shaun. *Remarkable, Unspeakable New York*. Boston: Beacon Press, 1997.

Ogle, Maureen. *Key West: History of an Island of Dreams*. Gainesville: University Press of Florida, 2003.

Ousby, Ian. *The Road to Verdun: France, Nationalism and the First World War*. London: Jonathan Cape, 2002.

Pizer, Donald, *Toward a Modernist Style: John Dos Passos*. New York: Bloomsbury, 2013.

Preston, Paul. *We Saw Spain Die: Foreign Correspondents in the Spanish Civil War*. New York: Skyhorse Publications, 2009.

Quintanilla, Paul. *Waiting at the Shore: Art, Revolution, and Exile in the Life of Spanish Artist Luis Quintanilla*. Brighton: Sussex Academic Press, 2014.

Reynolds, Michael S. *Hemingway's Reading, 1910–1940*. Princeton: Princeton University Press.

———. *The Sun Also Rises: A Novel of the Twenties*. Boston: Twayne Publishers, 1988.

Rhodes, Charles Elbert. *Old Testament Narratives*. New York: Scott, Foresman and Co., 1915.

Rideout, Walter B. *Sherwood Anderson: A Writer in America*, vol. 1. Madison, WI: University of Wisconsin Press, 2006.

Rollyson, Carl. *Nothing Ever Happens to the Brave: The Story of Martha Gellhorn*. New York: St. Martin's Press, 1990.

Sanderson, Rena. *Hemingway's Italy*. Baton Rouge: Louisiana University Press, 2006.

Sarason, Bertram. *Hemingway and the Sun Set*. Washington, DC: Microcard Editions, 1972.

Saroyan, William. *The Daring Young Man on the Flying Trapeze*. New York: New Directions Classic, 1997 (originally published in 1934).

Sawyer-Lauçanno, Christopher. *E. E. Cummings: A Biography*. Naperville, IL: Sourcebooks, 2004.

Scott, Phil. *Hemingway's Hurricane: The Great Florida Keys Storm of 1935*. New York: McGraw Hill, 2006.

Seed, David. *Cinematic Fictions*. Liverpool, UK: Liverpool University Press, 2009.

Segrave, Kerry. *Vision Aids in America: A Social History of Eyewear and Sight Correction Since 1900*. Jefferson, NC: McFarland, 2011.

Sokoloff, Alice. *Hadley: The First Mrs. Hemingway*. New York: Dodd, Mead, 1973.

Standiford, Les. *Last Train to Paradise: Henry Flagler and the Spectacular Rise and Fall of the Railroad That Crossed an Ocean*. New York: Crown Publishers, 2002.

Stein, Gertrude. *What Are Masterpieces*. Los Angeles: Conference Press, 1940.

Svoboda, Frederic Joseph. *Hemingway & The Sun Also Rises: The Crafting of a Style*. Lawrence: University Press of Kansas, 1983.

Thompson, J. Lee. *Never Call Retreat: Theodore Roosevelt and the Great War*. New York: Palgrave, 2013.

Walker, Robert W. *The Namesake: A Biography of Theodore Roosevelt, Jr.* New York: Brick Tower Press, 2008.

White, William, ed. *By-Line: Ernest Hemingway*. New York: Scribner, 1967.

Articles

Cannell, Kathleen. "Scenes with a Hero." *Connecticut Review* 2, no. 1, 1968, reprinted in Sarason, *Hemingway and the Sun Set*.

Carey, Craig. "Mr. Wilson's War: Peace, Neutrality, and Entangling Alliances in Hemingway's *In Our Time*." *Hemingway Review* 31, no. 2 (Spring 2012): 6–26.

Cordero, María Bautista. "The Spanish Translation of *Manhattan Transfer* and Censorship." *Estudios de Traducción* 3 (2013): 149–162.

Cowley, Malcolm. "John Dos Passos: 1896–1970." *Proceedings*, 1971.

Donaldson, Scott. "The Jilting of Ernest Hemingway." *Virginia Quarterly* 65, no. 4 (Fall 1989).

Fleming, Robert E. "The Libel of Dos Passos in *To Have and Have Not.*" *Modern Literature* 15, no. 4 (Spring 1989): 597–601.

Gallagher, Willliam. "Waldo Peirce and Ernest Hemingway: Mirror Images." *Hemingway Review* 23, no. 1 (Fall 2003): 24–41.

Hancuff, Rich. "John Dos Passos, Mike Gold, and the Birth of the New Masses." *Reconstruction* 8, no. 1 (2008).

Hays, Peter L. "Hemingway as Social and Political Writer." *Hemingway Review* 34, no. 2 (Spring 2015): 111–117.

Hughson, Lois. "Dos Passos' World War: Narrative Technique and History." *Studies in the Novel* 12, no. 1 (Spring 1980).

Lewis, Robert W. "Hemingway in Italy: Making It Up." *Journal of Modern Literature* 9, no. 2 (May 1982).

Livengood, Shelby. "Psychological Trauma: Shell Shock During WWI." *Journal of History and Social Science* (Fall 2011). https://hssjournal.files.wordpress.com/2012/01/shelby-shell-shock.pdf.

Ludington, Townsend. "Spain and the Hemingway-Dos Passos Relationship." *American Literature* 60, no. 2 (May 1988): 270–273.

Nolan, Charles J. Jr. "Hemingway's 'Out of Season': The Importance of Close Reading." *Rocky Mountain Review of Language and Literature* 53, no. 2 (Fall 1999): 45–58.

Pizer, Donald. "Hemingway in Action: A Dos Passos Painting from the 1924 Pamplona Fiesta." *Hemingway Review* 35, no. 1 (Fall 2015): 97–101.

———. "John Dos Passos in the 1920s: The Development of a Modernist Style." *Mosaic* 45, no. 4 (December, 2012): 51–68.

———. "John Dos Passos' 'Rosinante to the Road Again' and the Modernist Expatriate Imagination." *Journal of Modern Literature* 21, no 1 (Summer, 1997): 137–150.

———. "The Hemingway-Dos Passos Relationship." *Journal of Modern Literature* 13, no. 1 (March 1986): 111–128.

Putnam, Thomas. "Hemingway on War and Its Aftermath." *Prologue* 38, no. 1 (Spring 2006).

Rohrkemper, John. "Mr. Dos Passos' War." *Modern Fiction Studies* 30, no.1 (Spring 1984).

Schmidt, Amy. "Forty Plus Coats of Paint: Pauline Pfeiffer-Hemingway as an (Almost) Delta Debutante." *Arkansas Review: A Journal of Delta Studies* 45, no. 2 (August 2014): 87–100.

Seed, David. "Media and Newsreels in Dos Passos' *U.S.A.*" *Journal of Narrative Theory* 14, no. 3 (Fall 1984): 182–192.

Spindler, Michael. "John Dos Passos and the Visual Arts." *Journal of American Studies* 15, no. 3 (December 1981): 391–405.

Sterling, Robert E. "The Libel of Dos Passos in *To Have and Have Not.*" *Journal of Modern Literature* 15, no. 4 (Spring 1989): 597–601.

Stewart, Matthew C. "Ernest Hemingway and World War I: Combatting Recent Psychobiographical Reassessments, Restoring the War." *Papers on Language & Literature* 36, no. 2 (Spring 2000).

Wilson, Robert Forrest. "Paris for Young Art." *Bookman*, June 1925.

INDEX

+

To learn more about the two authors featured in this book, visit the websites maintained by the societies dedicated to their lives and works:

The Hemingway Society—https://www.hemingwaysociety.org/
John Dos Passos Society—http://jdpsociety.blogspot.com/

+